A DEMONSTRATION

OF THE

ERRORS OF A LATE BOOK.

THE WORKS

Of the REVEREND
WILLIAM LAW, M.A.,

Sometime Fellow of *Emmanuel* College, *Cambridge*.

In Nine Volumes.

Volume V.

I. A Demonstration of the Gross and Fundamental Errors of a late Book, called, *A plain Account of the Nature and End of the Sacrament of the Lord's Supper,* &c.
II. The Grounds and Reasons of Christian Regeneration.

Wipf & Stock
PUBLISHERS
Eugene, Oregon

Wipf and Stock Publishers
199 West 8th Avenue, Suite 3
Eugene, Oregon 97401

Vol. 5 - A Demonstration of the Errors of a Late Book & The Grounds and
Reasons of Christian Regeneration, vol. 5
By Law, William
Copyright© by Law, William
ISBN: 1-57910-619-6
Publication date 3/12/2001
Previously published by G. Moreton, Setley, 1892

Prefatory Advertisement.

A Demonstration of the Errors of a late Book, &c.

BETWEEN the publication of the 'Serious Call' and this Demonstration, WILLIAM LAW wrote his Reply to DR. TINDAL'S 'Case of Reason,' which appears in the second volume of this re-issue of Law's Works. He also wrote, during the years 1731-2, three Letters to a Lady inclined to enter into the Romish Communion. These Letters were not published until after his decease, nor with the collected edition of his Works, but separately: they will be found in the last Volume of this Edition.

The Demonstration was published in the year 1737, when William Law had left the *Gibbon* family; and was living in his late father's house at *King's* Cliffe. It was written—after WILLIAM LAW had become greatly influenced by the writings of JACOB BEHMEN—in repudiation of 'A Plain Account of the Nature and End of the Sacrament of the Lord's Supper' of which BISHOP HOADLY is supposed to have been the Author. The Demonstration, like all WILLIAM LAW'S works, contains many excellent and deeply instructive passages—that upon the Names or Titles given to the Sacrament being capable of very general application:

'WHATEVER *Names* or *Titles* this Institution is 'signified to you by, whether it be called a *Sacrifice* 'propitiatory or commemorative; whether it be 'called an holy Oblation, the *Eucharist*, the '*Sacrament* of the *Body* and *Blood* of Christ, the Sacrament 'of the *Lord's Supper*, the *Heavenly Banquet*, the *Food of Immortality*, or the *Holy Communion*, and the like, matters not 'much. For all these *Words* or *Names* are right and good, and

'there is nothing wrong in them, but the striving and contention
'about them. For they all express *something* that is true of the
'Sacrament, and therefore are every one of them, in a good Sense,
'rightly applicable to it; but all of them are far short of express-
'ing the whole Nature of the Sacrament, and therefore the Help
'of all of them is wanted. He therefore that contends for one
'*Name*, as the only proper one in Exclusion of the rest, is in the
'same Mistake, as he that should contend for one *Name* and
'*Character* of our Saviour, as the only proper one, in Exclusion
'of all the rest. For as all the *Names* and *Titles* by which
'Christ is described, from the *Seed of the Woman* in *Genesis*, to
'the *Alpha* and *Omega* in the last Chapter of the *Revelation*, are
'only to *help* us to know, believe, and experience more of him as
'our Saviour, than can be expressed by all these different
'Characters of him: So all the various *Names* and *Titles* given
'to the Sacrament, are only to teach us to know, believe, and
'find more of our Redemption and Salvation in the Sacrament,
'than can be pointed out to us by any or all of these Ex-
'pressions.'

To those who require Evidence of the Truth of the Gospel the following passage is commended:

'BUT it may be you will say, you would believe the Gospel
'if you could, but that its Evidence cannot have that
'Effect upon your Mind. You may say also, the Gospel
'is a Matter of Fact; you must examine into the
'Truth of it, as you do into the Truth of other Matters of
'History; and as both the internal and external Evidence of the
'Gospel is much defended and opposed by learned Men, its Evi-
'dence is so perplexed, and made a Matter of such laborious
'and intricate Enquiry, that your Mind cannot come at any
'Certainty of what you ought to believe concerning the Truth
'of it. I will therefore propose to you the *shortest*, and at the
'same time the *surest* of all Methods. . . . I don't recommend
'to you to lay aside Prejudice, and begin again the Controversy
'from the Bottom, and read all on both Sides with all the Im-
'partiality that you can. I would as soon send you on a *Pil-
'grimage*, to be a *Penitent*, as propose to you this Travel to be
'a Christian. The Truth of the Gospel lies much nearer to us
'than we imagine, and we only dispute and wrangle ourselves
'into a Distance from it. Do you think that you need many
'Books to show you that you are a *Sinner*, that you have the
'Disorder of almost all the *Beasts* within you; that you have
'besides this, such Passions and Tempers of Pride, Envy, Selfish-

Prefatory Advertisement. vii

'ness and Malice, as would make you shun the Sight of other
'People, if they could see all that passes within you? Need any
'Learning instruct you, that at the same time that you have all
'these Disorders, both of the Beasts and evil Spirits within you,
'you have a great Desire to seem to be without them, and are
'affecting continually to have, and appear in those very Virtues
'which you feel the Want of? When you are full of Hatred
'and Envy, you affect to be thought good and good-natured,
'when proud, to appear as humble. Now I desire you to know
'no Books, but *this Book* of your own Heart, nor to be well read
'in any Controversy but in that which passes *within you*, in order
'to know the Gospel to be the greatest of all Truths, and the
'infallible Voice of God speaking the Way of Salvation to you.'

II. *The Grounds and Reasons of Christian Regeneration.*

THIS remarkable Treatise, written by WILLIAM LAW and published in the year 1739, is based upon the teaching or revelation of JACOB BEHMEN. The influence of JACOB BEHMEN'S writings with WILLIAM LAW has proved fatal to *Law's* reputation as a Religious Teacher with many persons; and a great stumbling-block to those to whom the 'Christian Perfection' and the 'Serious Call' have been most convincing and productive of eternal benefit.

The general and erroneous supposition, that WILLIAM LAW, after leading from his youth upwards, not only an irreproachable, but a sanctified life; and having written such books as the 'Christian Perfection' and the 'Serious Call'—the most perfect religious guides, considered merely as such, that have ever appeared and a world-enduring honour to poor aspiring human nature—and after having displayed so strong and penetrating an understanding, free from any kind of error, in the detection and exposure of such fallacies as are set forth in the 'Bangorian Letters': 'Fable of the Bees': 'Case of Reason,' &c., should — with all his deep insight, intellectual power, and life's-devotion to the Truth—have become the victim of a delusion in adopting the ideas of Jacob Behmen, is a supposition which is perfectly incredible* to, and to be rejected by, an earnest Reader, who is possessed of any 'divine idea.'

---

* This appears to be the silent conviction of so able an Authority as the Rev. Dr. WHYTE upon this portion of WILLIAM LAW'S life.

Prefatory Advertisement.

'The Grounds and Reasons of Christian Regeneration' represents WILLIAM LAW'S earliest exposition and elucidation of JACOB BEHMEN'S ideas; and as an Introduction to the exalted sphere of thought and devotion upon which WILLIAM LAW was then entering, it is admirable.

Perhaps the most impressive idea that WILLIAM LAW sets before us in these new Studies, is that in which he approaches the subject of 'Universalism' and doctrine of 'Free Will.' BISHOP BUTLER has demonstrated almost to a certainty that we are 'Free Agents'; but WILLIAM LAW goes further and deepens that tremendous responsibility in a truly awful manner in the following passage:

'I WILL grant you all *that* you can suppose, of the Goodness of God and that no Creature will be finally lost, but what *Infinite Love* cannot save. But still, here is no *Shadow* of Security for *Infidelity;* and your *refusing* to be *saved* through the *Son* of God, whilst the Soul is in the *redeemable State* of this Life, may at the Separation of the Body, *for* aught you know, leave it in *such* a Hell, as the infinite Love of God *cannot* deliver it from. For, *first*, you have no *Kind*, or *Degree* of Proof, that your Soul is not that *dark, self-tormenting, anguishing* and *imperishable Fire*, above-mentioned, which has lost its *own proper* Light, and is only comforted by the Light of the *Sun*, till its Redemption be effected. *Secondly*, You have no *Kind*, or *Degree* of Proof, that God himself *can* redeem, or save, or enlighten this *dark Fire-Soul*, any other Way than, as the Gospel proposes, by the *Birth* of the Son of God in it. Therefore your own Hearts must tell you, that for aught you know, *Infidelity*, or the *refusing* of this Birth of the Son of God, may, at the End of Life, leave you in *such* a State of *Self-torment*, as the infinite Love of God can no way deliver you from.'

G. B. M.

A DEMONSTRATION

OF THE

Gross and Fundamental ERRORS
Of a late BOOK, called

A Plain Account of the Nature and End of the Sacrament of the Lord's Supper, &c.

Wherein also the Nature and Extent of the Redemption of all Mankind by JESUS CHRIST is stated and explained; and the Pretences of the *Deists*, for a Religion of *Natural Reason* instead of it, are examined to the Bottom. The whole humbly, earnestly, and affectionately addressed to all Orders of Men, and more especially to all the Younger CLERGY.

By *WILLIAM LAW*, M. A.

LONDON:
Printed for W. INNYS and J. RICHARDSON, R. MANBY and J. S. COX. 1737.

A DEMONSTRATION OF THE ERRORS *of a* LATE BOOK.

MY Design (worthy Reader) is not to lay before you all the Errors and false Reasonings of this Author throughout his whole Treatise. This would lead you into too much Wrangle, and the Multiplicity of Things disputed, would take your Eye from the chief Point in Question, and so make the Matter less edifying to you.

Many therefore of his lesser Mistakes I shall pass over, and only endeavour to discover such gross and fundamental Errors, as may justly pass for an entire Confutation of his whole Book.

The Foundation on which he proceeds, and the principal Matters of his Discourse, are not only notoriously against the Truth of the Sacrament, but plainly destructive of the principal Doctrines of the Christian Religion.

And if this Key of Knowledge, put into your Hands by this Author, is accepted by you, you will not only lose all the right Knowledge of this Sacrament, but be rendered a *blind, deaf*, and even *dead* Reader of all the other Doctrines of Scripture. For the Way he points out to find the Truth of the Doctrine of the Sacrament, is the only Way to lose the Truth of all the most important Parts of the Gospel.

Who this Nameless Author is, neither concerns the Truth, nor You, nor Me, and therefore I leave that Matter as he has left it.

He begins with giving us this Account of the Principles on which he proceeds. 'I have endeavoured to establish and 'explain the true Nature, End, and Effect of the Sacrament of 'the Lord's Supper. And this in such a manner, that all who 'are concerned may, I hope, be led into the right way of judging 'about it.* To this I have endeavoured to guide them, by 'directing and confining their Attention to all that is said about 'this Duty, by those who alone had any Authority to declare the

---
* Page 5.

'Nature of it: Neither on the one hand diminishing, nor on the
'other augmenting, what is declared by them to belong to it.—If
'therefore the Manner in which I have chosen to treat this
'Subject, should appear to some to stand in need of any
'Apology; this is the only one I can persuade myself to make,
'That I have no Authority to add to the Words of Christ and
'his Apostles upon this Subject; nor to put any Meaning or
'Interpretation upon these Words, but what is agreeable to the
'common Rules of speaking in like Cases, and to the declared
'Design of the Institution itself.*—All who (in the *Apostle's*
'Phrase) love our Lord Jesus Christ in Sincerity, and who desire
'to be no wiser about his Appointments, than he himself was;
'and are content to expect no more from his Institution than he
'himself put into it, will join with me at least in the one only
'Method of examining into the Nature and Extent of it.'†

Here he has given us a short, but full Account of the *Principles* on which he proceeds, which I shall reduce into the following Propositions.

First, That the *Nature, End,* and *Effects* of the Holy Sacrament can only be *so far* known, and apprehended by us, as the *bare* Words of Christ in the Institution of the Sacrament, related by the Apostles and Evangelists, have made them known to us.

Secondly, That no other Meaning or Interpretation is to be put upon these Words, but what is *agreeable to the common Rules of speaking* on the like Occasions.

Thirdly, That this Examination into the Meaning of the Words, according to the common Rules of speaking on the like Occasions, is the *one only Method of Knowing* what is meant by them.

Fourthly, That this Knowledge thus acquired from such a Consideration of the Words, is *all* the Knowledge that we can have of the *Nature, End,* and *Effects* of this Holy Sacrament.

Everyone must see that these Propositions are fairly taken from his own Words, and that they are the Foundation of his whole Discourse. He builds upon them as upon so many Axioms, or first Principles; and all he says from the Beginning to the End of his Treatise, is founded upon the supposed incontestable Truth of them.

Here therefore let me desire you to fix your Eye, for here I will place the Merits of the Cause with him: If this Foundation cannot be shaken, I will dispute nothing that he has built upon it.

But then let it be observed, that if these Propositions are

---

* Page 6.   † Page 7.

proved to be absolutely false, and most evidently repugnant to the repeated *Letter,* constant *Spirit,* and whole *Tenor* of Scripture, then all this whole Treatise, from the Beginning to the End, so far as he proceeds upon his own avowed Principles, is mere Fiction and Fable, a Castle in the Air.

I shall therefore in the plainest Manner show the Falseness of these Propositions, and that they are so far from being what He takes them to be, *viz., the only Means of arriving at the Fulness of Scripture Truths,* that whoever entertains them as Truths, and abides by them in his Search after Scripture Truths, is, and *must* be, so long as he continues in that Sentiment and Practice, *Stone-Blind* to all the Mysteries of the Kingdom of God, as related in Scripture.

And that, if it were anyone's Desire to do exactly what our Blessed Lord charges upon the Pharisees and Lawyers, ' That ' they shut up the Kingdom of Heaven, took away the Key of ' Knowledge, entered not in themselves, and those that were ' entering in, they hindered ': Were this the deepest Desire of anyone's Heart, the one only effectual Way of doing it, must be the Way that this Author has taken in this Treatise. For, it shall also be made appear, that these Principles of his are that *very Veil* which the Apostle says was upon the Hearts of the *Jews;* and that the Scriptures have never been *useless* to, *misunderstood,* or *rejected* by any People of any Age, but for this Reason, because their Hearts were blinded and hardened by this very Method of knowing Scripture Truths, which he proposes to us. All the Characters of ' stiff-necked, hardened, blind, carnal, ' and uncircumcised in Heart and Spirit,' which are in the Scriptures given to the unbelieving *Jews,* are only so many various Ways of describing that *State* of Heart, which these very Principles had produced in them.

Had they thought of any other Method of knowing their *Messiah,* but that of the *bare Letter* of Scripture, interpreted according to the *common Rules of speaking,* the greatest Occasion of their Infidelity had been removed.

But to begin in my proposed Method. The Holy Sacrament was instituted in these Words : ' And as they were eating, Jesus ' took Bread, and blessed it, and brake it, and gave it to the ' Disciples, and said, Take, eat, this is my Body. And He took ' the Cup, and gave it to them, saying, Drink ye all of it: For ' this is my Blood of the new Testament, which is shed for ' many, for the Remission of Sins,' Matth. xxvi. 26. In St. *Luke* the Words of Institution are : ' And he took Bread, and ' gave thanks, and brake it, and gave it unto them, saying, This ' is my Body which is given for you : This do in remembrance 'of me. Likewise also the Cup after Supper, saying, This Cup 'is the new Testament in my Blood, which is shed for you,' Luke xxii. 19.

Let us now apply the Doctrine contained in the forementioned Propositions to these Words of the Institution of the Sacrament. According to the Doctrine of those Propositions, the one only *Method of understanding* what is meant by these Words of the Institution, is to consider and interpret them 'according to the common Rules of speaking in like Cases.' But, pray Sir, where must a Man look for a *like Case?* Does the World afford us any Case like it? Have the *Speaker*, or the *Things* spoken, any Things in common Life that are alike to either of them? How vain is it therefore to refer us to the *common Rules* of speaking on the *like* Cases, when the whole World affords us neither any Person like him that spoke, nor any Thing, or Case, like the Things and Case here spoken of.

The Scripture saith, 'He spake the Word, and they were 'made; He commanded, and they were created.'* Has this Way of speaking any Parallel in the Language of Men? Do human Things and Transactions furnish us with anything like this?

Now the Word which *thus* speaking *created* all things, is not more extraordinary, more above the common Rules of speaking, or more without human Example, than that Word which, in the *Institution* of the Sacrament, *spake*, and it was *done;* commanded, and it was created. For it is the same Omnipotent Word that *here* speaketh, that spoke the Creation into Being; and the Effects of his speaking in the Institution of the Sacrament, are as *extraordinary*, and as much above the Effects of human speaking, as when the same Word *spake, and they were made; commanded, and they were created.* And it is impossible for anyone to show, that there is less of *Divine Power* and Greatness, less of Mystery and Miracle implied in these Words spoken by the Eternal Word in the Institution of the Sacrament, than when the same Eternal Word said, 'Let there be 'Light, and there was Light.'

All Words have a Meaning, a Significancy and Effect, according to the Nature of him, whose they are. The Words of God are of the Nature of God, Divine, Living and Powerful; the Words of an Angel are, as that Angel is in Power and Perfection; the Words of a Devil have only his Nature and Power, and therefore they can only and solely *tempt* to Evil; the Words of Man are, as Men are, *weak, vain, earthly*, and of a

---

* Psalm cxlviii. 5.

poor and *narrow* Signification. To direct us therefore to the common Rules of speaking amongst Men, as the *only Means* of truly knowing *all* that the Son of God spoke, when he spoke of himself, and on such an Occasion, and in such Circumstances as never did, nor ever can happen or belong to anyone but himself, is surely no small Mistake. The common Rules of speaking are like other things that are common amongst Men, *viz.*, poor, empty, and superficial, hardly touching the *Outside* of the mere human Things we talk about. If therefore what the Son of God said of himself in the Institution of this Holy Sacrament, must necessarily be supposed to have no *higher* Meaning or *deeper* Sense, than such as is according to the *common* Rules of speaking amongst Men ; it must necessarily follow, that he spoke as *meanly*, as *imperfectly*, and as *superficially* in what he said of himself, and the Matter he was upon, as when Men speak of themselves and human Things. For if there were not the same weak, empty, and superficial Meaning in his Words, as there is in the common Discourse of Men ; then the common Rules of speaking amongst Men cannot be a *proper*, much less the *only Means* of understanding *all the Truth* that is contained in them.

This Author seems to be in the same mistake concerning Jesus Christ and his Kingdom, as his Disciples were in, before they had *received Power from on high*. They had till then heard him only with their *outward Ears ;* conceived what he said, only according to the *common Rules* of speaking amongst Men, and so continued *perfect Strangers* to all the Mysteries and great Truths of the Gospel. But after the Descent of the Holy Ghost upon them, their Understandings were opened, and they saw all things with new Eyes, and in a new Light ; they then fully apprehended what their Lord meant by these remarkable Words, ' My Kingdom is not of this World.' Which is the same thing as if he had said, I speak not as a Person of this World, nor of the Things of this World, and therefore the Things which I say, can neither be understood by a *worldly* Mind, nor according to the *common Ways* of speaking amongst Men. And had this Author sufficiently attended to the Sense of these Words, and felt the Truth of them in his own Heart, it seems next to impossible for him to have fallen into his present way of Reasoning. For he that truly and fully believes that the Kingdom of Christ is not of this World, and that therefore *worldly Powers and Privileges* are not a proper Part of it, can hardly be so inconsistent with himself, as to affirm, that worldly Language, spoken on worldly Matters, is the *only proper* Key to the right Understanding the Truths and Doctrines of this

Kingdom, that is so out of, above, and contrary to this World.

And if he has but one just and good Argument to prove, that worldly Power is not the proper and only Power that belongs to this Kingdom, the same Argument will as fully prove, that worldly Language understood according to the common Rules of speaking, cannot be the proper and only Means of rightly apprehending the Truths of this Kingdom.

To proceed; he refers and confines us to the bare Words of the Institution, for the right and full understanding of *all* that is to be understood of the *Nature, End,* and *Effects* of the Holy Sacrament.

Here he throws an easy Deception into the Mind of His Reader, who because he may justly think he is right in declaring the Words of the Institution to be the only *true* and *full* Account of the Sacrament, as to the *outward Form* and *Matter* of it, suspects him not to be wrong, when he concludes from thence, that the Words are also the only *true and full* Account of the *Nature, End* and *Effects* of the Holy Sacrament. Whereas this is as false, as the other is true; for the Nature, and End, and Effects of the Holy Sacrament, neither are, nor possibly can be taught us (as shall be shown hereafter) from the bare Words of the Institution, considered by themselves.

Let us suppose that one of this Author's *rational* Men, of *clear Ideas,* but an absolute Stranger to the Scriptures, and to our Saviour's Doctrines, had been present only when he spoke the Words of the Institution; would his Knowledge of the Meaning of Words, according to the *common Rules* of speaking, have directed him to the true Sense of all that was implied by this Sacrament and the Observation of it? To say that such a Person thus qualified could have known the true *Nature, End,* and *Effects* of the Holy Sacrament, is surely too absurd to be imagined. And to say that he could not, is fully giving up this Author's *whole* Doctrine, namely, that the *bare understanding the Words of the Institution according to the common Rules* of speaking, is the *only Way* to understand *all* that is certain and true as to the *Nature, End, and Effects* of the Sacrament. For if this were so, it would evidently follow, that a perfect Stranger to all the other Doctrines and Institutions both of the Old and New Testament, would be as well qualified to understand all that was implied in the Words of the Institution, as he that had the fullest Knowledge of everything that ever had been revealed or appointed by God, either before or since the Birth of Christ.

But if some Knowledge of what God has revealed both in the Old and New Testament be required, for a right understanding what is implied in the Words of the Institution, then it is absolutely false, and highly blamable, to say, that the bare Words of the Institution, considered in themselves only, according to the common Rules of speaking, are the *only* Means or Method of understanding all that is implied in them.

Either this Sacrament has some relation to some other Doctrines of the Old and New Testament, or it has not; if it has no Relation to them, then it must be said to have no Agreement with any other Part of Scripture: But if it has some Relation to other Doctrines of Scripture, then it demonstratively follows, that this Institution must be interpreted, not according to the *bare Meaning* of the Words in the common Ways of speaking, but according to that *Relation* which it has to some other Doctrines of Scripture. This, I think, is incontestable, and entirely overthrows his only *Method* of understanding the Nature of the Sacrament.

Again, another Argument of still greater Force against him may be taken from the Apostles themselves. He confines us to the bare Words of the Institution related by the Apostles and Evangelists, as the *only Means* of knowing all that can be known of the *Nature, End, and Effects* of the Sacrament; and yet it is certain, beyond all Doubt, that the Apostles and Evangelists neither had, nor could possibly have this Design in relating and recording the Words of the Institution, namely, that we might thereby have the one *only Means* of knowing all that is to be understood by it.

For they very well knew, that they had received no such Knowledge themselves from the bare Words of the Institution, and therefore they could not relate them as the *only Means* of Instruction in that Matter to others. They very well knew, that if they had received *no other* Light, besides that which those Words conveyed, they had died in a *total Ignorance* of the whole Matter.

They very well knew, that though they had personally conversed with Christ, had heard from his own Mouth, Mysteries preparatory to their right Knowledge of their Saviour, that notwithstanding all this, when they heard and saw him institute the Sacrament in its outward *Form* and *Matter*, as they relate it, by the help of the bare Words of the Institution, they then neither *did*, nor *could* rightly understand the *Nature, End, and Effects* of the Holy Sacrament. And therefore it may be said to be *certain* beyond *all Doubt*, that they neither *did* nor *could* relate and record these Words of the Institution, as the *only Means* of rightly understanding all that is implied in the Sacrament, as to the Nature, End, and Effects of it. And yet this

Author takes all this for granted, and supposes that the Apostles had all their Knowledge of the Sacrament from the Words of the Institution, and that they have recorded the Institution for this End, and with this Design, that we might know all that they knew, and all that could be known concerning it.

That the Apostles themselves did not comprehend the Nature, End, and Effects of the Sacrament from the Words of the Institution, is plain; for they did not then know what *Person* their Saviour was, or *how* he was to save them, or *what* their *Salvation* in itself implied. They knew nothing of the Nature or Merit of his Sufferings, but thought all to be lost, when he suffered Death. They knew not how to believe in his Resurrection, and when they did believe it, they knew nothing of the Consequences of it; which is a plain *Proof* that they did not at all see into the *Meaning* of the Holy Sacrament, for had they known what was implied in it, they must have known their *Saviour*, and the *Nature* of their Salvation. And yet (what is well to be observed) it is also plain, that in this State of gross *Ignorance* and *Infidelity*, knowing nothing of their Salvation, they had *all* that Knowledge of the Holy Sacrament which this Author is recommending to the Christian World, as the only true Knowledge of it. For they must have understood the Words according to the *common Rules* of speaking, which is all that he allows to be understood by them. For any other Sense or Meaning, that is not literally expressed in the Words taken according to the common Rules of speaking, is by him called a being *Wiser* than Christ in his own Appointments, an *adding* to the Institution, or a *putting something* into it, which he has not put in. So that it is evidently plain, that this *Purity* of Knowledge concerning the Sacrament, which this Author has writ so large a Volume in Recommendation of, is that *very* Knowledge of the Sacrament which the Apostles had, when they had *no Faith* in Christ as their Saviour, nor any *Knowledge* of the Nature of Christian Salvation. Everyone must see that this Charge is justly brought against him, and that he cannot possibly avoid it. For if that is the only right Knowledge of the Nature, End, and Effects of the Holy Sacrament, which the bare Words of the Institution, understood only according to the common Rules of speaking, declare; if every other Sense and Meaning is to be rejected as a Criminal adding, or putting something into Christ's Institution, and a presuming to be *wiser* than he was; then it undeniably follows, that that *simple* and *pure* Knowledge of the Sacrament, which he lays so great Claim to, and so much contends for, is that very *gross Ignorance* of it which the Apostles were in, when they had *no Light* but from the bare Words of the Institution, and had all the Articles of the Christian Faith to learn.

Further, as the Apostles did not, so they could not *possibly* know the *Nature, End, and Effects* of the Holy Sacrament, from the bare Words of the Institution, nor is it possible for any *one* since their Time to know it by that Help alone.

The outward *Matter* and *Form* indeed, or that wherein the positive Institution consists (as I have already said) is sufficiently plain and intelligible from the *bare Words* of the Institution, and is by them made unalterable. This is the only Plainness of the Institution. But what Mysteries or Doctrines of Christian Faith are to be acknowledged or confessed by the *Words*, the *Form*, and the *Matter* of it, and what are not, cannot be known from the bare Words of the Institution, but are to be learnt by *that Light* which brought the Apostles and the Church after them into a true and full Knowledge of the *fundamental* Articles of the Christian Faith.

Take the Words of the Institution alone as the Apostles first heard them, understood only according to the *common Rules* of speaking, and then there is nothing in them, but that *poor Conception* which they had of them at *that time*, and such as did them no good; and then also we have that Knowledge of this Institution, which this Author pleads for. But, take the same Words of the Institution, understood and interpreted according to the *Articles* of the Christian Faith, and seen in that *Light* in which the Apostles afterwards saw them, when they *knew* their Saviour; and then everything that is great and adorable in the Redemption of Mankind, everything that can delight, comfort and support the Heart of a Christian, is found to be centred in this Holy Sacrament. There then wants nothing but the Wedding Garment to make this Holy Supper the *Marriage Feast* of the Lamb: And it is this Holy Solemnity, this Author is taking so much Pains to wrangle us out of, by so many dry Subtleties of a superficial Logic.

But I proceed to show, that neither the Apostles, nor any other Persons since them, could possibly know the Nature, End and Effects of the Holy Sacrament, from the bare Words of the Institution considered only in themselves, according to the common Rules of speaking. And this may be demonstrated from every Part of the Institution.

I shall begin with these Words, which are only a *Command* to observe the Institution, 'Do this in Remembrance of me': That is, let this be done as your *Confession* and *Acknowledgment* of the Salvation that is received through me. Does not every common Christian, that has any Knowledge of Scripture, know, that this is the plain Meaning of these Words? And that as often as he *does this*, he does it in Remembrance of his Saviour, in *Acknowledgment* and *Confession* of that *Salvation* which Mankind received through him? But now, that which is thus *plain* and *intelligible* in the Words of the Institution to a common Christian, knowing only the *chief Articles* of his Salvation, is altogether *unintelligible* to any Man that is left solely to the bare Words of the Institution; for unless he was instructed in the other Parts of Scripture, so as to know what he was to understand by the Words, they would signify no more to him than they would to a *Heathen*, who had by *Chance* found a bit of Paper in the Fields with the *same Words* writ upon it.

Now a *Heathen*, ignorant of all Divine Revelation, if he found such a Paper, could not know what it related to, nor what any of the Words signified; he could not know when he was nearer, or when he was further from a right understanding of them; the common Rules of speaking amongst Men, would be of no use to teach him, whether there was any *Truth* in such a Paper, or what kind of Truths were declared by it.

Now this is exactly the Case of him that renounces *all other Means* of knowing what is contained in the Institution, but that of the Words themselves, understood *only* according to the *common Rules* of speaking amongst Men. Such a one is only in the State of this Heathen, the Words of the Institution are as *unintelligible* and *useless* to him, as if he had found them by chance; they relate to he knows not what, they may be all *Fiction* and *Invention* for aught he knows, they cannot possibly be understood as having any Truth or Reality in them, till he that reads them, *knows more* than is related by them, till he knows the chief Articles of the Christian Salvation. For the bare Words of the Institution, considered by themselves, do not at all *prove, justify*, or *explain*, even that which they *literally* express; they are all but *empty, unmeaning Words*, till the *Proof*, the *Justification* and *Explication* of them, is learned from some other Parts of Scripture. They do not at all prove, justify, or explain, either that we *want* a Saviour, or *why* we want him, or that a Saviour is given us, and *how* he effects our Salvation; and yet *all* these things are *absolutely* necessary to a right understanding of this Institution; and as soon as these things are *proved, justified* and *explained*, as soon as we know that we *want* a Saviour, and that one is given to us; as soon as we know *who* this Saviour is, *how* he saves us, and the Nature and Manner of our Salvation, then, and not till then, all these Words of the Institution become clearly intelligible after a new Manner; then all the great Articles of our Salvation appear to be finely remembered, acknowledged, and set forth by them.

The short of the Matter is this; to understand these Words only by themselves, knowing no more in them or by them, than what the common Use of Words teaches us, is to understand them *only* in such a Degree as a *Heathen* may understand them, who knows nothing of the Scripture besides; and this is the Knowledge, or rather the *total Ignorance* of the Sacrament, that this Author is contending for.

But if these Words are but a *Part* of the Christian Religion, if they are to be understood *according* to that *Religion* of which they are a Part, if the Articles of our Christian Salvation have any *Concern* in them, and we are to receive them as Christians in *such* a Sense as our *Christianity* requires of us; then it is undeniably certain, that this Author refers us to an *Absurdity*, and *Impossibility*, when he refers and confines us to the bare Words of the Institution, understood only according to the common Rules of speaking, in order to have a *Christian* Knowledge of the Holy Sacrament.

Again, 'Do this in Remembrance of me': Now take these Words in what Sense you please, is it not *equally* and *absolutely* necessary for the right understanding of them, to know who and what kind of Person this ME is, who is here to be remembered? For if this is to be done in *Remembrance* of him, how can he be remembered, or acknowledged, unless it be known what *Qualities* and *Characters* of him are to be remembered and acknowledged?

But this is not done in the Words of the Institution; the *State*, *Nature*, and *Characters* of the Person to be remembered are not there *declared*, nor *proved*, and *explained;* therefore something of the *greatest Importance* to the Words, and that must have the greatest Effect upon the Sense of them, and that is absolutely necessary to the right understanding of them, is necessarily to be learnt elsewhere; and therefore it is again proved that he refers us to an *Absurdity* and *Impossibility*, when he refers and confines us to the bare Words of the Institution, to know all that a Christian can rightly know of them.

For if all that is done in this Sacrament, is to be done for the sake of *remembering* and *acknowledging* him as our Saviour, then surely it requires us to remember, and acknowledge him, according to what *he is*, with regard to our Salvation, and according to those Characters which are so plainly ascribed to him in Scripture, and on which our whole Religion is founded; and therefore it is also necessary, that we rightly know (what cannot possibly be known from the bare Words of the Institution) in what *Respects* and on how many *Accounts* he is our *Saviour*, before we can *rightly* make this Remembrance and Acknowledgment of him as such.

It was the want of *this Knowledge*, that made the Institution of the Sacrament useless to the Apostles when they first heard it; but when they had got this *Knowledge*, and knew all the *Characters* of their Saviour, and in how *many* Respects he stood as the *Mediator* and Redeemer betwixt God and Man, then the Institution became *highly* intelligible to them, and every Part of it plainly declared the Mystery that in a certain Sense was both concealed and expressed by it. Now the Addition of this Knowledge of the *Nature, Condition,* and *Characters* of the Person to be remembered and acknowledged by the Institution, is adding nothing to the Institution, but the *right Use* of it; it is bringing nothing to it, but a Mind capable of knowing and observing it.

He that is to understand a Proposition written in *Hebrew*, cannot be charged with adding to that Proposition, because he holds it *necessary* to learn the Hebrew *Language*, before he pretends to understand a Proposition written in Hebrew.

Now a Scripture-Christian Institution must as necessarily be understood according to Scripture and Christian Doctrine, as an Hebrew Proposition must be understood according to the Hebrew Language: And the making use of Scripture and Christian Doctrine, in order to understand a Scripture and Christian Institution, is no more an *adding* of something to the Institution, that need not, or ought not to be done, than the interpreting an Hebrew Proposition by the Hebrew Language, is an adding of something to it, that need not, or ought not to be done.

And, on the other hand, to confine us to the *bare Words* of the Institution, as they are in themselves, as they sound only in common Language, in order to understand a *Scripture-Christian Institution*, is exactly the same thing as to confine us to the *bare Words* of a Proposition written in Hebrew, considered only according to the common Rules of speaking, and not according to that Meaning they have in the *Hebrew Language* to which they belong, and of which they are a Part.

For a Scripture-Christian Institution must in the same manner have its Dependence upon, Foundation in, and Interpretation from Scripture and Christian Doctrine, of which it is a Part, and to which it belongs, as an Hebrew Proposition hath Dependence upon, Foundation in, and Interpretation from the Hebrew Language, to which it belongs, and of which it is a Part.

This Scripture-Christian Institution being thus interpreted, according to the Scripture and Christian Doctrine, of which it is a Part, is, when thus interpreted, left and kept in that *State*, in which Christ left it to be kept. Nay, the Institution itself cannot even *literally* be observed according to the bare Words of it, unless it be observed according to *this Knowledge* and *Acknowledgment* of all the Characters of Christ.

For though the bare Words of the Institution do not *express* or teach these Characters, yet the bare Words or Letter of it *requires* thus much: For since the Letter of the Institution requires us to *do this in Remembrance* and Acknowledgment of Christ, the bare Letter requires us in *doing this*, to acknowledge and remember all the Characters of Christ; therefore he that in *doing this* does not remember and acknowledge all the Characters of Christ, must be said not to observe the very Letter of the Institution. Hence therefore there arises another plain Demonstration against his Doctrine, *viz.*, that we are to know no more of the Nature or right Observation of the Sacrament, than what is expressly taught us in the bare Words of the Institution. For the very Letter itself of the Institution contradicts this; and if he will not directly refuse what the bare Words expressly command, he must seek for *something* towards the right Observation of this Sacrament, which is only required, but not taught in the Words of the Institution. For by the Letter of the Institution you are commanded to remember and acknowledge a Person, whose *Characters, Condition* and *Offices* to be acknowledged, are not taught in the Institution, but only to be found in other Parts of Scripture; and therefore the bare Letter of the Institution is grossly violated, if we look no further than to the Words of the Institution for a right Knowledge and Observation of the Sacrament.

Again, If the Scriptures *teach* and *prove* Christ to be the Sacrifice, Atonement and Propitiation for our Sins, as expressly as they teach us the *Institution* of the Sacrament, does not the Remembrance and Acknowledgment of him as the Sacrifice, Atonement and Propitiation for Sin, become a *necessary Part* of our right Observation of the Sacrament? For if the Sacrament is appointed for the Remembrance and Acknowledgment of Christ as our Saviour, and if as our Saviour he is the *Atonement*, the *Sacrifice*, and *Propitiation* for our Sins, is not the Remembrance and Acknowledgment of him as our Sacrifice and Atonement, *essential* to the Remembrance of him as our Saviour? If these Characters were mentioned in the Institution, I suppose they would be allowed to be an essential Part of it. But if the Letter of the Institution directly points to, and calls for the Acknowledgment of these Characters, then they are as essential to it, as if they were expressly mentioned in it.

Jesus Christ is not mentioned in the Institution as our *Saviour*, but I suppose it will not be denied that he is there by way of necessary Implication, since the Person there to be remembered, is declared by the Scripture to be our *Saviour*. But if we may be allowed thus to take our Saviour to be the Person that is to be remembered and acknowledged by the Sacrament, if this may be done without adding anything to the Institution, if it must be done as absolutely essential to it, then the Addition of *Sacrifice, Atonement,* and *Propitiation* for our Sins, may be added without adding anything to the Institution, and must be done as absolutely essential to it; because the Scriptures *teach* and *prove,* that Jesus Christ, as our Saviour, is the Sacrifice, Atonement, and Propitiation for our Sins. Therefore if the Remembrance of him as our Saviour is essential to the Sacrament, the Remembrance and Acknowledgment of him as the Sacrifice and Atonement, and Propitiation for Sin, is essential to the Sacrament.

And therefore it follows again, that the very Words of the Institution direct us to a *further Knowledge* of the Sacrament, than that which is *expressly* taught by them.

To proceed: *Take, eat; this is my Body.* Now what signifies it what anyone can make of these Words, understood according to the *common* Ways of speaking? For the Way itself is *singular* and *uncommon,* and has no certain Meaning according to the common Rules of speaking. He may as well read a Discourse upon *Truth,* to know whether these Words have *any Truth* in them, as consult the common Forms of speaking, to know what is meant by them. For if the things mentioned and expressed in these Words, were not made *significant* and *important* to us by *something* not mentioned in the Sacrament, if they were not asserted and explained in *other Parts* of Scripture, it could never be known from the Words themselves, that they were of any *Significancy* to us, or that there was any *Truth* and *Reality* in them. The short of the Matter is this: Either these Words are only a great Impropriety of Speech, darkly expressing only a common thing; or they are a figurative Form of Words, which by the Particularity of the Expression are to raise the Mind to a *Faith* and *Apprehension* of such Things, as cannot be *plainly* and *nakedly* represented by human Language. Now one of these two must necessarily be true, that is, they must necessarily be either a *dark Form* of Words with only a plain *common Meaning* of an ordinary Thing at the bottom, or they must be a mysterious Form of Words signifying *something* more than human. But now which of these two they are, cannot *possibly* be known from the Words of the Institution. For the Words in themselves prove nothing at all of this; from aught that appears in the Words themselves, they may be mere *Fiction* and *Impropriety* about a Trifle, or the *greatest* and most *important* of all Truths may be taught by them. But this can no other possible way be known, but by other Parts of Scripture. And if the Scriptures were as silent about the *Truth, Nature,* and *Extent* of the Things barely mentioned in the Sacrament, as the Institution itself is, it must be the same useless, unintelligible Form of Words to us, that it was to the Apostles when they first heard them, and had no Knowledge of their Saviour.

But, on the other hand, if the Things *barely mentioned* in the Words of the Institution, are *openly asserted*, and *variously explained* in other Parts of Scripture; if we are often told what the *Body* of Christ is in several Respects, of the *Necessity* and *Possibility* of Eating his Flesh, and Drinking his Blood; if the Scriptures abound with *Instruction*, showing us how we have *our Life* in him and from him, how we must be *born again* in him and through him, how he must be *formed* in us, and we *new Creatures* in him; then it follows, that to separate the *Institution* from these Scriptures that *variously unfold* its Nature, and to confine us to the *bare* Words of the Institution itself, in order to understand it *fully*, is the same *Absurdity*, the same Offence against Scripture and Reason, as it would be to confine us to the bare Words of the first Promise of a Saviour made in the third Chapter of *Genesis*, in order to know *fully* our Christian Saviour, and what our *Christian Salvation is*. For as that first Promise of a *Seed of the Woman that should bruise the Serpent's Head*, contained the *whole* Character of our Saviour, and all that related to him as such, and yet contained *nothing* of it intelligible *enough*, till further *Revelations*, *Doctrines* and *Facts* explained all that was *short* and *figurative* in that first Promise, and showed how every Part of our Salvation was promised by it; so the Institution of the Sacrament contained *every* thing relating to Christ as our Saviour, and yet contained *nothing* of it intelligible *enough*, till further *Revelations*, new *Light*, *Doctrines* and *Facts* explained all that was *short* and *figurative* in it, and plainly showed what it was in its *real* Nature, how it *stood* in the *Heart* of our Religion, fully attesting and representing the chief Characters of Christ, as he was our Saviour and Redeemer.

Therefore it is the same gross Error to confine the Words of the Institution to their *own literal* Meaning, and to understand them *only* according to the *common Rules* of speaking, as it would be to confine that *first Promise* of a Saviour to the *literal* Meaning of the Words in which it was expressed, understood only according to the *common Rules* of speaking. For as it was by the Scriptures speaking a Language *different* from the Expressions of the first Promise of a *Seed to bruise the Serpent's Head*, and giving *further* Revelations concerning the promised Saviour in *other* Words, that the Words of the first Promise itself came rightly to be understood and believed; so it is by the Scriptures speaking a Language *different* from that of the Sacrament, and by revealing *Doctrines* on which it is *founded*, that the Sacrament itself came rightly to be known and understood. And if the Scripture may and must be allowed to explain, confirm, and establish the true Meaning of the first Promise of a *Seed* to destroy the Serpent's Head, even where the *Words* of it are not *mentioned*, or *expressly* said to be explained ; then the Scriptures may and must be allowed to explain, confirm, and establish the *true Nature* of the Sacrament, even where the Words of it are not mentioned, or *expressly* said to be explained.

Yet this Author *poorly* and *vainly* supposes, that the *Nature* of the Sacrament, and the Things *meant* by it, are *nowhere* to be looked for in Scripture, but where the *Sacramental* Words, or the Manner of the *outward Institution* is repeated, or expressly said to be explained : Which is as just and solid, as if a *Jew* should from the same Skill in Words suppose, that the Explication of the first Promise of a *Woman's Seed* to bruise the Serpent's Head, was *nowhere* to be looked for in Scripture, but in *such* Places as spoke strictly the *Language* of the first Promise, and mentioned the express Words, *Seed*, and *Bruise*, and the *Serpent's Head*.

And indeed herein, in this *poor literal* Exactness lay all the *Infidelity* of the Jews, the *Blindness* and *Hardness* of their Hearts, and their *Incapacity* to receive their Saviour. Look at every Folly, Grossness, and erroneous Principle of the *Scribes* and *Pharisees ;* look through the whole of their false Religion, and you will find, that they fell into it all, because they had this Author's *Method* of finding the Truth. They placed *all* in the *Letter* of Scripture, as this Author does ; they understood that Letter only according to the *common Rules* of speaking amongst Men, as this Author does ; they looked upon and understood all the *Institutions* of their Religion, as this Author looks upon and understands the *Sacrament ;* they saw just so far into the *Law*, as he does into the *Gospel ;* they had his Degree of Knowledge, and he has their Degree of Ignorance. For take but away from the *Scribe* and *Pharisee* the Letter of Scripture, understood according to the *common Rules* of speaking, and you take away *all their* Religion ; they see *no more* of an inward Mystery, Spirit, or Doctrine in it, than this Author sees in the Sacrament.

Again, leave them but the *Letter* of Scripture, *understood* according to the *common Rules* of speaking, as this Author would have the Sacrament left, and then you leave them *all* that they would have ; and the Religion of the *Scribes* and *Pharisees* is in its *full Perfection*, and has *exactly* the Perfection of this Author's *plain Account* of the Sacrament.

This made me say above, that it would appear, that this

Author's *Method* of understanding the Scripture Doctrine of the Sacrament, was that *very Veil* which the Apostle said was upon the *Hearts* of the Jews; and that he was labouring to draw Skins over our Eyes, and to make our Ears gross and dull of hearing, that the *New* Testament might be as useless to us, as the *Old* Testament was to the unbelieving Letter-learned *Scribes* and *Pharisees*. For his excellent Method of understanding the Nature of the Sacrament, is to a *tittle* that very Method which kept them *totally* ignorant of the Nature of their Religion.

Every Prophecy of our Saviour, whether in the *Law*, or the *Psalms*, or the *Prophets*, served only to keep him more out of their Knowledge; because looking *only* upon it, as this Author looks upon the Words of the Institution, they were under a *Necessity* of understanding it *wrong*, and so the more Prophecies they had of him, the further they were carried from the true Knowledge of their promised Saviour. *Circumcision, Sacrifices, Washings, Feasts and Fasts, &c.*, which were intended and appointed as so many *School-masters* or *Guides* to Christ, were by them turned into *dead, carnal, earthly* Ordinances, that left them in their Sins, and *incapable* of acknowledging their Saviour, or so much as *feeling* any want of one; for this *very Reason*, because they saw no further into their Sacrifices, than this Author sees into the Sacrament; but thought that the whole *Nature* and *End* of a Sacrifice was fully observed, when they had *slain an Ox*, and not changed it into the *cutting off of a Dog's Head*. This was their *Great Point* in Sacrifice, just as this Author has found out the *Great Point*, as he calls it, of the Sacrament, which consists in a *bare Act of the Memory*, remembering Christ as a Teacher of *Religion* at the *Instant* you take the Bread or the Cup, and not remembering *Aristotle* or *Socinus, &c.*, as Teachers of *Logic* and *Criticism*.

When you have by this sole Act of your Memory thus *separated* and *distinguished* what is done in the Sacrament, from *that* which is done for *Food*, or *Mirth*, or in *Memory* of your Friends, then you have secured the *great Point* in the Sacrament, and are to look for nothing further as to the peculiar *Nature, End*, and *Effects* of it. Just as the Letter-learned *Pharisee* thought that the *whole Nature* and End of the Sacrifice was *fully* observed when he had *slain an Ox*, and not cut off a *Dog's Head*.

And if you are for adding anything to the Sacrament besides this *distinguishing* Act of the Memory, you are as blamable in the Sight of this Author, as the *Apostles* were in the Eyes of the *unbelieving* Pharisee, when they taught that the *Blood* of slain Beasts was, as to its Nature and End, a *Type* and *Application* of the Atonement of Christ's Blood. Thus does this Author stand in the very *State* and *Place* of the unbelieving *Pharisee*, teaching Christians the *Gospel*, as he taught the Jews the *Law*, and excluding the true Knowledge of Christ from Christian Institutions, just as the *Pharisee* excluded it from the *Jewish*.

And if you ask, or search ever so much into the *true Reason* why the Religion of the *Scribes* and *Pharisees* was so odious in the Sight of our Blessed Saviour, why he cast so many *Reproaches* upon it, why he denounced so many *Woes* against it; the one *true genuine* Cause was this, it was because they stood on the *Outside* of the Law, just as this Author stands on the *Outside* of the Gospel, and were content with such a *plain Account* of their Sacrifices and Circumcision, as he has given us of the Sacrament; it was because they stuck to the *bare Letter* of Scripture, only understood according to the *common Rules* of speaking amongst Men; it was this Fulness of a *false, empty*, and *dead* Knowledge, that made the Scriptures useless to them, that fixed them in a State of *blind Self-sufficiency*, and made it harder for the *Rational, Letter-learned* Pharisee, than for a *gross Sinner* to *see the Kingdom of God*, or to acknowledge him that preached it.

And here we may see the true and solid Meaning of the Apostle, when he saith, God had 'made them able Ministers of 'the New Testament, not of the Letter, but of the Spirit; for 'the Letter killeth, but the Spirit giveth Life.'*

For the Letter of Scripture, understood only according to the *common Rules* of speaking, is the *Letter that killeth*, the Letter that made the *Jews* Unbelievers in Christ, that makes *speculative* Christians, *Idealists, Critics* and *Grammarians* fall into Infidelity; but Scripture, interpreted not by *Lexicons* and *Dictionaries*, but by *Doctrines* revealed by God, and by an *inward Teaching* and *Unction* of the Holy Ghost, is that Spirit which giveth Life.

But this Author, according to his own Principles, is obliged to own himself to be an Anti-Apostle, and to declare, that not God, but *Logic*, and *much Attention* to human Words and Ways of Reasoning, have made him an *able Minister* of the New Testament, not of the *Spirit*, but of the *Letter*; and has convinced him, that it is the *Letter alone* that giveth Life. For he cannot allow the smallest Degree of sound Doctrine to be in the Apostle's Words; had he but dropped an Expression like it, or made the least Acknowledgment of a *killing Letter* of Scripture, till the Spirit gave Life to it, it must have passed for a full *Recantation* of all his *Plain Account*.

But to return to the further Consideration of the Words of the

---

* 2 Cor. iii. 6.

Institution: 'This is my Body, which is given for you; this is 'my Blood, which is shed for many, for the Remission of Sins.' Who can know what is *right* or *wrong* in these Expressions, or in what *Sense* they are to be received, if he look only to the Sound of the Words according to the common Rules of speaking? Or supposing he could guess out some *tolerable* Meaning; yet if the Scripture has *Doctrines* concerning these things, *teaching, asserting*, and explaining *how*, and in *what* Sense his *Body is given for us*, and *his Blood the Atonement for our Sins*, in a Way and Manner above all *human Thought and Conception;* then it follows, that *no Meaning* of the Words can be admitted, but that which is according to the Scripture Explication of the things mentioned by them.

Nothing therefore can be more unjustifiable and impracticable, than this Author's *only Method* of understanding the Nature of the Sacrament from the Words considered in themselves. For as this cannot be the Way of understanding the Truth of *any* Doctrines of Scripture, so least of all can it be the Way of understanding the true Meaning of the Words of the Institution; for these Words have a more than ordinary Relation to, and Dependence upon all the Scriptures. For as Christ is in some respect or other *represented*, and made *further* known what he is to us, in almost every Page of Scripture; so the *Sacrament*, which is to be done in Remembrance and Acknowledgment of what *he is* to us, must have its *Relation* to, and *Dependence* upon *all* those Places and Doctrines of Scripture, which teach what *he is* to us, and *what* we are to remember and acknowledge him to be. Therefore, *all those* Passages of Scripture, which teach and explain the *Nature*, *Office*, and *Condition* of Christ, directly and immediately teach and explain *what* we are to do, remember, and acknowledge in the Sacrament, and are in the same Degree *true* and *proper* Comments upon the Nature of the Sacrament, in which they are *true* Accounts and Descriptions of our Saviour. And that which we are to believe of our Saviour according to the Scriptures, that we are to remember and acknowledge of him in the Sacrament; and therefore the Scripture Explication of the Sacrament is not, as this Author extravagantly supposes, confined to *those Texts* that mention expressly the *Sacrament*, or the Words of the *Institution*, but is as *large* and *extensive* as the Scripture Explication of the *Nature*, *Office*, and *Condition* of Christ as our Saviour. Wherever we are taught anything concerning him *as such*, there we are directly taught something of the true *Nature* and *End* of the Sacrament, and what we are to remember and acknowledge of him in the doing it.

'Search the Scriptures,' saith our Blessed Saviour, 'for they 'are they which testify of me.' Is not this in the plainest Manner referring us to *all* the Scriptures that speak of him as our Saviour, to know what we are to *remember* and acknowledge of him in the Sacrament? For since he saith, Search the Scriptures, for they are they that *testify* of me; and in the Sacrament, Do this in *Remembrance* or *Acknowledgment* of me; is it not directly as full to the Purpose, as if he had said, Search the Scriptures, for they are they which testify *what* you are to *remember* and acknowledge concerning me in the Sacrament? For that which they testify of him, that they must testify of the *Nature* and *End* of the Sacrament, which is to be done in Remembrance and Acknowledgment of that which is so testified of him. Since therefore every Scripture that testifies anything concerning Christ, as our Saviour, testifies so much of that which is to be acknowledged of him in the Sacrament, it plainly follows, that the Nature and End of the Sacrament can only be so *far* known, as the Nature, Character, *Office* and *Condition* of Christ is known; and that all those Scriptures which teach us the one, in the same Degree teach us the other, and are as necessary to teach us the Nature of the Sacrament, as the Nature of Christ; for this plain Reason, because the Sacrament is to remember and acknowledge that which is taught us concerning the Nature of Christ.

Hence again it appears with how little Judgment and less Truth this Author affirms, that the Nature and End of the Sacrament is only to be known from the bare Words of the Institution, understood according to the common Rules of speaking.

Again, another Argument which will make the Absurdity of this same Error still further apparent, may be taken from the following Passage of Scripture. When our Saviour said in the 6th of St. *John*, that his 'Flesh was Meat indeed, and his Blood 'was Drink indeed;' and that unless a 'Man did eat his Flesh, 'and drink his Blood, he had no Life in him; his Disciples were 'astonished at his Discourse, and said, How can this Man give 'us his Flesh to eat?' To which, by way of Answer, he said, 'The Words that I say unto you, they are Spirit, and they are 'Life.' For if our Saviour had thought at all like this Author, and had intended to be understood according to the common Rules of speaking, he would have spoken only common Language; and upon their not understanding what he said, he must have directed them to the right Way, and have said, *Consider my Words only according to the common Rules of* speaking, and then you will know *all* that is to be known by them.

Least of all could he have said, to help their understanding of them in a common Way, 'The Words that I speak unto you, 'they are Spirit, and they are Life;' for surely such a Way of speaking could not be a directing them to the common Rules of speaking amongst Men. For if he had intended to show them in the strongest Manner, how much what he said was different from, and superior to all the *common Meaning* of human Words; how could he have done this in a higher Degree, than by saying as he did, 'The Words that I speak unto you, they are Spirit, 'and they are Life.'

Now, the Question put by his Disciples, 'How can this Man 'give us his Flesh to eat?' comes as *naturally* in the Case of the Sacrament, where we are to eat his Body, and drink his Blood, as in the forementioned Place of St. *John;* and as there is the same Foundation for the same Question, so there is strictly the same Foundation for the same Answer, *viz.*, 'The Words that I 'speak unto you, they are Spirit, and they are Life.'

And it is *absolutely* impossible for anyone to show, that the Words of the Institution are not as *truly* to be looked upon as *Spirit* and *Life*, as the other Words about eating his *Flesh*, and *drinking his Blood*. For surely, he that is obliged to own, that the Words in St. *John*, of eating his Flesh, and drinking his Blood, are *Spirit* and Life, cannot have any Proof that the Words in the Sacrament, of eating his Body and drinking his Blood, have *nothing* of that Spirit and Life in them. For if it be asked, Why the Words in St. *John* are Spirit and Life? The one *only* Reason is this, because they speak of eating Christ's *Flesh* and drinking his *Blood*, which is such a *spiritual, living Participation* of the Nature of Christ, or, in Scripture Words, such a *putting on of Christ*, as cannot be understood or obtained by *outward* and *dead* Words. And yet if the Words in the Sacrament must be said, *not* to be Spirit and Life, the *one only* Reason must be this, because they only speak of eating Christ's *Body*, and drinking his Blood.

But surely this is too great an Absurdity for anyone to hold; for it is saying, that the drinking his Blood, when joined with eating his *Body*, is only an *human* Expression, to be understood according to the *common* Rules of speaking; but that the drinking his Blood, when joined with eating his *Flesh*, is so *great* a *Mystery*, so above our *common Ways* of conceiving, that the Words expressing it, are said to be *Spirit* and *Life*.

But now if the Case be thus, if the Words in the Sacrament must be allowed to be *Spirit* and *Life*, for the same Reason that the Words in St. *John* are said to be Spirit and Life; then there is an End of this Author's poor Contrivance to enter into the whole Truth contained in the Sacrament, by only considering the Words according to the *common Rules* of speaking. It is a Contrivance as *unfit* for the Purpose, as *weakly* and improperly thought of, as an Iron Key to open the Kingdom of Heaven.

Again, If a Person hearing the Words of our Saviour, as recorded in St. *John*, had said to him, There is no more *Spirit* and *Life* in your Words than in the Words of anyone else, and they can mean *no more* than our Words according to the *common Rules* of speaking, such a Person might have been reckoned amongst those that blasphemed the Son of God.

Now if this Author will say the same thing concerning the Words of the Institution, of eating his Body and drinking his Blood, that they are no more *Spirit* and *Life*, than the Words of Men speaking of *human* things, and that nothing more is to be understood in them and by them, than according to the *common* Rules of speaking; I desire to know, how this could be a lesser Degree of Blasphemy, or a smaller Offence against the Son of God, than in the former Case? Or why it was not as *right* and *justifiable* for a Person to say, there was no *Spirit* and *Life* in the Words of our Saviour, speaking of eating his *Flesh* and drinking his Blood, as to say, there is no Spirit and Life in his Words, speaking in the Sacrament of eating his *Body* and drinking his Blood?

Lastly, Either therefore this Author must say with those that blaspheme the Son of God, that the Words of the Institution are not the Words of him, whose Words were *Spirit* and *Life*, or he must give up his only Method of understanding the true Meaning of them. For if they are *Spirit* and *Life*, then to seek for the Sense of such Words in the common Forms of speaking, is truly to seek the *Living* amongst the Dead.

From what has been said of the Words of the Institution, of their not being understood by the Apostles, of the Impossibility of their being understood according to the Sound of the Words in the common Ways of speaking; of the Impossibility of their being understood, till the great Doctrines and Articles of the Christian Faith were first known, and so became the plain and visible Explication of them; from these things we may sufficiently see the Falseness of this Author's *chief Propositions* concerning the Sacrament.

These *Propositions* are printed in a pompous Manner, with great Show of Significancy, as so many Pillars of Truth. The four first are the chief; if therefore they are removed, the others must go with them.

I shall begin with the fourth Proposition, because it is the chief; both those that are before, and those that follow it, depend entirely upon the Truth of it; and yet it has already appeared, and shall be made still more apparent, that there is not the least glimpse of Truth in it.

Speaking of our Saviour's instituting the Sacrament, he says as follows.

Proposition IV. 'It cannot be doubted, that he himself 'sufficiently declared to his first and immediate Followers, the 'whole of what he designed should be understood by it, or im-'plied in it.'

And yet it has been fully shown to be out of all doubt, by a Variety of Arguments, that the first Followers of Christ, neither *did*, nor *possibly* could understand the *whole Nature* of the Sacrament from the Words of the Institution; which is all that our Saviour himself declared to them about it, and also all that this Author appeals to, as a Proof of his having *sufficiently* declared the whole Matter to them.

Further, what is asserted in this Proposition, is as directly contrary to *Truth, Scripture, Fact*, and our Saviour's own *Declarations;* as if it had been asserted, that our Saviour did that *sufficiently* himself, which he declared he had *not* done sufficiently; and also *should* not be done, till after his leaving the World. For at the time that he was about to depart from them, he expressly says unto them, ' I have yet many things to ' say unto you, but ye cannot bear them now. Howbeit, when ' he the Spirit of Truth is come, he shall guide you into all ' Truth.'

From this Declaration of our Saviour, as well as from plain Facts recorded in the History of the Apostles, it is out of all doubt, that he left the Apostles in *great Ignorance* of the Christian Religion, and that it was not his Intention to deliver them out of this Ignorance by his *own personal* Instruction of them; but that they were to *continue* in this Ignorance till further *Revelations*, new Light, and *certain Fact*s which were about to happen, should open to them a clear and full View of the Nature of the Christian Religion.

For first, *here are many things* that they were yet to be taught, which they *then* had not been taught, and of which they were then to continue ignorant; therefore it is plain, that they could not *sufficiently* know *all* that they were to know, or *all* that our Saviour *designed* they should know of any *Article* or *Institution* of the Christian Religion; that is, they were so far from knowing the *whole Nature* and End of the Sacrament, that they knew the whole Nature of *nothing* else in the Christian Religion, but knew everything that they did know, in the most *imperfect Manner*. For surely, if *many things* relating to the Christian

Salvation were yet to be kept secret from them, the Christian Salvation was imperfectly made known unto them; and therefore they could only have been taught *in Part*, and had only seen as it were some first Sketches, or beginning Lines of what they were afterwards to see in its true Fulness.

And that *these many things*, of which they were kept thus ignorant, were many things of the *greatest Importance* and Signification to the right Knowledge of the Christian Salvation, is evident from the Reason given by our Saviour, why they were not then taught by him, *viz.*, 'But ye cannot bear them now.' For surely, if those *many things* were then not taught them, for this reason, *because they were not able to bear them then*; they must have been things of the *greatest* Importance, and most *uncommon* in their Nature; such things as were the *hardest* to be comprehended, the most *difficult* to be believed, and the most *contrary* to the common Conceptions of Men, and consequently such as were most necessary and essential to a right Knowledge of the Christian Salvation.

From this also it appears, how low a State of Knowledge the Apostles were in at the time of the Institution of the Sacrament, since they were not only ignorant of so *many things* of the greatest Importance to be known, but were in a State so *contrary* to this Knowledge, so full of Dispositions *contrary* to it, that they were then *incapable* of being taught it.

And though all this be declared by our Saviour himself, at the *End* of all his Instructions, when he was upon the *Point* of going from them; yet this Author, in *direct* and *full* Contradiction to *Scripture Facts*, and this express *Declaration* of our Saviour, says, 'It cannot be doubted, that he sufficiently declared ' to his Disciples the whole of what he designed should be under-' stood by it.'

Whereas, the contrary to this is as plainly declared by our Saviour himself, as if he had said in express Words, I have instituted a Sacrament to be observed by you hereafter; but *what* is to be understood by it, and implied in it, can *only* be known by you now, in that *poor, low,* and *ignorant* Manner, in which you know other things at present concerning me. But when the *many things* which ye now cannot *bear* to be taught, shall by my *Death, Resurrection,* and *Ascension,* and the *coming* of the Holy Ghost, be made truly intelligible to you, and become the real Light of your Minds, then shall ye clearly see and know the whole of that which I designed to be understood by, and implied in this Sacrament of my Body and Blood.

For what our Saviour has said concerning the *Imperfection* of their Knowledge then, and their *Unfitness* to be instructed further, and of their *Necessity* of being taught in *another* Manner, is as plain a Proof of this, as if it had in express Words been applied to the Sacrament.

For though it is too much for anyone to pretend to say exactly *what* or how *many* these Things were, that they were then not in a Condition and Capacity to understand; yet this may with great Assurance be affirmed, that the Doctrines concerning Christ's *Death*, the *Nature, Necessity*, and *Merits* of his Sacrifice and Atonement for the Sins of the World, the *Possibility* and *Necessity* of eating his Flesh, and drinking his Blood, were certainly amongst those many things; and therefore this Holy Sacrament, which hath its Foundation in this *Atonement for Sins*, and is itself instituted for the *eating his Flesh, and drinking his Blood* must of all necessity be amongst *those many things*, of which they were then greatly ignorant, because they were not in a Condition to receive a *right* and *full* Knowledge of them. Therefore there is the fullest Proof that can be desired, that our Saviour *did* not, and could not intend sufficiently to declare to them the whole of what he intended should be understood and implied in the Sacrament of his Body and Blood.

And for this reason also He saith unto them, ' It is expedient ' for you that I go away; for if I go not away, the Comforter ' will not come. But if I depart, I will send him unto you.' Again, ' These things have I said, being yet present with you; ' but the Comforter, which is the Holy Ghost, whom the Father ' will send in my Name, He shall teach you all things, and ' bring all things to your Remembrance, whatsoever I have said ' unto you.'

As if he had said, ' It is expedient for you that I go away, ' because so long as I thus stay with you in the Flesh, ye cannot ' know, nor believe, nor enter into the true Nature, End, Merits ' and Effects of my Death, Resurrection and Ascension; neither ' can the Holy Ghost come upon you *in my Name*, till my ' Kingdom is thus set up, and these things are accomplished in ' me. Therefore *these things I have said*, being yet *present with* ' *you;* that is, I have spoken *thus far* of these things in a way ' suited to your present State; not that they should be the ' Matter of your *present* Knowledge, whilst you know nothing ' *rightly*, nor apply anything that I say, to its *proper Object;* but ' I have said these things to you, that they may be laid up in ' your Minds, then and then only to be truly *understood*, rightly ' *remembered* in their proper Place, and duly applied to their ' *proper* Objects, when the Holy Ghost shall come in my Name, ' that is, upon the Foundation of my Death, Resurrection and

'Ascension, and shall teach you all things, and bring all 'things to your Remembrance, whatsoever I have said unto 'you.'

From all these things it appears sufficiently, that this Author's fourth and fundamental Proposition is absolutely false, and grossly contradictory to *Scripture*, *Facts*, and the express *Declaration* of our Saviour; and that our Saviour himself, in his own Person, before he left the World, did not, could not intend *sufficiently to declare* to his Disciples *the whole of what he intended should be understood by, and implied in the Sacrament*.

And here I must observe to you, that the Confutation of this fourth Proposition, is not to be considered as the Discovery of a *single Error* in this Author, but as a full Detection of the *general* Falseness, and erroneous Procedure of his whole Book; for everything, and every other Proposition of any moment, throughout his whole Book, is founded upon the supposed Truth of this fourth Proposition. He cannot take *one Step*, in the way he is in, without it. He has not an Argument but what is built upon it. And all his Treatise, from the Beginning to the End, is as idle and wandering as a sick Man's Dream, unless you grant him these two bulky Errors; 1*st*, That our Saviour himself, in the Words of the Institution, *sufficiently declared to his Disciples the whole of what he intended should be understood by, and implied in the Sacrament*. 2*dly*, That the only Method of understanding the *whole* of what he so sufficiently declared to them, is to interpret the same bare Words of the Institution, according to the common Rules of speaking.

But as both these Positions have, as I think, been already shown to be *gross Errors*, directly contrary to *Reason*, *Sense*, *Scripture*, *Facts*, and the express Declaration of our Saviour himself, so the whole of his Treatise is already in the fullest Manner confuted.

But I shall now proceed to consider some poor, little Pretences of Argument, which this Author brings in Support of this false Proposition. Which are as follow: ' For this being,' says he, ' a ' Positive Institution, depending entirely upon his Will; and not ' designed to contain anything in it, but what he himself should ' please to affix to it, it must follow, that he declared his Mind ' about it, fully and plainly,' p. 4.

This is his whole Proof, that our Saviour himself sufficiently taught his Disciples the *whole Nature* and Meaning of the Sacrament, and that they *wholly* understood it.

The thing that he would here speak to, is very improperly expressed, and ought to have proceeded thus: ' This being a

'positive Institution, by his Will and Pleasure introduced into a
'Religion, which contains the Means and Method of the Salva-
'tion of Mankind by himself the Institutor, cannot be designed
'by him to be any ways understood, or to have any other Nature,
'Meaning, and End in it, than such as is truly and fully accord-
'ing to the Doctrines of that Religion into which he has intro-
'duced it, and more especially according to that Part of Religion
'in which he has placed it.'

Whereas instead of this, this Author poorly says, *it was not designed to contain anything in it, but what he should please to affix to it.* For he put nothing to be contained in it, he affixed nothing to it, but only placed it in the *Heart*, or midst of a Religion; which Religion, as soon as it was truly known by his Disciples, would sufficiently declare and explain to them the whole Nature and End of this positive Institution. In consequence of what he had just now erroneously said, he proceeds thus: 'Because otherwise he must be supposed to institute a
'Duty, of which none could have any Notion without his
'Institution; and at the same time not to instruct his Followers
'sufficiently what that Duty was to be.' Whereas instead of this, it ought to have been expressed thus: 'Because otherwise, if he
'had not so instituted this Sacrament, as to have its Nature,
'End, and Effects explained and determined by that Religion,
'and chiefly by that Part of Religion, in which it was placed, it
'could never have appeared to any of his Followers, what they
'were to do in it, or that there was any Reason in its Institution,
'or any Benefit to be had from the Observance of it.'

As for instance; If the *Religion*, of which the Sacrament is a *Part*, did not teach us how his *Body is given* and his *Blood shed for us*, if it did not teach us something concerning the *eating his Flesh, and drinking his Blood*, what could the mentioning of these *two strange* things in the Sacrament signify to us, or how could we have any Notion of what was to be done or acknowledged by the Sacrament? For if the Sacrament speaks of *anything* that the Religion in which it is placed speaks *nothing of;* if it represents *anything* that that Religion *has not* to be represented, then it can signify no more in that Religion after its Institution, than it did before. But if to be a *Part* of that Religion in which it is appointed, it must speak the *Language* of that Religion; if the things that it represents, must be the *Things* of that Religion, then it plainly follows, 1*st*, That our Saviour himself in Person, at the Time, and by the Words of the Institution, *did not, could not fully and plainly declare* the whole Nature of the Sacrament; because the Language which it spoke, and the Things that it represented, were the Language and Things of a Religion, which was not, and could not then be known by his Disciples. 2*dly*, It follows also, that our Saviour had *fully* and *sufficiently* provided for their right Knowledge of this Sacrament, because it was so *worded* and so *placed* in their Religion, that the first true Knowledge of their Religion would become the full and clear Explication of it.

This Sacrament was instituted before the Religion, of which it was to be a Part, was known; is it therefore any wonder in itself, or any Matter of Accusation of our Saviour, that when he appointed this Institution, he left it to be *then* only understood, *when* the Religion, of which it was to be a Part, should be known? And if he left his Disciples in the *same* Ignorance of the Sacrament, as of the *Nature, Merits*, and *End* of his Death, Resurrection and Ascension, is there any more to find fault with in the one, than in the other?

And this Author might with the same show of Argument prove, that he did declare unto them, fully and plainly, the *whole Nature, Merits*, and *End* of his Death. For it may as well be said of that, as of the Sacrament, that he must have *fully and plainly declared his Mind about it;* otherwise he must be supposed to have instructed them of a Matter of Faith, which, without his Instruction, they could have no Notion of, and at the same time not to instruct them fully about it.

Now if anything may be said in defence of what our Saviour did to his Disciples with regard to that imperfect State in which he left them, as to the Knowledge of the *Nature, Merits*, and *End* of his Death; if he might justly leave the *true* and *full* Knowledge of it, to its only proper *Time*, and only proper *Manner* of being fully known; namely, till the Consequences of his Death, till his Resurrection, Ascension, and coming of the Holy Ghost, should prove the *Nature, Power, Merits,* and *End* of it; then the same may and must be said in defence of our Saviour's leaving his Disciples so ignorant of the *Nature, End*, and *Effects* of the Holy Sacrament. It was not because he was *deficient* in instructing them, but because he instructed them with the *greatest Wisdom*; not giving them *verbal* Explications of Things which *could not* so be understood by them, but leaving them to be informed in the one only proper *Time*, and the only proper *Manner;* namely, when by the Knowledge of his Death, Resurrection, and Ascension, and by the coming of the Holy Ghost, they should *truly* and *fully* know the whole of that Religion, of which this Sacrament was appointed to be a Part.

All therefore which this Author saith of the Necessity of their knowing sufficiently at first from the Words of the Institution, the whole Nature of it, because it was a *Positive Institution*, and could have no more in it than he intended should be in it, are mere empty Words; for it is granted on all Sides, that the Institution can be *only* that which Christ intended it should be, and can imply no more than he designed should be implied in it. But the Question is, how we are to know all that he designed should be understood by, and implied in it.

This Author says, this can only be known from the *bare Words* of the Institution considered *in themselves*, according to the *common Rules* of speaking. Therefore, according to this Author, had *Socrates* said the same Things that Christ said, the Institution had been just the same thing as it is; it had had the same Meaning, and there had been neither *more* or *less* in it. This cannot be denied: For if the Words of the Institution are only to be understood according to the *common Meaning* or Sound of Words in common Life; then they must have the same Meaning, and signify neither more or less, whether they be applied to Christ, or *Socrates*.

On the other hand, we say, since Christ appointed this Institution to stand in a *certain Place*, to be a *certain Part*, and to have *Relation* to *certain Doctrines* of a Religion *not* known, when this Institution was appointed; that therefore what Christ meant by it, and would have implied in it, can then *only* be *fully* known, and when that Religion in which it was to have a certain Place, and of which it was to be a certain Part, and to whose Doctrines it was to be related, came to be fully known and understood. In short, that a Christian Institution, ingrafted into the Christian Religion, and connected with its chief Doctrines, could then only be fully known, when the Christian Religion was fully known.

Thus for Instance: Let it be supposed that at the Time of instituting the Sacrament, the Apostles had no other Way of knowing what was meant by it, but by considering the Words in *themselves*, according to the *common Sound* of the Words. Yet, if after the *Death*, and *Resurrection*, and *Ascension* of our Saviour, and the coming of the *Holy Ghost*, they *knew* a Religion, which they knew *nothing* of before, and saw this Sacrament to be a *Part* of that Religion; had they not then got a *new* and *sure* Way of understanding what our Saviour meant by it? And had they not this *very new* Means of understanding it from our Saviour himself? Did not he teach them *all* that they were taught by his *Death, Resurrection,* and *Ascension,* and by the coming of the *Holy Ghost?* And was not that which he thus taught them in this manner, to be as *sacred* with them, and as much to be *adhered* to, as when he only taught them the *Words, outward Form,* and *Matter* of the Sacrament? And if he thus led them into the Possession and Knowledge of every *Truth* and

Doctrine upon which this Sacrament was founded, and to which it was related ; is he not *still* the Teacher of the Sacrament, as well as he was the Teacher of it in the Words of the Institution ?

Vainly therefore doth this Author thus further argue, that seeing 'no one can be a Judge, but the Institutor himself, of what 'he designed should be contained in it ; therefore, supposing him 'not to have spoken his Mind plainly about it, it is impossible 'that any other Person should make up the Defect,' p. 5.

Vainly, I say, is all this argued, because here is no Defect charged upon the Words of the Institution, nor any *other Person* appointed or appealed to, to *make up* the Defect. The Words of the Institution are allowed to be *full* and *plain*, as to all that is *positive* in this Institution, both as to the *Matter* and *Form* of the Sacrament : They were as plain at the *first* as they are now, or ever can be. But that Part which is *not* positive in this Institution, which is the *greatest* and *chiefest* Part of it, namely, the *Truths* signified and represented, and acknowledged by the outward *Form* and *Matter* of the Sacrament ; as the *Body of Christ given, and his Blood shed* for the Sins of the World, *and the Eating his Flesh and drinking his Blood* were not then, are not *now*, nor ever *can* be truly and rightly known from the Plainness of the Words of the Institution alone. Yet here is not the *smallest Defect* either in the Institutor or the Institution. For since the Institution was not an independent thing, made for itself, and on its *own* Account, nor to be practised at the *Time* it was appointed ; it was no *Defect* in it, that it did not explain itself, or was not then known, when it was not to be practised. And seeing the Institution was appointed for the *Sake* of a Religion, that then was *not*, but soon should *be*, it could be no *Defect* in the Institutor, that it was not known *sooner* than it was wanted, or *till* the Time came, that everything else that was to be practised with it, or for the Sake of it, were fully and truly known.

It was no Defect in our Saviour as a Teacher of Religion, that his Religion was not known nor understood, till after his *Ascension* into Heaven, and the *Coming* of the Holy Ghost ; because his Ascension, and the coming of the Holy Ghost, were to be fundamental *Articles* and principal *Parts* of his Religion.

So also it was no Defect in him, as an Institutor of the Sacrament, that the true Nature and End of it was not known, when he first instituted it, or from the bare Words of the Institution ; or that it was not to be known, till such things as were to be the *principal Parts of it* came to be known.

And as that which was *further* and *fully* known of the Christian Religion, after our Saviour's Death, was not by anyone's *making up the Defect* of his teaching, but was *solely* done by his *own Power*, and in his *own Name;* so all that which was further and fully known of the Sacrament after the Death of Christ, was not by anyone's *making* up the Defect of his Institution, but was his *own further* teaching them by his *Death, Resurrection,* and *Ascension,* and by the coming of the *Holy Ghost.* For as he thus by his own Power set up his own Kingdom, so all that which was plainly shown and declared by his Kingdom, was strictly shown and declared by himself.

And as it necessarily followed, that they must know more of Christ as their *Saviour,* and the *Manner* of their Salvation, after his Death, Resurrection, and Ascension, and Mission of the Holy Ghost, than they did before; so also it necessarily follows, that they must have exactly the *same Increase* of Knowledge at that Time, concerning the Nature of the Sacrament, which they had concerning their Saviour; because the Sacrament is expressly appointed to *do that* which it does, in *Remembrance* and *Acknowledgment* of that Saviour *so* made known. And therefore the more they knew of him as their Saviour, the more they must know of that which was to be remembered and acknowledged of him in the Holy Sacrament.

All therefore which this Author says, of the *making up the Defect*, if Christ did not at first make the *whole* of the Institution plain, is of no Significancy; for what they further knew rightly of it, when they knew their Religion, and saw *how* and in what *manner* it was a Part of it; all this further true and real Knowledge of it, came as *plainly* and *undeniably* from him, as the Words of the Institution did; and what they were taught by his Death and Resurrection, and the Consequences of them, was as truly from him, as what they were taught by his *Birth* and *Incarnation*, and miraculous Conversation with them.

Having thus despatched this Author's Fourth and chiefest Proposition, and his Proof of it; I shall now go back to his First, which stands thus.

Proposition I. 'The partaking of the Lord's Supper, is not a 'Duty of itself, or a Duty apparent to us from the Nature of the 'thing; but a Duty made such to Christians, by the positive 'Institution of Jesus Christ,' p. 2.

There is a great deal of Error and Deceit proposed to the Reader in this Proposition. For it is to make him believe, that the *Nature* and *End* of the Sacrament is *wholly positive*, and that all that we are to mean, and intend, and do by it, is *something* that we are only obliged to do by virtue of the *Institution:* All which is absolutely false.

For the Institution, as to its *Nature* and *End*, is so far from being *wholly positive*, that its Nature and End hath *nothing positive* in it. And all that which it is our Duty to *intend* and do by the Sacrament, is to be intended and done for *itself*, on its *own Account ;* and that which is positive in the Sacrament, is only as a *Means*, or *Mark*, or *Sign* of our doing it. That which is *positive* in this Institution, and not to be done but because of the *Will* of the Institutor, is something entirely *distinct*, and *different* from the Nature, End and Intent of the Institution. And that in which the *whole Reason, Meaning, End and Intent* of this Institution essentially consists ; is something that is to be done for *itself*, and does not take its Reason of being done from the Institution.

Now if all that is to be *done*, *implied* and *intended* by our celebrating the Lord's Supper, was, and is *absolutely* necessary to be done, though the Way of doing it by the Sacrament had never been instituted ; then the *Meaning, End* and *Intent* of the Sacrament cannot be *positive ;* and if our Obligation to do *all* that is contained in this Meaning and Intent of the Sacrament, is an Obligation arising from the Thing itself, then this is not a *positive Duty*.

Now the Meaning, End and Intent of the Sacrament, is to *remember*, *acknowledge* and *profess* Christ to *be* our Saviour, and the *Manner* in which he is our Saviour ; but all this is to be done on its *own Account*, from the Nature of the Thing itself, and must have been done, though the Sacrament had not been instituted ; therefore the *Meaning*, End and Intent of the Sacrament has nothing *positive* in it, and contains only our *natural Duty* to Christ, arising from the Relation between him and us. For to acknowledge and profess Christ to be our *Saviour*, and in all the Respects in which he is our Saviour, is no more a *positive* Duty, than it is a *positive* Duty to acknowledge and profess the Goodness of God towards us; but is a Duty of itself, of the same Nature, and of the same Obligation, as *Faith* and *Love*, and Adoration of our Creator and Redeemer are.

But to show still more plainly, that the Nature, End and Intent of the Sacrament, is not positive, but entirely distinct and different from that which is positive in the Sacrament; take the following Instance.

Let it be supposed, that God by a positive Command enjoined the People of one Age to build an *Altar* for his *Honour* and *Worship ;* the People of another Age to set up a *Tabernacle*, and a third to build a *Temple* for the same End and Intent ; namely, for his *Honour* and *Worship*.

Now here are three positive *Appointments*, and three positive *Duties ;* and all that is positive in the one, is very different from that which is positive in the other; yet the *Meaning*, *End* and *Intent* of all three is the *same*, namely, the *Honour* and *Worship* of God; therefore the Meaning, End and Intent of positive Appointments, is something not positive, but *entirely different* and distinct from that which is the positive Part of it.

Now this is exactly the Case of the Sacrament: Bread and Wine appointed to be used in *acknowledgment* of Jesus Christ as our Saviour, is as the *Altar* or *Tabernacle*, appointed to be built for the *Honour* and *Worship* of God. And as it was purely depending upon the Will of God, whether it should be an *Altar* or a *Tabernacle*, or a *Temple*, that should be built for his Honour and Worship; so it was solely depending upon the Will of Jesus Christ, whether it should be *Bread* and *Wine*, or any other thing else that was to be used in Remembrance and Acknowledgment of him. And as the Honour and Worship of God, which was the sole *Meaning*, *End* and *Intent* of building either *Altar* or *Tabernacle*, was a natural Duty, founded in the *Relation* between God and *his* Creatures, and was something that was to be done, though no Altar or Tabernacle had ever been built; so the Remembrance and Acknowledgment of Jesus Christ as our Saviour, which is the *End* and *Intent* of our using Bread and Wine in the Sacrament, was a *natural* Duty, founded in the Relation between Christ and us, and was something that was to be done for itself, though the Use of Bread and Wine in the Sacrament had never been appointed. It is therefore an unpardonable Error in this Author, to represent the Sacrament, as containing nothing in its *Meaning*, *End* and *Intent*, that was a Duty *itself*, or to be done upon its *own Account;* but that everything implied by it, was only a Duty by virtue of the Institution. For the Reverse of all this is the very Truth; for *all* that is *meant, implied* and intended by the Sacrament, is as much our Duty to do on its own Account, as it is our Duty to *believe* in God; and the positive Part, the Use of Bread and Wine in this Sacrament, is only an *appointed Way* of our expressing, acknowledging and doing that, which it was *our Duty* to express, acknowledge and do, though we had never been taught to use Bread and Wine for that End.

And indeed this is the Case of all positive Appointments and Institutions of Revealed Religion; the *Meaning*, *End* and *Intent* of them, was always something *entirely different* from that which was *positive* in them; for the same Reason, that an *Idea* or *Sentiment* is entirely different from that *English* or *Latin* Word by which you are to express it, or to put yourself, or another Person in mind of it. For the *positive* Part of an Institution has much of the Nature of *Language* in it, and is to express and teach something by *Symbols* and *outward* Things, better than it could be expressed or taught by mere Words ; but that which is *meant, implied,* and *intended* by the Symbol, is as different from it in its *whole* Nature, as the *Idea* of *Sentiment* meant and intended by an *English* or *Latin* Word, is different from it in its whole Nature. To look therefore, as this Author doth, for the *whole Nature, End and Intent* of the Sacrament, in the *positive Part* of this Institution, is as absurd, as to look for the true Knowledge of God and the Divine Attributes from the *English* Word, *God*. For the Things meant and intended by the Sacrament, are as entirely and wholly different from that Use of Bread and Wine by which they are expressed, as the Divine Nature is entirely and wholly different from that *English* or *Latin* Word, which is to express or remind us of that Divine Nature.

Great Part of the *Jewish* Religion consisted in positive Appointments and Institutions ; but the *Meaning, End and Intent* of them was entirely of another Nature, and consisted of such things as were Duties of themselves, and of the highest Necessity to be done. For the End and Intent of their Institutions were either to keep up and exercise their *Faith* and *Hope* of a Redeemer, or to set forth the *Characters* and Marks by which they should know him, or to represent to them the *Nature* and *Manner* of their expected Redemption, or to teach them some *inward dying* unto Sin, and inward living unto God, or some other Truth, *Doctrine* or *Practice*, that was to be acknowledged and done for itself, though no positive Institution had ever been made on its Account. And the one only Reason why the greatest Part of the *Jews* lived in such a *total* Ignorance of their Religion, was, because they had learned it in the *same Manner* as this Author has learned Christianity ; they would *see nothing* in their Institutions but what a *Heathen* might as well have seen, nothing but what could be seen in the *Outside* of them ; just as this Author will see no more in the Sacrament, than what a *Heathen* that knows only the Words of the Institution may see in it. They were too learned and rational to allow of any Mysteries at the Bottom of their *Services*, as this Author is too sober a Critic to allow of any Mystery in the Institution of the Sacrament. And as they, through a blind Zeal for the *Letter*, and to show their Fidelity to them, lost all that which was truly *meant* and *intended* by them; so this Author, full of the same Zeal for the *Letter* and *Plainness* of this Christian Institution, is doing all that he can to make us lose all that is truly meant and intended by it.

The Sacrifices of the *Jews* were at the bottom, only so many *Representations* and *Applications* of that great Sacrifice for the

Sins of the World, first promised to all Mankind, in these Words: ' The Seed of the Woman shall bruise the Serpent's Head ;' but because this was not *expressly* said in the Institution of any of their Sacrifices, *this is done in consequence of that first Promise*, or this is to show you *how and in what manner* you are to seek and find your Redeemer, because the Letter was not thus adapted to these carnal Men, they contented themselves with the *Religion of slaying Beasts*. Just as this Author is only a *bare Eater* of Bread and Wine in the Sacrament, because it is not there *expressly said*, what great Mysteries of Christ as our Saviour are represented by it. The *Jews* had many Passages in their Scriptures that called them to the *Spirituality* of their Religion, and showed them the inward *Meaning, Spirit* and *Intent* of all their Institutions ; but because it was not expressly said, *This is* an Explication of *such an Ordinance*, or this that is *here* said, relates to the true Meaning and Intent of *such an Institution*, all these Passages of Scripture were neglected by them, and not applied to their proper Objects. It is just thus with this Author; the New Testament abounds with Passages that prove, teach and explain the true *Meaning, End* and *Intent* of the Holy Sacrament; but because those Passages don't expressly say, *This is the Proof or Explication* of what is said in the Institution, they are by him overlooked and rejected, as having nothing to do with it. The learned *Pharisee*, in order to know the Meaning and Intent of *killing a Heifer* in Sacrifice, or of *circumcising* the Flesh, would only look for *such Places* of Scripture, as *appoint* the killing of an Heifer, and the circumcising the Flesh ; just so this Author, to know the true Meaning and Intent of the Institution of the Sacrament, only searches the Scripture in the *same manner*. He seeks only *such Places* as expressly mention the Institution, or repeat the Words of it.

The *Jews* neither expected nor allowed any *Benefits* and Merits of Christ to be obtained by *means* of their Sacrifices ; because such Benefits were not *literally* mentioned in the Institution of their Sacrifices ; just so this Author, neither expects nor allows the *Merits* and *Benefits* of Christ's Passion to be applied to us by the Holy Sacrament, because the Application of such Benefits and Merits is not expressly mentioned in the Words of the Institution. Thus was it that the *Jews* never found their Saviour in the Old Testament ; and thus it is, that this Author has lost him in the New.

And indeed, upon his Principles, it is *impossible* that anyone should ever know anything of the *real* Nature and *Truth* of the *Jewish* or *Christian* Religion. For let anyone but search into the Nature, Meaning and Intent of the *Jewish* Institutions, as this Author doth into the Nature and Intent of the Sacrament; and he must, as I said above, be rendered *stone-blind* to all the Mysteries of the Old Testament as well as of the New.

For as Christ was the *Substance*, the *Heart*, and true *Meaning* of all their Ordinances, though not mentioned *expressly* in the Letter of their *positive* Institutions, they were obliged by this Author's Principles, not to acknowledge him to be in them, and to reject all such Interpretations as led to him; and to allow nothing to be meant by their positive Institutions, but that which the Words of them understood, according to the common Rules of speaking, declared to be in them: Therefore every *Jew* that had this Author's *Principles*, was under a *Necessity* of being stone-blind, or *totally* ignorant of the real Nature and Truth of the *Jewish* Religion.

Again, the Apostle saith, ' He is not a Jew which is one out-'wardly, neither is that Circumcision which is outward in the ' Flesh; but he is a Jew which is one inwardly, and Circumcision ' is that of the Heart, in the Spirit, and not in the Letter.'*

But according to this Author's Principles, you are to maintain, that he *only* is a *Jew*, which is one *outwardly*, and that *only* is Circumcision which is *outward* in the Flesh; for to allow *Judaism* to have anything inwardly more than is in the *outward Letter*, or Circumcision to be anything else than that which is *expressed* in the Words of the Institution, is a thing not lawful to be done upon this Author's Principles. This I think may sufficiently show you the Truth of what I said to you in the Beginning, that if you accept of this Author's Key of Knowledge, for the right understanding the Nature of the Sacrament; you will not only lose all the right Knowledge of the Sacrament, but be rendered a *Blind, Deaf* and *Dead* Reader of all the other most important Doctrines of Scripture. For, according to his Principles, you are to see no more Spirit, Life, or Mystery in any other Sayings of our Saviour, than in that of the Sacrament; and low as he had reduced that, it is full as high and mysterious, and deep in its Meaning, as anything in the whole Nature of the Christian Religion can be allowed to be by this Author.

But to return; There are plainly two distinct and essential Parts of the Sacrament, which constitute its whole Nature. The first is in these Words, ' This is my Body which is given for you, ' this is my Blood which is shed for the Remission of Sins.'

What is here said by our Lord Christ, we are to acknowledge to be true; therefore we are to own and acknowledge this great Truth, that this Bread and Wine are made Symbols and Me-

---

* Rom. ii. 28.

morials of, *viz.*, that his Body is given for us, and his Blood shed for the Remission of Sins; and consequently all that the Scripture teaches concerning the Truth, Reality and Manner in which he is the Sacrifice, Atonement and Satisfaction for our Sins, is in this Sacrament to be of all necessity acknowledged and confessed by us. And we cannot perform this Sacrament according to what it is, unless we see and own all that to be in it, which Christ saw and owned to be in it; unless we present it to him in the same Meaning, as he presented it to his Disciples. For if Christ has declared this *Nature* and *Meaning* to be in it, we cannot perform this Sacrament according to Christ's Declaration, unless we also in our Peformance of it, declare that same *Nature* and *Meaning* to be in it. Therefore the Acknowledgment of Christ's being the Atonement and Satisfaction for our Sins, is an essential and important Part of the Sacrament. If we were to mistake or neglect something in the right Use of Bread and Wine in the Sacrament, such Mistake would only relate to the outward positive Part of this Institution, which has no Obligation upon us but from Divine Appointment; but if we refuse to own and confess Christ to be the *Atonement* and *Satisfaction* for our Sins, we sin against God and the Nature of things, as those Atheists do, who refuse to own that it was the Goodness of God that created them.

Secondly, The other essential, and no less important Part of the Sacrament is, *the eating the Body, and drinking the Blood of Christ.* This is plainly another essential Part of the Sacrament, *entirely distinct* from the other. The one respects Christ, as he is the *Atonement* and Satisfaction for our Sins; the other shows that he is to be owned and received as a *Principle of Life to us.*

The other Words, 'Do this in Remembrance of me,' relate equally to both these Parts, and are only as if our Saviour had said after the Institution; Let this, which I have thus appointed to be done, be *your Acknowledgment* of that Salvation which is received through me, both as I am the *Atonement* and Satisfaction for Sin, and a *Principle of* Life to all that lay hold of me.

You cannot help seeing that all this is plain, easy and natural in this Explication of the Words of the Institution, and that I have used no Art or Force to come at it, and that no one can find any fault with it; but he that is unwilling to own these *two great Truths* of Scripture, that Christ as our Saviour is the *Atonement* and Satisfaction for our Sins, and a *Principle* of Life to us. The short of the Matter is this; the Scriptures are full of Proofs of these two great and fundamental Characters, that he is in one respect the Atonement and Satisfaction for our Sins, and in another, a *Principle* of a new Life to us; if therefore these two essential Characters of our Saviour, which contain all that is said of him as such, are not to be acknowledged by us in the Sacrament; then the Sacrament must be said to be instituted for the Denial of Christ; and the Words, 'Do this in 'Remembrance of me,' must have this Meaning, *Do this in Denial of me:* For if he is not to be remembered, as the Atonement and Satisfaction for Sin, and as a Principle of new Life to us; then he is not to be remembered and acknowledged as he is, and therefore in the strictest Sense is to be *denied*.

Hence it appears, that this Author's *Plain Account* can have no Truth or Reasonableness in it, but upon this Supposition, that Christ Jesus is not a real *Atonement* and *Satisfaction* for our Sins, nor a real *Principle of Life* to us. For if these things were true of Christ as our Saviour, then the Sacrament, which is done in Acknowledgment of him, as such, must also of necessity acknowledge these Truths. Therefore this Author's *Plain Account*, which does not acknowledge these things of Christ, can have no Truth or Reasonableness in it, but upon this Supposition, that these things are not true of Christ.

For if these things were real Doctrines of Scripture, it must follow, that they were to be acknowledged in the Sacrament, even though they were not expressly mentioned or pointed at in the Words of the Institution. For since the Sacrament is to be done in Remembrance and Acknowledgment of Christ, it necessarily follows, that that which the Scriptures teach us concerning the Nature and Character of Christ, is to be remembered and acknowledged of him *in* and *by* the Sacrament, because the Sacrament is appointed for that End. And therefore, since this Author will not allow our Saviour to be thus acknowledged in the Sacrament, he must deny that he is thus described in Scripture.

Now deny either of these Characters of our Saviour, and you deny all the Christian Religion; the Words, *Saviour, Salvation, Redemption,* and such like, have no proper *Meaning, Truth* or *Reality* in them.

But if you allow these Characters of our Saviour, that he really is, what he said he was, and what all the Scriptures affirm of him; namely, the *Atonement* for Sins, and a *Principle* of a new Life to us; then the Sacrament, which is the Representation and Acknowledgment of these two great Truths, has all that is great, mysterious, and adorable in the Christian Religion, centred in it. And had this Author believed these two great Doctrines concerning our Saviour, it had been as impossible for him to have his present poor Notion of the Sacrament, as it was impossible for St. *John*, who knew that the *Word was God*, and that the same *Word was made Flesh*, to have had so poor a Notion of Jesus Christ, as those *Jews* had, who took him to be only the Carpenter's Son.

Hence also it plainly appears, that seeing these two great Truths are the essential Parts of the Sacrament, and that it is appointed to *express* our *Faith* of them ; that the *Nature* and *End* of the Sacrament is not, as this Author teaches, to turn an *Act* of our Memory upon Christ ; but that it is to exercise our *Faith* in Christ, and to be our *open* Profession of these *two great Truths ;* and also that our Faith is thereby exercised in this *twofold* Manner ; 1*st*, In believing Christ to be the *true Atonement* for our Sins, and a real Principle of Life to us : 2*dly*, In believing that this Atonement, and his being a Principle of Life to us, is made *certain* and *confirmed* to us, by taking the Bread and Wine to be the true Significations of them.

For when our Saviour says, *Do this*, it is the same thing as if he had said, Do these *two Things* appointed in the Sacrament, as your *Act of Faith*, that I am both the Atonement for your Sins, and a *Principle* of Life to you. Don't say bare and empty outward Words, when you say, ' This is my Body which is given ' for you, and this my Blood which is shed for the Remission of ' Sins ;' but let *Faith* say them, and acknowledge the Truth of them : When you eat *my Body*, and drink *my Blood*, don't let your Mouth *only* eat, or perform the *outward* Action ; but let *Faith*, which is the *true Mouth* of the inward Man, believe that it *really* partakes of me, and that I enter in by *Faith;* and when you thus by Faith perform these *two essential* Parts of the Sacrament, then, and then only may what you do be said to be done in *Remembrance of me*, and of what I am to you. For nothing *remembers* me but *Faith*, nothing *acknowledges* me but Faith, nothing *finds* me, nothing *knows* me but Faith.

I appeal to the most ordinary Understanding for the Truth of all this ; for it is so plain and visible, that nothing but *Art* or *Prejudice* can avoid it. For since our Saviour says, This is *my Body* which is *given for you*, this is *my Blood* which is shed for the Remission of Sins, what he says, that we are to say ; and what we say, that we are to believe ; and therefore what we are here to do, is an *Act* or *Exercise* of *Faith*. And since in these Words he says *two* Things, the one, that he is the *Atonement* for our Sins ; the other, that this Bread and this Wine are the *Signification* or Application of that Atonement, or that which we are to take for it ; therefore we in *doing this*, are by Faith to say and believe these *two Things ;* and therefore all that we here *do*, is *Faith*, and Faith manifested in this *twofold* manner.

Again, seeing our Saviour commands us to *eat* his Body, and *drink* his Blood, we are to *say* and *believe*, that his Body and Blood are there *signified* and *exhibited* to us; and that his Body and Blood may be *eaten* and *drank*, as a *Principle of Life* to us; and therefore Faith is *all*, or all is Faith in this other essential Part of the Sacrament; and we cannot possibly *do that* which our Saviour commands us to do, unless it be done by *Faith*.

But now this Author, in his *Plain Account*, takes no more notice of these *two great essential* Parts of the Sacrament, than if there was not *one Word* about them: And yet they are *so much* there, that in the whole Institution, there is not a Word about anything else. For the Words, 'Do this in Remembrance of me,' are as entirely distinct from the Institution, as a Command to do a thing, is distinct from the thing that is to be done. They enter no more into the Nature of the Institution, nor any more teach us *what* is to be done in it, than if Christ had only said, ' Do this as your Duty to me.' Had he said thus, it would easily have been seen, that the Institution must be entirely distinct from such a Command to observe it. And yet his saying, 'Do 'this in Remembrance of me,' has neither more nor less in it, than if he had said, ' Do this as your Duty to me.'

The plain Truth is this; The Institution consists of those two essential Parts just mentioned; that is, in *offering, presenting*, and *pleading* before God, by *Faith*, the Atonement of Christ's Body and Blood, and in *owning* him to be a Principle of Life to us, by our *eating* his Body and Blood: This is the entire, whole Institution. The words, 'Do this in Remembrance of me,' are only the *Command* to observe the Institution. *Do this*, is a Command to *do all* that had been mentioned in the Institution; and the Words, *in Remembrance of me*, don't show *what* the Institution is, or what is to be *done* in it, but only the Reason, why such an Institution, whatever it is, was commanded to be observed.

The Words therefore, in *Remembrance of me*, are not a Part of the *Institution*, but are only a Part of the *Command* to observe the Institution, and only show the Reason why such an Institution is commanded to be observed.

And yet this Poor Man (for so I must call one so miserably insensible of the Greatness of the Subject he is upon) can find nothing in the Institution, but, first, *Bread* and *Wine*, not placed and offered before God, as first *signifying* and *pleading* the *Atonement* of his Son's Body and Blood, and then *eaten* and *drank* in *Signification* of having our Life from him: But Bread and Wine *set* upon a *Table*, to put the People, that see it, in *mind*, that by and by they are to exercise an *Act of the Memory*. And then, secondly, this same Bread and Wine afterwards brought to everyone in particular, not for them to know, or believe that they are receiving anything of Christ, or partaking of anything from him; but only to let them know, that the *very instant* they take the Bread and Wine into their Mouth, is the *very time* for them *actually* to excite that *Act of the Memory*, for the exciting of which, Bread and Wine had been before *set* upon a Table.

This is this Author's *Great Point* in the Observance of the Sacrament, and what he calls the *peculiar* Nature of this Duty. And this he teaches, not because the *Church*, or *Saint*, or *Father* of any Age since Christ, has taught him so; but because being a serious Man, and of great *Exactness* in weighing of *Words*, he has found out, that the Words, *in Remembrance of me*, which are only a Part of the *Command* to observe the Institution, are the *whole* of the Institution itself; and that therefore nothing is to be admitted into it but an *Act of the Memory*, and Bread and Wine taken into the Mouth to *excite that Act of the Memory;* because *Remembrance* which is the whole of this Duty, neither is nor can be anything else but an *Act of the Memory*.

Thus by making first the Words, *in Remembrance of me*, the whole Essence of the Institution, when they are as distinct from it, as they are from these Words, 'This is my Body which is given for you;' and teach us only the reason why we are commanded to do that which is to be done in the Institution :

And then, 2*dly*, By limiting the Word *Remembrance*, and allowing nothing to be meant by it, but an *Act of the Memory :* By the help of these two equally *false* and *shameful* Steps, this Author has stripped the Institution of every Mystery of our Salvation, which the Words of Christ show to be in it, and which every Christian that has any *true Faith*, though but as a *Grain* of Mustard Seed, is sure of finding in it.

God, we know, made a certain great Promise to *Abraham;* now let it be supposed, that God, after the making of this Promise to him, had enjoined him to come frequently to that Place where the Promise was made to him *in Remembrance of it:* Could it be supposed, that the Remembrance here spoken of, could signify anything else, but an Exercise of his *Faith* in that Promise; and as an outward *Sign* of his declaring to God his full Belief of it? Or could anything be more extravagant, than to say that God here only required of *Abraham* an *Act of his Memory*, because the word Remembrance relates only to the Memory?

Now this is strictly the Case of the Sacrament. In the Institution our Saviour has said, 'This is my Body and Blood, which 'is given and shed for you, for the Remission of Sins;' in the

Institution he has bidden us to eat *his Body*, and drink *his Blood*. All this is proposed to our *Faith*, just as the Promise was proposed to *Abraham's* Faith. When therefore he bids us to *do* this, that is, do these two things in *Remembrance* of him ; can it be supposed, that the *Remembrance* of him can be anything else but an Act of Faith in him, believing and owning all that concerning him, which we *say* and *do* in and by the Sacrament ? For nothing but Faith can *see*, or *hear*, or *understand*, or *do* that which is to be done in the Sacrament : Nothing but Faith can say, that this his Body and Blood are the Atonement of our Sins : Nothing but Faith can say, that the Bread and Wine are his Body and Blood : Nothing but Faith can eat his Body, and drink his Blood : Nothing but Faith can say, that his Body and Blood are a Principle of Life to us : Therefore the Command to *do these Things*, is a Command to exercise so many *Acts of Faith;* because the Things commanded can only be done by Faith ; and the Person, in *Remembrance* of whom these Things are to be done, can only be remembered by *Faith*. For to *remember* him, neither is nor can be anything else, but to have *Faith* in him.

And therefore it is out of all doubt, that when he said, 'Do 'this in Remembrance of me,' nothing more nor less can possibly be meant by it, than if he had said, Do *all this*, as your *Act of Faith* in me.

Since therefore this is so plainly the Nature of the Institution, which is solely appointed to express our Faith in these two great Characters of our Saviour, both as he is the Atonement for our Sins, and a Principle of Life to us ; you may well ask how it was possible for this Author, with his Eyes open, and the Scriptures before him, to give us so *false* and so *poor* an Account of it.

Now the *one only* Reason why the Scriptures are thus useless to him, and why he is forced to find out a Doctrine that is not in them, is this, it is because he is *blinded* with a Philosophy, and Science *falsely so called*, which will not allow him to believe, that Jesus Christ was *truly* and *essentially* God, as well as a perfect Man : For the Foundation and Possibility of Christ's being a *real Atonement* and Satisfaction for our Sins, and a *real Principle* of Life to us, was his *Divine Nature ;* but as this Author cannot be suspected to believe this great Foundation Doctrine, that Christ was *truly* and *essentially* God, *very God of very God*, so he could not believe him to be a *true* and *real* Atonement for Sins, or a true and real *Principle* of Life to us, and therefore could admit nothing of *these Truths* into his Account of the Sacrament.

The way therefore that this Author came by his *Plain Account* of the Sacrament, was not, as he would have you believe, from a *bare impartial Consideration* of the Words of the Institution, but from his wrong Knowledge of the Christian Faith. He had first *lost* and *renounced* all the right and true Knowledge of our Saviour in the Scriptures, and therefore was obliged not to *find* it in the Sacrament. And because it would be openly confessing to the World, that he was in the Sense of the Scripture an *Antichrist*, if he should plainly have told you, that he did not believe Christ to be *truly* and *essentially* God, or the *Atonement* and *Satisfaction* for our Sins, or a *Principle* of Life to us; therefore he only tells you, that he has been led into this Account of the Sacrament, by a *bare Consideration of the Words of the Institution*, according to the common Rules of speaking.

Now if this Author will declare, that he sincerely believes Jesus Christ to be *truly* and *really* God by *Nature*, and the true real *Atonement* and *Satisfaction* for our Sins, and a true and real *Principle* of Life to us; I shall be glad, and he ought to be glad, that I have been the Occasion of his declaring Things so important to himself, and to the Matter in hand. But this I may still say, that he could not have had *this Faith*, when he wrote his *Plain Account*, unless he may be supposed to have had it, but would not write of the Sacrament conformably to it.

And, Secondly, If he will now declare, that without any Equivocation or mental Reserve, he fully believes these great Truths, no further a Recantation of his whole Book need to be desired.

For if these Things are true and undeniable Characters of our Saviour; then it follows, that the *Nature* and *End* of the Sacrament must be *essentially* concerned with them, since it is the confessed Nature and End of the Sacrament, to remember and acknowledge Christ to be *that* which the Scriptures testify him to be.

The short of the Matter is this; either this Author will plainly own a sincere Belief of these Doctrines, or he will not: If he will not own the Belief of them, you have no reason to consider him as a *Christian* Writer upon this Subject; and so ought no more to learn from him, than from a *Jew*, the Nature of the Sacrament. But if he will declare his full Belief of these Doctrines, then you have the fullest Assurance from himself, that his *Plain Account* cannot be *Christian:* Because if these Things are true of Christ, they must be remembered and acknowledged in that Sacrament, which is appointed for the Remembrance and Acknowledgment of him.

Now these two *essential Parts* of the Sacrament, relating to this twofold Character of our Saviour, as he is the Atonement and Satisfaction for our Sins, and as he is a Principle of Life to us, contain the whole *Nature, End,* and *Effects* of the Sacrament. You are to look nowhere, nor in anything else, for the right Knowledge of this Sacrament, but in the right Faith and Knowledge of these two great Points. And everything that they teach you, and everything that the Scripture teaches you of these two great Points, is the *only true* Doctrine of the Sacrament.

All that you know of Christ, as the Atonement for our Sins, all that you know of him, as a Principle of Life to us, is neither more nor less than that which you are to *know*, and *confess*, and *appeal* to, in and by the Use of the Sacrament. And indeed these two great Points do so plainly show themselves, at first Sight, to be in the Words of the Institution, that any Man upon the bare reading of them, without any further Knowledge, might justly say, If Christ is not an Atonement for our Sins, why is his Body said to be *given*, and *his Blood shed for our Sins?* If he is not a *Food* to our Souls, or a *Principle of Life* to us, why are we commanded to *eat* his Body, and *drink* his Blood?

So that though a Man could not say, that these Things were certainly true, or in what Sense they were true, merely from the mention of them in the Sacrament, yet he might justly say, that the Words of the Institution pointed at such Truths, and could have no *Foundation*, unless these Things barely mentioned in it, were in the Scriptures proved and declared to be true Doctrines of the Christian Religion.

And as these two great Points are so visibly plain in the Sacrament, and constitute its *whole Nature;* so as soon as we rightly understand what the Scripture has taught concerning these Points, they make known to us, in the shortest and plainest Way, all the *Merit, Dignity,* and *Value* of this Sacrament, all the Blessings and Advantages derived to us from it, and all the pious Dispositions with which we are to approach it. Hence it was that the Apostles, after the Day of Pentecost, when they had all their Ignorance dispelled, yet gave us no further or particular Explications of the Nature of the Sacrament; because as soon as it was known, that Christ was a real Atonement and Satisfaction for Sins, and a real Principle of Life to us; as soon as these two great Doctrines were known, the Sacrament had all the Explication it could possibly have.

For no more can be known of the Sacrament, than is signified by them. All that is great, mysterious, and adorable in these Doctrines, as found in the Scriptures, is equally great, mysterious and adorable in them as they are found in the Sacrament.

Needless therefore would all Books be upon the Nature of

the Sacrament, and the right Preparation for it, did we but truly know and believe Christ to be the Atonement and Satisfaction for our Sins, and a Principle of Life to us; for the Belief of these things in the Sacrament, would like the *Unction*, spoken of by St. *John, teach us all things* concerning it; and we should have no need of other teaching.

No one need then, as this Author vainly does, enquire for some *Promise of Scripture annexing a Benefit to this Sacrament*, to know what Good we receive by it. For the Knowledge of these two great Parts of the Sacrament, would sufficiently show us the inestimable Benefit that we receive by it.

For if this Sacrament is appointed by Jesus Christ, as the *Acknowledgment* of his being the Atonement of our Sins, and a Principle of Life to us; if it is appointed to *stand* between him and us, as a *declared Proof* on his Side, that he is thus our Atonement and Life; and as a *declared* Proof on our Side, that we *own*, *seek*, and *apply to* him as such; and if this is not set as a Mark *once* for all, but as a Proof that is to be *repeated continually*, and that is to be made good to us, not by our once having done it, or he once owned it, but to be *perpetually* owned and done, both on his Side and ours, can we want any other Assurance of the Benefit and Advantage of observing this Sacrament, than the thing itself by its own Nature declares?

For if we are in Covenant with Christ, and have an Interest in him, as our *Atonement and Life;* not because he once said, That this was his Body and Blood, given and shed for our Sins, or because we once owned it, and pleaded it before him; but because he continues to say the *same thing* in the Sacrament, and to *present* himself there to us as our Atonement and Life, and because we *continue* to own and apply to him as such; it necessarily follows, that the Sacrament rightly used, is the highest Means of finishing our Salvation, and puts us in the fullest Possession of all the Benefits of our Saviour, both as he is our *Atonement and Life*, that we are *then* at *that time* capable of.

For if the Atonement of our Sins by Christ, and that Life which he communicates to us, is not to be considered as a *transient Matter*, as something that is *done* and *past*, but as something that on the Side of Christ is *always* doing, and never will be done, till the Consummation of all Things; if our applying to, and receiving Christ as our Atonement and Life, is not to be considered as a *transient* Act, as something that is *done* and *past*, but as something that is *always doing*, and never will be done, till we depart out of a State of Trial; then it follows, that *that* which is the appointed *Means* or *Proof* of Christ's *continuing* to communicate himself to us, as our *Atonement and Life*, and of our *continuing* to apply to, and receive him as such, is in its *own Nature*, and unless hindered by us, a *certain Means and Instrument* of conveying and imparting to us all the Benefits of Christ, both as he is our *Atonement* and Life. To ask therefore for a *particular Promise* annexed to this Institution, which in its Nature communicates to us *all* that *ever* was *promised* to us in a Saviour, is highly absurd.

But after all, it can be truly said, that the Scriptures are very full and particular in setting forth the Benefits and Advantages of the Holy Communion, to all those that have Eyes that see, and Ears that hear. For do not the Scriptures plainly enough tell us of the *Benefit* of believing, seeking, and applying to Christ as the Atonement for our Sins? And is not the Benefit of *this Faith* the Benefit of the *Sacrament*, if Christ is there *believed*, sought and applied to as our Atonement?

And is it not the sole End of the Sacrament to *continue, confirm* and *exercise* this Faith, to which all the Blessings of our Salvation are annexed? Therefore, all that the Scriptures say of the Riches and Blessings, and Treasures, which *Faith* in Christ as our Redeemer, can procure to us, *all that* they say of the Benefit of that Faith, which is absolutely required and exercised by this Sacrament.

Again, do not the Scriptures plainly and frequently enough tell us of the Benefit of the *New Birth* in *Christ*, of the *putting on* Christ, of having Christ *formed in us*, of Christ's being *our Life*, of our having *Life in him*, of his being that *Bread from Heaven*, that Bread of *Life*, of which the *Manna* was only a *Type;* of his Flesh being *Meat indeed*, and *his Blood Drink indeed;* of our *eating* his Flesh, and *drinking* his Blood, and that without it we *have no Life in us;* and are not all these things so many *plain* and *open* Declarations of that which we seek and obtain, ' by eating the Body and Blood of Christ?'

For we eat the *sacramental* Body and Blood of Christ, to show that we *want* and *desire*, and by Faith lay hold of the *real, spiritual Nature* and Being of Christ; to show that we want and desire, the Progress of the *New Birth* in Christ; to *put on* Christ, to have Christ *formed* and revealed in us, to have him *our Life*, to *partake* of him our second *Adam*, in the same *Fulness* and *Reality*, as we partake of the Nature of the first *Adam:* And therefore all that the Scripture says of the Benefits and Blessings of *these things*, so *much* it says of the Benefits and Blessings that are sought and obtained by the eating the Body and Blood of Christ in the Lord's Supper. For to eat the *Body* and *Blood* of Christ, is neither more nor less than to *put on Christ*, to receive Birth and Life, and Nourishment and Growth from him; as the

the Errors of a late Book.

Branch receives its Being and Life, and Nourishment and Growth from the Vine. And because Christ is *that* to us, which the Vine is to the Branches, therefore there is a strict Truth and Reality in these Expressions ; and the *same Truth* and *Reality*, whether it be expressed, by saying, that we eat the *Flesh* and *Blood* of Christ, or that we *put on Christ*, or that Christ is *formed*, manifested or revealed in us.

For if you could bid the *Branch* to *eat the Substance* and *Juice* of the Vine, the same must be intended, as if you had said, that the Vine must be *formed* in the Branch, or must *manifest* itself in the Branch. So when it is said, that we must eat the *Flesh and Blood* of Christ, it is the same thing as saying, that Christ must *be formed in us*, or manifested in us.

But you will perhaps say, How does it appear, that these Expressions of *putting on Christ*, of Christ's being *formed in us*, of his being *our Life*, the *Bread of Life*, and his Flesh *Meat indeed, and his Blood Drink indeed ;* How does it appear, that these and the like Places of Scripture are to be understood *Sacramentally ?*

I answer, it does not appear. And the Question itself is as absurd, as if it was asked, How does it appear, that the Scriptures are to be understood *Sacramentally?* Whereas, if the Question began at the right End, it should proceed thus, How does it appear, that the Sacrament is to be understood *Scripturally*, or according to the plain Doctrines of Scripture ? Was the Question thus put, as it ought to be, it would fall of itself. For surely it need not be proved, that the things spoken of Christ in the Sacrament, are to be understood according to that which is spoken of Christ in the Scripture. When our Saviour said in the sixth of St. *John*, ' That his Flesh was Meat indeed, and his ' Blood Drink indeed, and that except a Man eat his Flesh, and ' drink his Blood, he hath no Life in him; and that he who eateth ' his Flesh, and drinketh his Blood, dwelleth in him, and he in ' him ;' he did not speak of the Sacrament, nor could possibly speak of it, for this plain Reason, because he spoke of the *Truth*, the *Reality*, and the *Thing* itself ; for the *sake* of which, and for the *Application* of which to ourselves, he afterwards instituted the Sacrament.

But if the Sacrament was instituted for the sake of that *Truth* and *Reality*, of which he then spake ; then the Sacrament must be *essentially* related to that which he then said, and must have its *Meaning* and *End* according to it.

And if what he then said, was that *Truth* and *Reality* of the Thing itself, and the Sacrament was instituted as an outward Sign, Proof or Declaration of it ; then what he said in St. *John*, he spoke not of the Sacrament ; and yet what he instituted in the Sacrament, has *all its Meaning* according to that which he said in St. *John*.

To ask, whether our Saviour meant the *Sacramental Bread and Wine*, when he said, my Flesh is Meat indeed, and my Blood is Drink indeed, is as absurd as to ask, whether he did not mean the Flesh and Blood of some other Person, when he said, *my* Flesh and *my* Blood?

And, on the other hand, to ask, whether the Sacramental Bread and Wine does not *signify* to us that Flesh and Blood which is our Meat indeed, and Drink indeed, is as absurd, as to ask, whether the appointed Sign of a thing, does not signify that which it is appointed to signify?

These two things therefore are evidently plain: First, That our Saviour in the sixth of St. *John* did not, could not possibly speak of his Sacramental Body and Blood, or Bread and Wine, because he spoke of *himself*, of his real, natural, and true Life, of which we must partake: Secondly, That what he calls his Body and Blood in the Sacrament, or has appointed to be the Signs of his Body and Blood, must be understood according to that which he has said in St. *John*, of his Flesh which is Meat indeed, and his Blood which is Drink indeed; for this plain Reason, because the appointed Sign of a thing must signify that which it is appointed to signify.

Therefore in St. *John* there is nothing said of the Sacrament; and yet what is said in the Sacrament, is to be *necessarily* understood of that *very thing* which is said in St. *John*. And the Reason is plain; for the *Thing* is essentially different from that which is appointed to be a *Sign* of it; therefore, he that speaks of the *Thing*, cannot in speaking of that, speak of the *Sign*. But the Sign, as such, has all its Nature from the Thing that it is to signify; and therefore the *Thing* itself must be *meant* by that which the Sign speaks of.

To say, as some do, that our Saviour could not speak of that in St. *John*, which is *intended* by the Sacrament, because the Sacrament was not then instituted, is very weak and unreasonable; for it is saying, that he could not then speak of a *Thing* or *Doctrine*, because he afterwards appointed something to be a *Sign* or outward *Declaration* of it. For if he had appointed an Institution, or *positive Rite*, which related to nothing that he had before taught, it must have been very unaccountable. Thus to command us to eat his Body and Blood in the Sacrament, if he had not beforehand taught that we had *our Life* from him, and that his *Flesh* was our *Meat indeed*, and his Blood our *Drink indeed*, had been very unaccountable. But seeing he had in the openest, plainest Manner declared, that he was the *Life of Men*, and that except we eat his *Flesh and drink his Blood* we have no Life in us; the Command to eat *Bread and Wine* as his *Body and Blood*, is plain and intelligible; and we have the fullest Assurance of the Meaning of it, for this reason, because Christ had often, and long beforehand taught *that Truth*, of which he afterwards appointed the Sacrament to be an *outward Sign*, and an outward *Means* of our owning, confessing, and embracing it. Thus all the Controversy about this Place in St. *John*, and other like Passages of Scripture, is at an end, and has the most plain and satisfactory Solution; such Passages do not speak of the Sacrament, because they speak of the *thing itself*, of which the Sacrament is an appointed outward Signification; but the Sacrament *directly speaks* of, and *points* to those Passages, because they contain that *Truth* and *Reality* which the Sacrament is appointed to signify.

For were not Christ our *real* Life, there had not been any *outward Figure* or Declaration of it appointed; was there not a *real* Eating the Flesh and Drinking the Blood of Christ, was there not a *true* substantial *putting on* of Christ, or partaking of the Nature of Christ, the *Sacramental* Eating and Drinking of his Body and Blood, had not been appointed; there could have been no Foundation for it; or if appointed, it could have had no Meaning suitable to the Words. But since *That* which is Sacramentally *figured* or *signified*, by the Eating and Drinking the Sacramental Body and Blood of Christ, is in the Scriptures declared to be a *real* Truth, since its *Reality* is taught, declared and explained by various Ways and Manners of Speech, it is undeniable, that the Sacrament, which is an appointed Figure, must be explained and asserted according to *that Truth* and *Reality*, of which it is the appointed Figure.

When our Saviour said, 'he that eateth my Flesh, and drinketh 'my Blood, dwelleth in me, and I in him': When he said, 'I am 'the Life'; and again, 'I am the true Vine, and ye are the 'Branches,' &c., he spake as much *strict* and *real* Truth, and as much according to the *Letter*, as when he said of himself, he came down from *Heaven*, or that *he is in* the *Father*, and the *Father in him*. What is there said, is no more to be considered as a *Metaphor*, or *Figure of Speech*, than when it is said, that *God* is our *Father*, or that in God we *live, move*, and *have our Being*.

For what is said of Christ, *as our Life*, is as strictly true, as when it is said, *that in God we live*, and *move, and have our Being;* and what is said of Christ's being the *true Vine*, has the same *real* Truth in it, as when God is said to be *our Father*.

Had Christ indeed said, *This Vine is me*, and *these Branches are* ye, what he said must then have been as *figurative*, as when he said of the Bread, 'This is my Body;' and his speaking so of a Vine, must have been only a Sign to us, that he was in Truth and Reality that to us, which the Vine is in a poor, *earthly, perishable* Manner to its Branches. But seeing he does not speak of a *Vine*, but speaks directly of *himself*, and says, that I am *the true Vine;* it is as if he had said, I am the Vine in Truth and Reality, as God is the Father of you all in Truth and Reality, because I am that in a *true* and *real*, and *living* Manner to you, which the Vine is in a poor, earthly, perishable Manner to its Branches.

Therefore all that is here said, is the *real Truth*, as far as human Words can set it forth; and when it is said, that we must *put* on Christ, or that *Christ* must be *formed* in us, or that he is the *true Vine, and we are the Branches*, there is the same *literal, real, immutable* and eternal Truth in these Expressions, as when it is said, that 'in God we live and move, and have our being,' or that God is our *Father*, and we his Children.

Now to deny that Christ is thus *our Life*, is as great a Denial of him, as to deny him to be the *eternal Word*, or the Son of God, or the *Light that lighteth every Man that cometh into the World*. And to deny that we receive our Life from him, or eat his Flesh and Blood in the same Reality as the Branch *eateth* of the Substance and Juice of the Vine, aud receiveth what it hath from it, is as great a Denial of him, as if we deny that he *came from Heaven, and was in Heaven*, even when he was upon Earth.

But if we own these great Truths, which are the very Heart and Substance of Christianity, if we know and acknowledge that we are thus of him, and by him, that our *inward Man*, which is all that is Christian within us, has all its *Birth, Life*, and *Growth* from Christ, as its Principle, *eating, drinking*, and *drawing* in Life from him, as the *Branch* eats, drinks, and draws its Life and Substance from the Vine; then we cannot be at a Loss either to know what is meant by the Sacrament, and the Benefits we receive thereby, or to know what Parts of Scripture explain those Benefits to us. Since it must appear to us beyond all doubt, *that* all *that* which the Scriptures speak to us of Christ, as the Atonement for our Sins, and our Peace with God, and all that they speak to us of *our Life* in Christ, of his *forming* and *manifesting* himself in the Birth and Growth of our inward new Man; is that which it speaks to us of the *Meaning* and *Benefits of* this Holy Sacrament, which is solely appointed as the Figure of all this, as the *Application* of all this to us, and as an established Means of exercising, increasing and strengthening our Faith in him, as he is *all this* to us.

Here therefore is full *room* for all our Devotion, and at the same time a full *Security* against all Delusion. For whilst we believe nothing of the Sacrament, seek nothing in it, nor plead anything by it, but such Scripture Truths and Benefits as we are obliged to believe, own and plead, though the Sacrament had not been appointed, all the Devotion which the Sacrament thus raises in us, is as secure from Delusion, has as much the Stamp of Truth upon it, and is as proper an Exercise of solid Piety, as when any Thing or Occasion excites us to an Act of loving God with all our Mind, and Heart, and Strength. For as we cannot too much esteem, love and adore our Saviour, both as he is the *Atonement* for our Sins, and a *Principle* of Life to us; so if the Use of the Sacrament quickens, nourishes, keeps up, and increases this Esteem, Love and Adoration of him, as such, it cannot do this too much.

For as we do nothing in the Sacrament, but what is our natural Duty, and good and right in itself; as we seek to Christ, trust in Christ, rely upon his Merits, desire to have Life in and from him, only in such a Manner as we ought to do, though we were not assisted in it by the Sacrament; so all this Faith and Hope, and Love and Desire, and Devotion which we practise by means of the Sacrament, has everything in it, that can prove it to be right, and just, and good. And the want of this Faith, Hope, Love, Desire, Adoration and Devotion, is more blamable in the Use of the Sacrament than anywhere else, because it is there more properly required, and has the most proper Object and Occasion to excite it.

You must therefore consider the Sacrament purely as an *Object* of your *Devotion*, that is to exercise all your *Faith*, that is to raise, exercise, and inflame every holy Ardour of your Soul that tends to God. It is an *Abstract*, or *Sum* of all the Mysteries that have been revealed concerning our Saviour, from the first Promise of a *Seed of the Woman* to bruise the *Serpent's Head*, to the Day of Pentecost.

As you can receive or believe nothing higher of our Saviour, than that he is the *Atonement* for our Sins, and a *real Principle* of Life to us; so every Height and Depth of Devotion, Faith, Love, and Adoration, which is due to God as your Creator, is due to God as your Redeemer.

Jacob's Ladder that reached from Earth to Heaven, and was filled with Angels ascending and descending between Heaven and Earth, is but a small Signification of that Communion between God and Man, which this holy Sacrament is the Means and Instrument of.

Now here it may be proper for you to observe, that whatever *Names* or *Titles* this Institution is signified to you by, whether it be called a *Sacrifice* propitiatory, or commemorative ; whether it be called an holy Oblation, the *Eucharist,* the *Sacrament* of the *Body* and *Blood* of Christ, the Sacrament of the *Lord's Supper,* the *Heavenly Banquet,* the *Food of Immortality,* or the *Holy Communion,* and the like, matters not much. For all these *Words* or *Names* are right and good, and there is nothing wrong in them, but the striving and contention about them.

For they all express *something* that is true of the Sacrament, and therefore are every one of them, in a good Sense, rightly applicable to it ; but all of them are far short of expressing the whole Nature of the Sacrament, and therefore the Help of all of them is wanted.

He therefore that contends for one Name, as the only proper one in Exclusion of the rest, is in the same Mistake, as he that should contend for one *Name* and *Character* of our Saviour, as the only proper one, in Exclusion of all the rest. For as all the *Names* and *Titles* by which Christ is described, from the *Seed of the Woman* in *Genesis,* to the *Alpha* and *Omega* in the last Chapter of the *Revelation,* are only to *help* us to know, believe, and experience more of him as our Saviour, than can be expressed by all these different Characters of him : So all the various *Names* and *Titles* given to the Sacrament, are only to teach us to know, believe, and find more of our Redemption and Salvation in the Sacrament, than can be pointed out to us by any or all these Expressions.

If you have yet known Christ in any true Degree, what must you think of him, who should contend that the *Lamb of God* was the only proper Character of our Saviour, and that therefore those other Names, *Seed of the Woman, Root of David, Bright and Morning Star, Bread of Life, Tree of Life, Son of Man, Firstborn of all the Creatures, Word of God,* could not belong to him as our Saviour, because of the Disagreement there is between a *Lamb,* and the *Bread of Life,* or a *Tree of Life ?*

Now this is the Learning this Author is full of ; from this scrupulous *Attention* to Words, and the Ideas annexed to them, he rejects almost all the *Names* by which the Sacrament has ever been expressed.

He is able to prove, that the Sacrament is not a *Commemorative Sacrifice,* because it is the *Supper* of the Lord ; just as another by the same Skill in Words, might prove, that the *Lamb of God* is not the *Tree of Life,* or the *Bread* that *came down from Heaven,* because of the great Difference there is between a *Tree, Bread,* and a *Lamb.*

Now the Reason why our Saviour is described under this vast Variety of Characters, is this, because no one Phrase or particular

Form of Expression can truly describe him to us; therefore that is to be done as well as it can, by different and seemingly contrary Characters.

Thus he is called the *Seed of the Woman* that was to bruise the Serpent's Head, in another respect the *Lamb of God*, in another the *Desire of all Nations*, in another the *Son of Man*, in another the *Brightness of his Father's Glory*, in another the *Bread that came down from Heaven*, in another the *Tree of Life*, the *Alpha and Omega*. Now it is the exceeding Difference, and even literal Contrariety of these Expressions, that makes them proper and useful to us; and we have the more true Knowledge of our Saviour because of these Characters, which, considered in themselves, seem to have no Agreement with each other.

Thus the *Lamb of God*, and the *Bread of Life*, are Characters of our Saviour, that have no Connection with each other, and yet they teach us the greatest Truths concerning our Saviour, because they are thus without Connection, and so unrelated to each other.

It is just thus with the Sacrament; the different and seemingly incoherent *Characters* and Expressions by which it is signified to us, help us to know more Truth of it, merely because of their Difference, than could be taught us by such Expressions as had a literal Agreement and Connection with each other.

Do you therefore reject this Author's *Wisdom of Words* which he proposes to you, and be content to be devout without it. Be glad to know, that as the Nature, Office, and Condition of our Saviour could not be made known to us, but by a Variety of different *Names* and *Titles* ascribed to him; so the *Nature* and *End* and Effects of this Holy Sacrament could not be made known to us, but by a Variety of different Names and Titles ascribed to it; that in one respect it is a *Propitiatory* Sacrifice, in another a *Commemorative* Sacrifice; in one respect it is the *Seal* and *Renewal* of the Covenant between God and Man, in another the *Food of Immortality*, the *Life of the Soul*, the *Bread* that came down from Heaven, the *Tree of Life;* that in one respect it is the Holy *Eucharist*, in another the Holy *Communion*.

And be assured, that he who tries to set these Expressions at Variance with each other, and would persuade you that if one is a true Account of the Sacrament, the others cannot be so, is as vain a *Disputer of this World*, as he that would persuade you, that if our Saviour be the *Seed of the Woman*, he cannot be essentially the Son of God; or that if he be the *Lamb* of God, he cannot be the *Bread of Life*.

The reason why this Sacrament is said in one respect to be a *Propitiatory*, or *Commemorative* Sacrifice, is only this, because you there *offer, present,* and *plead* before God, such Things as are by Christ himself said to be his *Body* and *Blood given for you*: But if that which is thus *offered, presented*, and *pleaded* before God, is offered, presented, and pleaded before him only for *this Reason*, because it signifies and represents both to God, and Angels, and Men, the *great Sacrifice* for all the World, is there not sufficient Reason to consider this *Service* as truly a *Sacrifice?* Or even supposing, that the calling this *Service* a Sacrifice, is no more according to a certain *literal Exactness* of some *Critics*, that when our Saviour says of himself, 'I am the 'Resurrection;' or that a *Quibbler* in Words may be able to object as much against it, as against our Saviour's saying of himself, 'I am the Resurrection and the Life,' have you any reason to dislike it on that Account, or to wish that such *little Critics* might find more of their empty, superficial, worthless Niceties in the Language of the Church, than in the Language of Scripture?

The miserable Use which this Author makes of this Kind of Learning may be sufficiently seen by the following Instances: 'To say,' says he, ' that this Communion *is the actual* partaking ' of all the Benefits of Christ's Body broken and Blood shed for ' us, or of his Living and Dying for our Good, has this peculiar ' Absurdity in it, that in this Rite, which was instituted *for the* ' *Remembrance of* Christ, it destroys that very Notion of *Remem-* ' *brance*, which is the *Essence* of it. The great Design of this ' Institution is to call to mind the *Remembrance* of Christ, and to ' *commemorate the Benefits* accruing to Christians *from it*. To ' make it therefore the *actual partaking* of these Benefits, is ' altering the Nature of it, as much *as actual partaking of* any-' thing is different *from* remembering it.'* Many other Passages like this are to be found in this Author.

Now to see the Truth and Sense of this Doctrine in its proper Light: Let it be supposed, that our Saviour, after the Institution, had thus added, ' Observe well what it is that I have taught ' you to understand and do by this *Rite:* I have indeed said, ' This is my Body which is given for you; but the Meaning ' of my Institution does not lie in these Words, nor are you to ' think that I am any way present in that which I call *my Body*, or ' that you are to present, and show, and plead it before God *as* ' *my Body*, which is *given* for you; for this is not my Intent, ' though I thus speak. I have also said, This is my Blood ' which is shed for the Remission of Sins, and have ordered ' you to *say so* of it before God, and Angels, and Men in the ' Church; but what I have taught has nothing to do with this

---

* Page 158.

'Institution, nor is it any Part of it; there is no Remission of
'Sins to be *thought of* in it, or *pleaded* by it. I have also bid you
'to *eat* that which I have declared to be *my Body*, and to drink
'that which I have declared to be *my Blood ;* but you must not
'therefore imagine, that you receive *anything* of me, or of my
'*Nature*, into yourselves, or that I am a *Principle* of Life to you.
'For though I thus speak so fully and plainly of eating my *very*
'*Body* and *Blood*, yet nothing is meant of any *real partaking* of
'anything from me. For this is *no Part* of my Institution, nor
'is it appointed for you to *receive* anything from me, nor for me
'to *communicate* anything to you. And to prevent your Appre-
'hension of anything of this kind, and to secure you from
'the dangerous Error of supposing that any *Benefits* and Bless-
'ings are received by your receiving my Body and Blood; I
'have added, Do this in Remembrance of me; which Words
'sufficiently show, that neither *Me*, nor the *Benefits* of me, as
'your Saviour, can here be received, because that which is
'appointed here to be *remembered*, cannot, without great
'Absurdity, be supposed to be *present*. Had I indeed said, Do
'this in *Acknowledgment* of me, or of that *Salvation* which is
'*received* through me; or had I said, Do this as an Act of *Faith*
'in me as your Saviour, then indeed you must have believed
'that there were *great Benefits* and Blessings presented to you by
'this Institution; for ye could not by *Faith* appeal to this my
'Body and Blood as given for you, and by *Faith* eat this as my
'Body and Blood, without the actual partaking of my Benefits
'and Blessings, both as I am the Atonement for your Sins, and
'a Principle of Life to you: But as I have chosen the Word
'*Remembrance*, you must see that it is only an *Act of your*
'*Memory* that is required of you; for this is the *great Point*
'in this Institution, perform but this and you have performed all
'that the Nature and End of this Institution requires of you.
'Take care therefore that you keep strictly to this *bare Act* of
'the Memory, and that you don't *add* anything to it; for the
'*Essence* of this Institution consists in this *simple Act* of the
'Memory. But above all, take heed of such *Faith, Devotion,*
'and *Desire* of me, as may lead you to *hope* or *believe* that you
'partake of my Benefits by the partaking of this holy Rite; for
'such a *Faith* and *Hope* are so *inconsistent* with this Institution,
'that they would *destroy* the very Nature and Essence of it, which
'is to be the *Remembrance* of my Benefits, and therefore cannot
'possibly be the actual partaking of them. Nor can you think of
'partaking of them by this holy Institution, but by making it
'an Institution of your own, directly contrary to that which I
'designed it to be.'

Everyone, I believe, must at first Sight perceive, that to put this Paraphrase upon the Sacrament into the Mouth of our Saviour, would be Profaneness and Blasphemy; and yet everyone must plainly see, that profane and blasphemous as it would be, there is not a Thought or Word in it, but what is strictly according to this Author's Doctrine.

Secondly, Let it be supposed that instead of 'Do this in 'Remembrance of me,' our Saviour had said, *Do this* as a Means of *partaking of all my Benefits to Mankind:* This Author's *Criticism* would prove it *absurd* to make the Sacrament even then an *actual* partaking of those Benefits. For he must say, that the great Design of it, was to be a *Means* of partaking of those Benefits. To make it therefore the *actual partaking of those Benefits, is altering the Nature of it, as much as actual partaking of anything is different from the Means of partaking of it.* Such is his Wisdom of Words!

Thirdly, If it were true, that the *actual partaking* of Christ's Benefits was not only not intended by, but also *inconsistent* with the right Observance of this Institution, so as to *destroy its Essence, and alter its Nature,* if such actual partaking was thought of by it; then it would follow, that no good Christian ought to observe this Institution, or act according to the Nature and Intent of it.

For it is as unlawful and even atheistical for any Christian to think himself not an *actual Partaker* of the Benefits and Blessings of Christ, as to think himself not an *actual Partaker* of the Benefits and Blessings of a God and Providence. 'Without me,' says our Blessed Lord, 'ye can do nothing.'* But, according to this Author, we not only can, but *must* do all that is done in this Sacrament *without him,* and must look upon the Sacrament as instituted for this *very End,* to keep up a *Sense* and *Belief* of our being *without him,* and to assure us, that we are not *actual Partakers* of him, that he is not *present* with us, nor acting in us. Again, saith our blessed Lord, 'Abide in me, and I in you; as 'the Branch cannot bear Fruit, except it abide in the Vine; no 'more can ye, except ye abide in me.'

But, according to this Author, he that would rightly perform this Institution, must, every time he performs it, come *out* of Christ as perfectly as he can, and make himself as separate from Christ, as the *withered Branch* that is separated from the Vine; that having no *actual Possession* of the Benefits and Blessings of Christ, he may be qualified to *do this in Remembrance of them.*

Further, no one can believe in Christ, love Christ, adore him,

---

* John xv. 5.

and hope and trust in him, without being an *actual Partaker* of the Benefits of Christ by so doing; if therefore to the due Observation of the Sacrament, and to preserve its *Nature* and *Essence*, there must be no *actual partaking* of the Benefits of Christ allowed in it, or by it; then it must be performed without Faith or Love of Christ, and without any Devotion towards him, or Adoration of him; for if these accompany that which we do in the Sacrament, and attend our reception of it, the Benefits of Christ must be *actually* received by it.

Fourthly, To see still more of the Absurdity and Impiety of this Author's Observation on the *Remembrance in the Sacrament*, we need only apply it to this parallel Text of Scripture, 'Remem-'ber thy Creator in the Days of thy Youth.'* For, according to our Author, he that would not alter and *destroy* the Nature and Essence of this Duty of *remembering* God, must not pretend, or hope, or believe, that by the Observance of this Duty, he is made an *actual Partaker* or Sharer of the Goodness, Perfections, and Attributes of his Creator, or of anything that belongs to his Creator, or that can be remembered of him: Because so long as he keeps strictly to the true Nature of this Duty, and continues to *remember* his Creator, so long every Thing, or Attribute, or Perfection that belongs to his Creator, must be considered as at a *Distance* from him, as *unenjoyed* and unpossessed by him, because that which is to be *remembered*, cannot be *present*. And therefore the Command *to remember our Creator*, is, according to this Doctrine, a Command to look upon our Creator as at a *Distance* and far from us, and is inconsistent with our believing, that 'in him we live, move, and have our Being'; because we cannot *remember* a *Creator* so present with us, and of whose Perfections we are *actual Partakers*.

If therefore this Author has found out the right Way of remembering God as our *Redeemer*, he ought to have told us, that the same Way of remembering God as our Creator was wrong, and tended to *Atheism*. For to remember God as *absent*, is but a very little way from *Atheism*.

Lastly, If, as this Author teaches, the *atual partaking* of the Benefits of Christ's living and dying for us, by means of this Sacrament, is an Absurdity that cannot be supposed, without destroying the Nature and Essence of the Sacrament, for this Reason, because that which is possessed as present, and *actually partaken* of, cannot be *remembered;* then it follows, that no Man can fully perform this Duty, that is, make it a Remembrance of *all the Benefits* of Christ, but he that is *actually* dispossessed of

---

* Eccles. xii. 1.

all of them. Because he cannot remember *all*, if any of them are then present with him, and enjoyed by him.

Secondly, It follows, that he who daily grows in the Gifts and Graces of Christ, and in whom Christ is every Day more and more formed, must, in proportion as the Strength, and Spirit, and Power of Christ is revealed in him, daily be less qualified to do perfectly that which is to be done in the Sacrament; because being daily more and more possessed of the Benefits and Blessings of Christ, he has every Day less and less to commemorate in and by the Sacrament.

Thirdly, It follows, that he who falls from his State of Grace in Christ, who becomes every Day more and more empty and destitute of his Gifts and Graces, who daily loses something of the Sense and Taste of the *heavenly Gifts, and the Powers of the World to come*, and finds himself less animated, assisted and strengthened by the Power and Spirit of Christ, must in proportion, as he becomes every Day more earthly, sensual, carnal, blind and weak, and wretched, and dead, and fallen from Christ, be more and more qualified to do that, which, according to this Author, is to be done in the Sacrament; for losing every Day something of the Benefits of Christ, and being daily a less Partaker of them, he is daily qualified to commemorate more of them, and so to perform that which is to be performed in this Sacrament in a more perfect manner.

Again, the Apostle saith, 'Know ye not that Christ Jesus is in 'you, except ye be Reprobates'*? But this Author must say, Know ye not that Christ Jesus is not in you, nor can be in you, if the Sacrament is to be observed in *Remembrance* of him? For how can ye without Absurdity *commemorate* that which is not absent from you?

Lastly, He who can say with the Apostle, 'the Life that I now 'live is not mine, but Christ that liveth in me, *is utterly* incapable of remembering Christ in the Sacrament; for he cannot commemorate an *absent* Christ, and therefore cannot commemorate him, till Christ has done living in him.

But there is no end of exposing all the impious Consequences of this Author's learned Account of the Word Remembrance. Which, monstrous as it is, is only founded upon a little *Criticism*, that the word Remembrance can only signify an *Act of the Memory* upon something that is *absent*. And yet it is certain that it does not, cannot signify so, when you are to remember your Creator, and therefore need not signify so, when you are to remember your Redeemer. And if you do but suppose it pos-

---

* 2 Cor. xiii. 5.

sible, that 'Do this in Remembrance of me,' may only signify, *do this* in *regard* of me, as your Act *of Faith* in me; then all this extraordinary Doctrine of the Impossibility and Absurdity of partaking of the Benefits of Christ by partaking of the Sacrament, has not so much as one of his Quibbles to support it.

Further, this Author's absurd Interpretation of the word *Remembrance* in the Sacrament is founded on this gross Error, that the things to be remembered, are things *done* and *past*, and therefore only capable of being remembered by an Act of the Memory. This he expressly says in many places. Thus, *They*, says he, *could not do the Actions here named, in remembrance of anything which was not done and past.** And in other Places, that the *Benefits cannot be present that are to be commemorated.*

And therefore the whole Support of this arguing is founded on this Error, that the things to be remembered, are *done* and *past*. Which is an Error, that he could not have fallen into, if he had but moderately understood the Nature either of the *Jewish* or *Christian* Religion.

Now that which is to be remembered in the Sacrament is Christ, or the Benefits and Blessings of Christ as the Saviour of Mankind; but neither Christ, nor his Benefits and Blessings have the Nature of things *done*, or *gone*, and *past*, but are always present, always in being, always doing, and never done.

'Jesus Christ, the same yesterday, to-day, and for ever,' always was, now is, and ever will be present as the Saviour of the World. He is the *Alpha* and *Omega*, the *Beginning and the End*, and therefore equally present in and through all from the Beginning to the End. 'Behold,' saith he, 'I stand at the Door, and knock; 'if any Man hear my Voice, and open the Door, I will come into 'him, and will sup with him.'† Thus he stood at the Door of *Adam's* Heart, as near as he stood to the *Apostles'*; and thus he stands, and will stand knocking at the Door of every Man's Heart, till Time shall be no more. Happy he that does not consider this Christ as absent, and is only for such a *Supper of the Lord*, as will not admit of his Presence.

The Benefits and Blessings of Christ as the Saviour of Mankind, began with the first Promise of a *Seed* of the *Woman to bruise the Serpent's Head;* they have continued with this Promise, they are the Benefits of every Age, they will never be at an End, till all that was implied in that Promise shall have its full Completion in the utter Destruction of the Serpent. Jesus Christ was the *Lamb slain from the Foundation of the World;* and the first

---

* Page 30. † Rev. iii. 20.

Sacrifice of the first Man, and every Sacrifice since, that hath been accepted of God, has been made solely acceptable through the Benefits and Blessings of Christ.

All the Shadows and Types, Sacrifices and Ceremonies of the *Jewish* Religion were only so many Ways of applying the Benefits of Jesus Christ to that People. 'Jesus Christ, the same yester-'day, to-day, and for ever,' is the same in and through all Ages; he was the Saviour of *Adam*, the *Patriarchs*, and the *Jews*, just as he is our Saviour. His Body and Blood, offered in their Sacrifices, was their Atonement, as it is ours, offered upon the Cross. His Flesh and Blood was Meat and Drink, or a *Principle of Life* to them, as it is to us.

Jesus Christ was theirs, as he is ours; he was the Life, and Substance, and Spirit of the Law, as he is the Life, and Substance, and Spirit of the Gospel; only with this Difference, that then Christ was covered, and received under more outward Figures and Ceremonies than he is now; we do that more openly, which was then done more covertly by the *Israel of God*.

His Atonement for our Sins is not a *transitory* Thing, that *began* and *ended* with his Passion and Death, but it began with the *Lamb that was slain from the Foundation of the World;* for he was the Lamb of God slain in all their *Types* and *Sacrifices* through every Age, till he became the *real* expiatory Sacrifice on the Cross for the Sins of the World.

When he died upon the Cross, his Atonement did not then become a thing that was *over*, or *past*, and *done*, that was only to be remembered by an *Act of the Memory*, but continued increasing in its Power and Virtue.

As Christ by his Death put an end to nothing in Religion but Types and Prefigurations; so by his Death he put an end to nothing of his Atonement, but that which was typical and prefigurative of it. And as he arose from the Grave with greater Power and Strength, and became instead of a *meek* and *suffering* Lamb, a *powerful* Conqueror over Death, a *Royal Priest* over the House of God, so his Atonement went on increasing in Strength and Virtue.

His Atonement was so far from being a Thing then *done* and *past*, when his Blood was shed upon the Cross, that it was shed for this very End, that he might for ever do that in the *Reality*, which the High Priest did in the *Type*, when with the Blood of the Sacrifice he entered once a Year into the Holiest of all, to make the *highest Atonement* for the People.

Thus Christ, to perform, and to continue for ever the most powerful Way of atoning for us, *by his own Blood he entered once into the Holy Place*—now to appear in the Presence of *God for us.** Where he continueth for ever, and *hath an unchangeable Priesthood;*† and therefore our Atonement is never *done* and *past*, but is just as *perpetual* and *unchangeable* as his *Priesthood.* For he can be no longer a Priest, than while he maketh an Atonement and Intercession for us. And from this his *unchangeable Priesthood*, the Apostle thus argues, 'wherefore he is able also 'to save them to the uttermost, who come unto God by him,‡ 'seeing he ever liveth to make Intercession for us.'

But if he is 'able to save them to the uttermost, who come 'unto God by him;' then his Atonement is not something *done* and *past*, but always in being, always present, always doing, and always presenting itself everywhere, and to every Man; and if he is *ever living to make Intercession* for us, then we have a *Propitiation* that never ceases, that is as *near* to us as it was to the Apostles, and will be as *present* to those that shall be born two thousand Years after Christ, as it was to those who stood by his Cross when he died. Agreeable to this, St. *John* saith, 'We have 'an Advocate with the Father, Jesus Christ the Righteous: And 'he is the Propitiation for our Sins.' He does not say, we have had an Advocate in this World, but that we *have* one *with* the Father, nor that Christ was our Propitiation some time ago, but that he *is* the Propitiation for our Sins.

And indeed Jesus Christ is the Atonement for our Sins, in that same *unlimited universal* and *omnipresent* Manner, in which he is the *Life* and *Light* of the World. And as he is the *Light which lighteth every Man that cometh into the World*, and is not an *actual present* Light to some, and a *distant unpossessed* Light to others, only to be remembered by an *Act of their Memory;* so he is the Atonement for every Man that cometh into the World, and is not an *actual, present* Atonement to some, and a *distant* Atonement to others, only to be remembered by an *Act of their Memory;* but is an Atonement *actually* and *really* present to all, as he is a Light actually and really present to all, and every Man that cometh into the World.

Therefore this Author's Account of the *Remembrance* in the Sacrament, has not only those Absurdities in it demonstrated above, but is also solely founded upon this grossest of all Errors, that the Benefits and Blessings of Christ, as the Saviour of Mankind, are something *done* and *past;* which is an Error that no one could have fallen into, that had but a common Knowledge of the first and plainest Principles either of the *Jewish* or *Christian* Religion. For both these Religions are founded upon this *great Truth*, and suppose it in every Part, that the Benefits and

---

* Heb. ix. 24.   † Heb. vii. 24.   ‡ Heb. vii. 25.

Blessings of Christ were always in *being*, always *doing*, always *present* in and to every Age, as well *before* as *since* the Incarnation and Death of Christ.

And as this Author has been forced to assert, they were things *absent, done*, and *past*, in order to make the Sacrament to consist of an Action of the *Memory* upon those absent things; so seeing it is an undeniable Truth, that they are not things absent, done, and past, but are as actually present, as ever they were, or ever could be, it follows, according to his own Principles, that the *Remembrance* spoken of in the Sacrament, cannot possibly signify only an *Action of the Memory*, but must necessarily signify such *Faith* and *Acknowledgment* of Christ, as when we are bid to *remember our Creator, or believe* in God.

Further, this Author proceeds thus: 'To say that the Communion is the actual partaking of all the Benefits of Christ's living and dying for us, is to put that upon one single Act of Obedience, which is by our blessed Lord made to depend upon the whole System of all Virtues united.'* And again, 'Such a Doctrine as this would, in my Opinion, be not only inconsistent with the plainest Declarations of the Gospel, but directly contradictory and destructive to the main Design of it.'†

What this Author calls here a *single Act*, and a single *Instance* of Obedience, is true only of his own Sacrament, which consists only of a *single Action* of the *Memory* cast upon Christ at a *certain Instant* of Time, and to which single Action, this Author expressly says, that no Prayer is necessary,‡ not even necessary to *attend* upon it, either as *going before, or following after it*. That in its own *proper and peculiar Nature*, it has nothing to do with Prayer or Devotion of any kind, can have no Perfection from it, nor be in any Degree imperfect as to its *Nature* and *Essence*, for want of any Prayer, because its *Essence* is entirely distinct from Prayer.

And therefore all *Prayers, Thanksgivings* and *Devotions*, are to be considered as things distinct from this Sacrament, that have no Relation to the *peculiar* Nature and *proper* Essence of it.§

Hence it is plain, that we do not overcharge this Author, when we say, that he places the whole Nature of the Sacrament in a *bare single Action* of the Memory. For if, as he says, no kind of Prayer, Devotion or Thanksgiving, is of the Essence of this Sacrament, or can be an essential Part of it; then it has all its Perfection within itself, as it is a bare Act of the Memory, and

---

* Page 58. † Page 144. ‡ Page 160. § Page 173.

cannot, as to its own *proper* Nature or Essence, have anything added to it by Prayer, or taken from it by the want of Prayer. Hence it is also undeniable, that this Author's Sacrament is not so much as a *bare Act* of Religion, nor can have any more Religion in it, than if it was the Act of a *Parrot.* For no Act can be a religious Act, but so far, and in such Degree, as it is an Act of *Faith*, and *Love*, and *Devotion* to God. But this Author's Sacrament will not, as it is a Sacrament, allow Faith, or Love, or Devotion to be any *Part* of it, therefore it cannot be so much as a *bare Act* of Religion.

Nay, it may and must be said, that the right Observation of this Author's Sacrament is directly an Act of *Atheism.* For if it is an Act, that in its *own Nature*, and according to its *peculiar Essence*, cannot be performed according to what it is, unless it be done without *Faith*, and *Love*, and *Devotion* towards God; then it is directly an *Act of Atheism*, because *Atheism* is nothing else but a Cessation of Faith, Love and Devotion towards God. But the Essence of this Author's Sacrament cannot be preserved, unless you keep *Prayer*, *Devotion* and *Thanksgiving* out of it. Therefore to perform it rightly according to what it is, is to perform an Act of *Atheism.*

And if at the taking of the Bread and Wine, you should suffer Faith, or Love, or Adoration of God, or Thanksgiving, to take up your Mind, you might as well have let the Sacrament alone, for you have neglected *all that* in which its whole Nature consists; and have only been in such a State of Devotion, as has nothing to do with it, nor can *possibly* be a *Part* of it. And therefore, if you will perform this Sacrament rightly according to this Author, you must perform it *Atheistically;* you must excite such a Remembrance as *excludes* Faith, Love, Devotion and Thanksgiving, from being a Part of it. And your Remembrance is not performed, unless it be such a Remembrance as these things cannot be a Part of.

The Devils are said to *believe a God;* but why is it that their Faith is no *religious Act*, nor of any Benefit to them? It is because their Faith is only a *bare Act* of *believing*, just as this Author's Sacrament has only a *bare Act of remembering;* and that which is the Perfection of his Sacrament, is their Wretchedness.

If you ask this Author, why Faith, and Prayer, and Adoration, and Thanksgiving, are not of the Essence, or cannot be essential Parts of the Sacrament: All he has to say is this, that the *Duty of Prayer is a Duty absolutely distinct from the Participation of the Lord's Supper.**

---

* Page 160.

It may and must be granted, that Prayer, Humility, Faith, Hope, Charity, &c., are absolutely *distinct* from each other; that Humility is not Prayer, nor Faith in its proper Idea Prayer, and so of the rest. Yet notwithstanding this Distinction between them, they are all of them essential to each other. Faith is of the Essence of Prayer, Hope is of the Essence of Faith, and all of them are essential Parts of Prayer. Therefore when this Author asserts that Prayer is not an essential Part of the Communion, he is just as much in the right, and has as much Truth on his Side, as he who says, that Humility, Faith and Hope are not essential to Prayer, because Prayer is distinct from Humility, Faith and Hope.

What this Author saith of the Sacrament, that it is one *single Act*, or one *single Instance of Obedience*, is only true of his *own Fiction* of a Sacrament, which he makes to consist in a single Act of the Memory; and indeed it would be highly inconsistent with the Gospel, to make such a Sacrament a Means of obtaining the Benefits of Christ. But this is not the Sacrament of Christ, nor the Sacrament which the Church of Christ observes.

For all that relates to our Salvation, either on the Part of Christ, or on our own Part, is plainly united in that Sacrament which Christ has instituted. All that relates to our Salvation on the *Part of Christ*, is in the Sacrament, because he has said, that his *Body and Blood* are *there for the Remission of our Sins*, and that his Body and Blood are there to be *eaten and drank*, as the Food and Life of our Souls, therefore Christ as our Saviour is *wholly* there.

And all that relates to our Salvation on our own Part, is there; because we cannot *come* to Christ, or find him to be there, as he has said he is, unless we come to him with all those Qualities and pious Dispositions that *correspond* to him, as he is an *Atonement* for our Sins, and a Principle of Life to us; therefore all that relates to our Salvation, either on the *Part of Christ*, or on our *own Part*, is plainly united in the Sacrament. And to call such a Communion *one single Act* of Obedience, is just the same Absurdity, as to say, that the *Baptism* of a *Heathen* converted to Christianity, is but *one single Instance of Obedience*. For everything that is implied in such a *Conversion* and *Baptism*, whether it be on the Part of Christ, or on the Part of the Person baptized, is implied in this *Communion*.

And as the Baptism of such a Person contains *all* in it that *relates* to his Salvation, either on the Part of Christ, or on his own Part, and therefore cannot without great Ignorance be called a *single Instance* or Act of Obedience: So it is with the Sacrament, it is *all that* to the pious Communicant, both on the

Part of Christ, and on his own Part, that Baptism is to the true converted Heathen; and he is made an actual Partaker of all the Benefits of Christ by it, as the *Convert* is made so by *Baptism;* and therefore it is the same Absurdity to call it a single Act, or Instance of Obedience.

And as it would be vain and groundless to say, that it was *inconsistent with the main Design of the Gospel*, to make such Baptism the *actual* partaking of all the *Benefits* of Christ; so it is equally, if not more so, to say the same thing of Communion; because every pious and holy Disposition is to be supposed to be in an *higher* State, in the pious Communicant, than in the pious Desirer of Baptism; and therefore, it cannot without much Absurdity be supposed, that the Sacrament is not as beneficial to the pious Communicant, as Baptism is to the pious Convert.

For if Christ has appointed this Institution, to assure us, that he is *there*, both as the *Atonement* for our Sins, and a *Principle of Life to us*, and we come to it with such pious Dispositions as *correspond* and *answer* to him in both these Respects, and make us capable of him; it must be great Absurdity to say, that we find him *not* there as our Atonement, *nor* receive him as a Principle of Life to us, *nor* are made Partakers of these Benefits of him.

If we stand before this Atonement, *without* such Dispositions as *correspond* to it, we are as *absent* from the *Sacrament of Christ*, as they are that refuse to come to it; if we eat that which is before us in the Sacrament, without such *Faith* and *Purity* as qualify us to receive the Flesh and Blood of Christ, we are only eating *that*, which *might* have been the *Bread of Life* to our Souls.

But if we, according to the Condition of our Humanity, are *that* which these two *essential* Parts of the Sacrament require us to be, then we may and ought as firmly to believe, that we are by this Sacrament made *actual Partakers* of all the Benefits of Christ, as that we are saved through Christ, and not by ourselves.

This Author makes great Complaint of ascribing these Benefits to the Reception of the Communion, because *it is*, as he says, *to put that upon a single Instance of Obedience, which our blessed Lord has made to depend upon the whole System of all Virtues united in us:* That is, Christ has made the System of all Virtues united in us, to be the *only Qualification* for the *actual* partaking of his Benefits; which is not only utterly inconsistent with the Gospel, but nonsensical in itself; for it is saying that we are then *only qualified* for the Benefits of our Saviour, when we have *no need* of them; for if all Virtues were so united in us, all that our Saviour could do for us, would be done beforehand.

But let us take an Instance or two from our Saviour's own Words, and then we shall best see how truly this Author has said, that he has made the actual partaking of his Benefits, *to depend upon the whole System of all Virtues united*. When our blessed Lord stood by *Jacob's* Well, talking with the Woman of *Samaria*, he said to her, ' If thou knewest the Gift of God, and ' who it is that saith to thee, give me to drink, thou wouldst have ' asked of him, and he would have given thee living Water; a ' Water which shall be in him that drinketh it, a Well of Water ' springing up into everlasting Life.'*

Here, I suppose, are offered to this poor Woman *all the Benefits* of the Saviour of Mankind. Our Lord does not say to her, If thou hadst the *whole System of all Virtues united in thee*, then thou mightest be made a Partaker of all my Benefits; I could make the Water of eternal Life perpetually spring up within thee.

No, there is no such Jargon as this in the Gospel: But as he came as a compassionate Saviour, to make the Blind to see, the Deaf to hear, and the Dumb to speak, and the Dead to awake; as he came as a good *Shepherd* to seek that which was lost, and as a *Physician* to heal the Sick; so he only says to the Woman, if she had *asked*, that is, if she had felt the *Want* of a Saviour, as the Blind feel the want of Sight, and her *Heart* had only *desired* this Gift of God, he would then have bestowed this greatest of all Gifts upon her.

But surely, if this Desire in the Woman would have made her thus capable of *all the Benefits* of our Saviour, it cannot be inconsistent with the Gospel, to make the *same Desire* as beneficial to a *true* and *pious* Christian, as it would have been to an *unbaptized Samaritan*.

Again, our Lord saith, 'All things whatsoever ye shall ask in ' Prayer, believing, ye shall receive.'† Here you see, *all things*, and therefore *all the Benefits of Christ*, are ascribed to *Faith*, and we have everything that we can desire or pray for, by virtue of it. Does not our Lord here ascribe as much *Benefit* to Faith, as ever anyone ascribed to the holy Communion? Or who ever said that of the Power, or Benefit, or Efficacy of the Sacrament, which our Lord here says of the Benefit of *Faith* in Prayer?

Is not this as inconsistent with the Gospel, as the actual partaking of Christ's Benefits, by the *single Duty* of receiving the

---

* John iv. 10.   † Matt. xxi. 22.

Sacrament? Is not this Benefit of the Prayer of Faith as contrary to this Author's *whole System of Virtues united in us*, as the other Benefit of the Sacrament? Is it not as just to say, that this *Prayer* of Faith is only *a single Instance* of Obedience, as to say so of the Sacrament? And is not the *main Design of the Gospel* as much destroyed by making *Faith* to be thus beneficial, as by making the Communion to be so beneficial?

Or can it be supposed, that when our Lord, who ascribes thus much to the *Prayer* of Faith, when it is *alone*, would think it *too much* to be ascribed to it, when the Holy Sacrament is *united* with it? Or must it be supposed, that this *Prayer* of Faith loses its Virtue and Power, is deprived of its excellent Effects, *only then*, when it is a Part of the Communion of Christ's Body and Blood.

Again, our Lord saith, 'Verily, verily, I say unto you, What-'soever ye shall ask the Father in my Name, he will give it you.' Must not this Author have as much to complain of in this Doctrine, that ascribes so much to Prayer in the *Name of Christ*, as in that Doctrine, that ascribes so much to the Sacrament? Must he not say, that the praying in the *Name of Christ*, is but *one single Instance of Obedience;* and that to say, we are thereby made Partakers of all the Benefits of Christ, is *putting that upon one single Act of Obedience*, which our blessed Lord has *made to depend upon the whole System of all Virtues united in us?* Must he not say, that this Account of the Power and Efficacy of Prayer in *Christ's Name*, is a Doctrine destructive of the main Design of the Gospel?

For everything that this Author objects against this Doctrine of the Sacrament, must with the same Strength be objected against these, and many other the like express Declarations of our Saviour.

Everyone must know that it would be very easy to produce various Passages of the Gospel, that teach the same Doctrine, as these do that I have quoted; and that when this Author said, our Saviour *made the partaking of his Benefits to depend upon the whole System of all Virtues united in us*, he had just the same Reason and Authority from the Gospel to say so, as he has to say, that Christ declared he came to *seek* that which was *not lost*, to *heal* those which were *not sick*, and *save* those who stood in *no need* of a Saviour.

But now, seeing this is the Nature, Power, and Efficacy of the Prayer of *Faith*, and of Prayer in the *Name of Christ;* seeing he himself has assured us, that they make us actual Partakers of everything that we can ask of the Father, or that he through Christ can give us, we have the fullest Assurance, that if we do that which the Sacrament requires to be done; if we don't separate *Faith* and Prayer in the *Name of Christ* from it, but perform it in *this Faith and Prayer,* or make it as it ought to be, a *real Exercise* of this Faith and Prayer, then we receive in and by it all the Benefits of our Saviour.

But because this Author seems entirely out of his Element, when speaking of the Benefits of Jesus Christ, and not to be able to speak an intelligible Word about it, as to the true Grounds and Nature of it, but only to puzzle himself and the Reader with an empty superficial Way of arguing from the Sound of Words: I shall therefore, in a word or two, endeavour to lay before you the true Grounds of the Benefits of Jesus Christ, as he is the Saviour of *all Mankind.*

It is the fundamental Doctrine, or rather the *known* Foundation of all *revealed* Religion, and the *known* Foundation of all natural Piety and Goodness, that Jesus Christ is the *second Adam:* That he is a *common Head,* or *Parent,* or *Person* to all Mankind, in the same manner as *Adam* is the common *Head,* or *Parent,* or *Person* to all Mankind.

That a real *Birth, Life, Nature,* and true *Man,* is in the same *Truth* and *Reality* derived to us from this our *second Adam,* as a real Birth, and Life, and Nature is derived to us from our first *Adam.* And that as without any *Figure* or *Metaphor* of Speech we are all said to be born of *Adam,* and descended from him; so we are all in the same Dependence upon our *second Adam,* really and not figuratively born of him, and have our Descent from him; Spirit of his Spirit, Life of his Life, in the same Truth and Reality, as every Man has the Nature of the first *Adam.*

And herein is seen the infinite Depth of Divine Love and Goodness to Mankind, who though they were by the Condition of their Creation to be derived from one *Head* or *Parent,* and to take his *State* of Perfection or Imperfection; yet were by the Goodness and Care of God for them, provided from the very Beginning with a *second Parent,* or common Head, who after the *Fall* of the first, and the fallen State that he had brought upon his Posterity, should be a *common Restorer,* and put it in every Man's Power to have the same Choice of Life and Death, as the first Man had; that so, they who were lost before they were born, and were made Inheritors of a miserable Nature without their Choice, might have a Divine Life restored to them in a *second* Parent, which should not be in the Power of anyone to lose for them, but should depend entirely upon their *own Will and Desire* of it, upon their *own Faith,* and *Hope,* and *Hungering* after it.

This eternal and immutable Truth, worthy of being written in capital Letters of Gold, is the Foundation of all revealed and natural Religion: and a standing Monument of God's universal Goodness and Love to all Mankind, and such as is sufficient to make all Men rejoice and give praise to God.

For by this Truth, all that seems hard and cruel to human Reason, that the Posterity of *Adam* should be involved in the Consequences of their first Father's Fall, (yet how could it be otherwise?) all this, I say, is made a wonderful Scene of Love, as soon as we consider, that all Mankind were redeemed as soon as they were lost, and that their Redemption was as *early*, as universal, and as extensive in its Effects, as the Fall was. And that no Son of *Adam* is left to inherit a *poor, earthy, perishable, corrupt* Nature from him, without having it in his Choice to be *born again* of a second *Adam*, and restored, with Advantage, to all the Riches, and Treasures, and Blessings of a divine and paradisiacal Nature, which were lost without his Consent.

There is something so amazingly loving and merciful in this Conduct of divine Providence over Mankind, that I cannot help thinking, no one can calmly consider it in the Quiet of his Mind, without having all his Infidelity melted down by it. And that such an *Act of general Pardon*, as early as the first Sin, and a new Parent provided for us, to be our Parent by *Choice and Faith*, as soon as our first Parent had undone us without our Consent: Such an Act of Pardon being the Beginning and Foundation of all revealed Religion, and of everything that is afterwards revealed in it, has surely enough in it, if once known, to make revealed Religion the Joy, and Comfort, and Desire of every Man's Heart. What would I give that I could but dart one Ray of this Truth into every Unbeliever's Heart; for the smallest Ray of it would do to everyone as the *Light that fell from Heaven* did to St. *Paul*, it would make as it were *Scales fall from his Eyes:* And he would find that all *Books* and *Systems* of Infidelity were as unreasonable in themselves, and as hurtful to him, as those Commissions were which *Paul* had *from the High Priest to bind all that called on the Name of Christ*.

But to proceed: That Jesus Christ is thus the Saviour and universal Redeemer of all Mankind, that he is this second *Adam* or Parent, giving a new Birth and Life to all that which was extinguished and lost by *Adam;* restoring *Adam* himself, and in him all Mankind to a Possibility of being born again, by their own *Will, Choice, Faith,* and *Desire;* and that revealed Religion *began* with the *Declaration* of this Redemption, and has revealed nothing but for the Sake and Support of it, is a Truth sufficiently attested by Scripture.

The Declaration which God made to *Adam* immediately after his Fall, of a *Seed of the Woman to bruise the Serpent's Head*, was a Declaration of *Pardon* and *Redemption* to *Adam*, and in him to all Mankind; for what he said to *Adam*, that he said to all that were in the Loins of *Adam;* who, as they fell in his Fall before they were born, without the Possibility of any one Man's being exempted from it; so were they all put into his State of Pardon and Redemption before they were born, without the Possibility of any one Man's being excluded, or left out of it.

Thus revealed Religion *begins* with an Offer of a *second Adam*, and upon the Foot of an *universal* Pardon and Redemption to all Mankind. Every Son of *Adam* is in the same Covenant with God that *Adam* was, and has the same *Bruiser* of the Serpent as *near* to him, as he was to *Adam*, and declared to be his Redeemer, in the same Degree as he was declared to be the Redeemer of *Adam*.

And who would seek for Arguments against such a Saviour? Or who would cavil at a *revealed Religion*, that has no other Beginning or End, but to reveal an *universal Redemption?* Or who can enough call upon all the Creation, Heaven and Earth, Angels and Men, and everything that hath Breath, to praise the Lord for such Salvation? You must forgive these little Digressions; for I want so much to touch the Heart of my Reader, and make him in love with God, and his own Salvation in Christ Jesus, that I know not how to content myself with bare Arguments.

Now this Declaration of God to *Adam*, of his pardon and Redemption by the Seed of the Woman, is not to be considered, as we consider the *Declaration* of a *Pardon* made by some great *Prince* to an offending *Subject*, which is only a Declaration of *Words*, that are heard only with our outward Ears, and of a Person that is entirely distinct from us.

God's pardoning a Sinner, or redeeming fallen Man, has nothing like this in it. If this offending Subject had his *Life*, and *Breath*, and *Being* in and from this great Prince, or could be said to *live, and move, and have his Being in him;* it would be easy, nay, necessary to believe, that his Declaration of Pardon to him, must be something very different from a Pardon of Words, and must signify some *inward Effect*, or *Change*, or new *State* of Existence in his Prince.

Now this Declaration of God's Pardon and Reconciliation to *Adam*, and in him to all Mankind, is not the Declaration of a Being that is *out* of, or *separate* from us, but of a God in whom *we live, and move, and have our Being;* who is the *Centre* of that which is most *Central* in us, the Life of our Life, the Spirit of our Spirit: His Declaration therefore of Pardon is not a Declaration of *Words*, or of a Being that is separate from us; but must signify some inward *Change*, or new *State* of our Existence in him, or that *he is* to us, and in us, that which *he was not* before he pardoned us. For his Words are Power, and what he speaks he acts; and what he acts, he acts not *out of us*, but in the *inmost Essence* of our Being, because so we exist in him, and he in us.

If God at the Fall had said, *Let us save Man*, the same had been effected, as when he said, 'Let us make Man.' When therefore God said to *Adam* and *Eve*, 'The Seed of the Woman shall 'bruise the Head of the Serpent,' what was said, was done; and it was the same Thing, had the same Meaning and Effect, as if he had said, 'Be ye henceforth in a State of Salvation, and let 'the redeeming, conquering Seed of the Woman from this time 'begin to have Power in you, and to be in you a Strength and 'Might against the Serpent.' And what he said was done, as when he said, 'Let there be Light, and there was Light.'

Thus this Declaration of Pardon and Redemption made by God to *Adam*, and, in him, to all his Posterity, was not *solely* a Promise of something to come, or of a Pardon that was at a Distance, no more than it was the Promise of a God that was at a Distance from him; but the Declaration of something then *inwardly done* and *given*, by a God inwardly present in him, and signified no less than God's *seeking* and *manifesting* himself again to a Creature, that had *lost* him as his *God* and *only Good*.

For how can the Anger of that Being, 'in whom we live, and 'move, and have our Being,' be only an Anger of *Words*, or made known to us only by Words? Or how can it be anything else, but some *inward Loss* of that which is our *Good* in him?

Or how can his Pardon be only a Pardon of *Words*, or something heard only with our Ears? Or how can it be anything else, but his *restoring* that to us, or his *reviving* that in us, which makes us again capable of *finding* him our *God and only Good?*

Therefore God's Declaration of Pardon to *Adam*, was not barely a Promise of something to come, but the Pardon itself; and was the *real Communication* of something to *Adam*, which made him *capable* of enjoying God as his *Good*, which he had not when he *wanted* to be pardoned, and which he could not have, if God was in a State of *Anger* with him.

Now had not God spoken this Pardon and Reconciliation to *Adam* after his Fall, he had been in the Condition of the *Deep*, when it was said, *Darkness was upon the Face of the Deep*.

Nay, it had been much worse with him; for had not God made this Declaration of Pardon and Redemption to him at that time, that is, had he not done *inwardly* in the *Depth* of his

Soul, something like that which he did to the Darkness of the Deep, when he spoke Light into it, *Adam* and *Eve*, and *all* their Posterity, had been inwardly mere *Devils*, and outwardly mere *Beasts*, a motley Mixture of both, till the Beast fell into the Earth, and the Soul to the State of Devils.

For had not God thus in the Beginning of the Fall, before any Man was born into the World of *Adam* and *Eve*, had he not spoken Pardon and Redemption unto *Adam* and *Eve;* neither they, nor any of their Posterity had been *capable* of any *Faith*, or *Hope*, or *Desire* of God, but had lived as much without all *Conscience*, or *Instinct* of Goodness, as the Beasts of the Earth and Devils do.

Therefore God redeemed Man, that is, restored to him a Power of being again his Creature, or a Power of *knowing* and *finding* him to be his *God*, when he said, the 'Seed of the Woman shall 'bruise the Serpent's Head.' He redeemed him by *communicating* to him a *Sense*, a *Feeling*, and a *Desire* of God, by communicating to him a *Capacity* to enjoy him as his *only Good*, by sowing into him a *Seed* of the Woman, a *Spark* of Life, an *Instinct* of Goodness, a *Taste* of Heaven, a *Principle* of Holiness, a *Touch* of Love, the *Pearl* of the Gospel, the *Pledge* of Immortality, the *hidden Kingdom* of God.

For all these Expressions of a Seed, a Spark, an Instinct, a Principle, a Pearl and Kingdom, are insufficient to express *that inward Treasure* of the Soul, and *Fund* of everlasting Happiness, which God in the Beginning of the Redemption, or as his Act of Redemption, communicated to Man.

Now in this Degree of Redemption is every Creature that is born of *Adam;* he has this Kingdom of God in his Soul, as a *Grain of Mustard Seed*, as a *Spark* of Life, as a *Pledge* of Immortality, as his *Attraction* to God: If he *tramples* this *Pearl* under his Feet, if he will *choke* this Word, if he will *put out* this Spark, if he will *resist* this Attraction, then his Destruction is from himself; and when the Carcass of Flesh and Blood falls off from him, he must find himself in his *own Hell*, and must have the Misery of a *darkened, anxious, fiery, self-tormented* Nature for ever, that would not suffer itself to be redeemed.

But if he will consent to his Redemption, and co-operate with that *inward Redeemer* which God has put into his Soul; if he will suffer his Spark to *kindle*, his *Instinct* of Goodness to *spread* itself, the Light of the Life to *arise* in him, the Voice of God to be *heard* in him; then will the *Divine* Life, the *inward* Man, be brought forth in him; and when his Body breaks off, Heaven will be made *manifest* in his Soul, and he will fall into all the Fulness of God. The *Son* of God will be his *Light*, the *Holy*

Spirit will *breathe* in him, and the Power and Omnipotency of the *Father* will be Life and Strength in him; and thus, in the completest Sense of the Words, shall he *ever live, and move, and have his Being* in God.

And now, my dear Reader, what shall I say to you? How shall I do that, which I most of all desire to do, touch your Heart? Or how can your Heart be untouched with this affecting View of the Mercies of God in Christ Jesus, and of the Riches and Treasures which lie hid in your own Soul, wanting nothing but your own Consent and good Wishes to be manifested in you?

But it may be, modern *Infidelity* has stolen into your Heart, and so you lie starving in the midst of Plenty, choosing rather to famish on the *dry Husks of Reason, Dispute*, and *Infidelity*, than to have this Divine Life, this Riches of your own Soul, discovered to you on the Terms of the Gospel. It may be you have buried this *Spark* of Life, this *inward Man*, and have heaped all the Earth upon him that you can get, that you have *sealed* the Stone of his *Sepulchre*, and have set your greatest Enemy, a *reasoning Infidelity*, upon the *Watch*, to dispute, wrangle, and deny every Doctrine of Scripture, *that* as a *good* Angel would roll away the Stone of the Sepulchre, and let your *inward Redeemer* arise in you.

If this is your Case, if you have let a *reasoning* Infidelity into your Heart, you know not what Mischief you have let into it; for the Denial of the Gospel reaches much further, and is more extensive than you imagine.

For to deny Jesus Christ, is to deny *your Share* in the first Pardon of God to Man; it is returning into the first State of the *Fall*, and refusing to be a Partner with *Adam* in his State of Forgiveness; it is going over to the Side of the Serpent, and declaring that you will not enter into Peace with God on the Terms of *bruising his Head;* for Jesus Christ that calls upon you in the *Gospel*, is that same Christ which became *Adam's* Pardon; and if you reject him in the Gospel, it is rejecting him from the Beginning: and is saying, that you will have no Share in that Salvation which was granted to *Adam*, and in him to all Mankind. Nay, what is still more, if you reject the *Saviour* offered to you in the *Gospel,* you reject *all that* which makes you differ from a *Devil;* for that Saviour which speaks to you in the Gospel, is that very same *inward Light of your Mind*, which makes you now differ from a Devil; for had you *nothing* of that Jesus Christ in you, whom you reject in the Gospel, you would be in the same *dark* Malignity, and *self-tormenting* Wretchedness, in which every diabolical Nature is.

To refuse him that speaketh to you in the Gospel, is not barely to renounce a certain *particular Religion* revealed by God at a certain Time, it is not barely to reject Christ as *come* in the *Flesh;* but it is rejecting *all* that God has ever *transacted* with Man, it is renouncing all that is *Divine* and *Good* within you, all that God inwardly speaks and teaches in the Depth of your Soul; it is saying that you will have no Benefit from the *good Workings* or Motions of your own Heart, or the *Instincts* of Goodness that are stirring in it; for Jesus Christ that calls you to Repentance in the Gospel, is the *very same* blessed Saviour, that *warns, reproves,* and *preaches* Repentance in the inmost Essence of your Spirit. For it is a Deceit of the grossest Kind, to think that Christ came only as our Saviour, when he came in the *Flesh,* or that he only speaks to us that which is *outwardly* spoken in the Gospel; for he always was *that* in every Man that *saved* him from being entirely a diabolical Nature, and was as really the Teacher and Mover of all that is good *within* you, as he was the Teacher of the *Gospel.* Therefore to reject him as your Saviour, to refuse him as such, and to desire to be without him, is in reality to desire to be in *Hell,* to have the *Darkness* and *Distress* of diabolical Beings; it is desiring to be without any *Light of God* upon your Mind, or any *Instincts* of Goodness stirring in your Heart.

And if this is not the *immediate Effect* of your Infidelity, if you don't immediately find that the Denial of Christ is *putting out* all the Light within you; 'tis because Christ is Love, and will be so good towards you, as to continue his inward Light to you, though you reject his outward Light of the Gospel.

But, my Friend, be wise in time, for this Goodness will continue but a Time; don't let a *poor worthless* Infidelity beguile you to *eat the Dust* of the Earth with the Serpent, when God has provided for you the *Bread of Life.* For this Time of Goodness and Forbearance will soon be over; and if the End of it finds you in your Infidelity, rejecting the Benefits of Christ, you will then see the whole of all you desired, you will be without Christ, you will find that all is gone with him, and that you will have nothing left, but that Nature which is the Torment of Hell.

You now think, that because you can frame *Ideas* of Virtue, and exert some *Acts* of Goodness, though you reject all Faith in Christ, that therefore he is not *necessary* to your Virtue and Happiness; but your miserable Mistake lies here, that you think Christ is only he that preached the Gospel, and that it is not him that speaks and moves every good Thought or Word that is spoken in you, but that you have a Light and Goodness of your own. But when this Time is over, and you have spent your Hour of Grace, Christ will no longer stand knocking at the Door of your Heart; and then you will find, that you are as empty of all *inward Light*, as you are of the Gospel, and that by rejecting him as your Saviour, you have rejected all that was *Divine* and *Good* within you.

Infidelity therefore is a much *deeper* Evil than you may imagine, it denies and rejects more than you think of; you may intend by it only to change the Light of the *Gospel* for the Light of *Reason*, but Christ will not be divided by your Intention; he is the *one only* Light of Men, the same in the *Heart* that he is in the *Gospel;* and though you may now think that you have *two Teachers*, because he teaches in two Places, and therefore may adhere to one, and reject the other; yet this is a Deceit that can last no longer than the Disputings of this World last with you.

When the Veil of Flesh and Blood is pulled off, and you must stand in the Nakedness of your Soul before God; then you will know, that these *two Lights* are only one, and that neither of them can be rejected by itself. These Lights appear now as two, only because God is so good as to leave no Part of you *untried*, but presses the Kingdom of Heaven upon you, both from within, and from without.

The eternal *Word*, the *Son* of God, took human Nature upon him, worked all his Miracles, taught all his Doctrines, underwent all his Sufferings, to make that Light of the Mind, which *every Man that cometh into the World* had received from him, effectual to their Salvation; therefore the Light of the Gospel, and the Light of the Mind, are one, as Christ is one, whether he speaks to you inwardly or outwardly. If therefore you reject Christ in the utmost Efforts of his Goodness to save you, you will find that the renouncing of Christ, is renouncing all that you have from him, and that all the good Light of your Mind, call it what you will, as it was his, is all rejected with him, and that nothing is left in that Soul, where he is not, but mere Darkness.

But to return to my Subject; what I have said above of God's Covenant with *Adam*, and the Redemption granted to him, is God's Covenant with all Mankind, and therefore thus far all Mankind are the redeemed of Jesus. There is no Partiality in God, no Election of one People to Salvation, and Dereliction of another to their own Misery. As all *fell* and *died* in *Adam*, so all were *restored* in his Restoration.

Thus says the Apostle, ' As by the Offence of one, Judgment ' came upon all to Condemnation; even so by the Righteousness 'of one, the free Gift came upon all Men unto Justification of 'Life.'*

But you will perhaps say, how does it appear, that this first Covenant of God with Mankind, or Redemption of all Men in the Redemption of *Adam*, is the Redemption in and by Jesus Christ.

I may better ask you, Where you can have the smallest Reason even to suspect the contrary? For is not the *Seed of the Woman*, Jesus Christ? And if our Salvation then began, when God made Declaration of the *saving Power* of this Seed, it is plain, that Christ's Redemption then began in Mankind, that he was thenceforward in every Man as a *Spark* of Life, that as a *secret Power*, should bruise the Serpent, and support us against him, till he, in the Fulness of Time, should, in the *Fulness of the Promise*, become such a Seed of the Woman, as should openly triumph over Death and Hell, and all the Kingdom of the Serpent. For if it were Christ that became *Adam's* Redeemer in the promised Seed; if he had actually the Power of that Salvation manifested in his Soul, and was in a State of Redemption, because Christ was become the Ransom and Life of his Soul; then all the Sons of *Adam*, from the first to the last, are in *Adam's* state of Covenant with God through Jesus Christ, and have the Seed of the Woman doing *all that* for them, which it did for *Adam*.

Again, Does not the Gospel expressly say, that Jesus Christ is the *True Light, which lighteth every Man that cometh into the World?* Therefore Jesus Christ is in every Man that cometh into the World, and every Son of *Adam* is in a State of Redemption in and by Jesus Christ, and every Son of *Adam* has received *that same* from Jesus Christ, which *Adam* received from him, *viz*., an *inward Light* of Life, a *Beginning* of his Salvation, an *actual Power* or Strength to resist the Serpent; therefore Jesus Christ, as he is the Light and Life of Men, as he is the Bruiser of the Serpent, as he is the Power of Salvation, is and ever was the *Free Gift of God unto all Men*.

Again, does not the Scripture teach us, that God is as well the God of the *Gentiles*, as the God of the *Jews?* But if he is their God, then they are his People. And as we know that God is not the Creator of any Beings, but in and by Jesus Christ, by whom everything was made, that was made; so he is not the God of any People, but in and by Jesus Christ, who is the Reconciler of all Things unto God, by whom alone all Things and Persons are made acceptable to him; therefore if he is the God

---

* Rom. v. 18.

and Father of the *Gentiles*, then the *Gentiles* have an Interest in Jesus Christ, have all their Access to God, as their Father and Creator, in and by the Benefits and Merits of Jesus Christ; or, in other Words, are actual Partakers of the Benefits of Jesus Christ, as he is the Saviour of Mankind.

Which is a Privilege or Blessing that this Author will not allow Christians to have, even when eating the Flesh and drinking the Blood of Christ; so little does he know what he speaks of, when he speaks of the partaking of the Benefits of Christ.

But you will perhaps further ask, How can the *Gentiles* have an Interest in the Benefits of Jesus Christ, since they know him not, nor ask anything in his Name. May you not as well ask me, How they can be said *to live, and move, and have their Being in God*, who know not what it is to have *Life*, and *Motion*, and *Being* in him, nor ever confessed it in a true Manner, or under a right Sense of it? For if they can have the Benefit of a Life in God, and be blessed by it, who are either totally, or much ignorant of it; then Christ, as he is the Atonement and Life of *Adam* and his Posterity, may be a Benefit and Blessing to those who are totally ignorant of it, or at least know nothing of him, as he is Christ, or the Son of God manifest in the Flesh.

Again, the Scripture says of Jesus Christ, that he came *unto his own, and his own received him not,* that is, *they knew him not:* Now if he could come unto his own, though they knew him not, then it is plain, that they may be *his*, who know him not, that is, they may have some Interest in him, be purchased by him, have received much from him, be greatly related to him, who yet are insensible of it.

Lastly, You might much better ask me, How can they, who never knew anything of Christ, as their *Mediator* and *Atonement*, be judged by him at the last Day? For if they were altogether Strangers to Christ, had no Relation to him, had received nothing from him, or by means of him, he could not be their *Judge*. For Jesus Christ cannot do anything as a *Judge*, till he has done everything as a *Saviour;* nor be anywhere a Judge, but where he has first appeared as a Saviour.

Therefore it is an evident Truth, that had not *all* Nations, and every *individual* Man, received a *certain* Means of Salvation through him, he could not be the *Judge* of *all*.

Heathens, Jews, and Christians differ not thus, that the one have a *Saviour* and are in a *redeemed* State, and the other are not; or that the one have *one* Saviour, and the other have *another;* for the *one Judge* of all, is the one Saviour of all: but they only differ in this, that one and the same Saviour is *differently* made known to them, and differently to be *obtained by them.* The Heathens knew him not as he was in the numerous *Types* of the *Jewish* Law, they knew him not as he is gloriously *manifested* in the Gospel; but they knew him as he was the *God* of their *Hearts,* manifesting himself by a *Light* of the Mind, by *Instincts* of Goodness, by a *Sensibility* of Guilt, by *Awakenings* and *Warnings* of Conscience; and this was their *Gospel,* which they received as truly and really in, and by, and through *Jesus Christ* as the Law and Gospel were received through him.

Therefore it is a great and glorious Truth, enough to turn every Voice into a Trumpet, and make Heaven and Earth ring with Praises and Hallelujahs to God, that Jesus Christ is the Saviour of all the World, and of every Man of every Nation, Kindred, and Language. Therefore saith St. *John,* ' They sung ' a new Song, saying, Thou art worthy to take the Book, and to ' open the Seals thereof; for thou wast slain, and hast redeemed ' us to God by thy Blood, out of every Kindred, and Tongue, and ' People, and Nation.'* And again, ' After this I beheld, says ' he, and lo, a great Multitude, which no Man could number, of ' all Nations, and Kindreds, and People, and Tongues, stood ' before the Throne, and before the Lamb, clothed with white ' Robes, and with Palms in their Hands, and cried with a loud ' Voice, saying, Salvation to our God which sitteth upon the ' Throne, and unto the Lamb.'†

I must, before I proceed further, put in here a Word of Caution to two Sorts of Readers. If you are in such a State, as I supposed one to be above, touched with modern Infidelity, having your *Reason* set upon the *watch* to guard you against the Gospel, it may here do its Office, and will perhaps tell you, that what I have here said in favour of the *general Light,* or *Seed* of Life that is in all Men, is much the same thing that you say in Defence of *natural Reason,* or Religion, only with this Difference, that I mention it as coming from Christ, and you consider it as the bare Light of Nature.

Now if this were all the Difference, is not this enough to show you, that my Opinion is the very *Denial* of yours; for if I proved that what you called the natural Light of Men, was wholly derived from the *divine Revelation,* would not that be a sufficient Proof that I denied and disproved your Religion of natural Reason? And have I not done the same thing, if I have asserted the Light of Men to be a Light derived from Christ? And how can such an Assertion be made in the least favourable to your Opinion, that such a Light is *natural?*

---

* Rev. v. 9. † Rev. vii. 9, 10.

But to prevent all Misapprehension, I now declare to you, and will show you in the most explicit manner, that that which I call the Light of Men, or the Seed of Life sown into all Men by Jesus Christ, is as wholly different from that which you call *natural Reason*, as Light is different from Darkness; and that they stand in that same State of *Contrariety* to each other, both as to their *Original*, their *Nature* and *Qualities*, as our Saviour and *Pontius Pilate* did.

I must therefore assure you, that as I fear God, and wish your Salvation, so I can no more say a word in favour of what is now called the Religion of *natural Reason*, than I would recommend to you the ancient *Idolatry* of Heathens. And yet at the same time, I am no more an Enemy to *Reason*, than I am an Enemy to the Light of the Sun, and as freely wish you all the Benefits of the one, as of the other.

But if you do by *Reason*, as they did by the *Sun*, who thought it to be *divine, fell down* before it, and expected *all* from it; then I must speak as plainly to you of the *Inability* of Reason to do you this Good, as I must have spoken of the *Inability* of the Sun to such *Idolaters* of it.

And if I should have told them, that the Sun was no more their God, than the poorest *Worm* upon Earth, and that it could no more make those to be divine that worshipped it, than a Storm of *Hail* could make those to be divine that it fell upon, I should have told them a great Truth. So if I say to you, that *Reason*, or the *Faculty* of Reasoning, is no more the Religion of Man, than the Faculty of *doubting* or *erring* is; and that it can no more make those to be divine who place their Trust in it, than a great *Error* can make those to be divine who abide by it, I should tell you a great and useful Truth.

For Reason, or a Faculty of Reasoning upon the moral Habitudes and Relations of Things and Persons, or upon the *moral Proportion* of Actions, has no more of the Nature and Power of Religion in it, than so much Reasoning upon the Relations of *Squares* and *Triangles*. And if a Man had this Religion of *Reason* only when he was dreaming in *Sleep*, it would be the same good thing to him, as it is to those who make it their Religion when they are awake.

For the *Good* of Religion, is like the Good of *Food* and *Drink* to an hungry and thirsty Creature; and if instead of giving such a one Bread and Wine, or Water, you should teach him to seek for Relief, by attending to clear Ideas of the Nature of Bread, of different Ways of making it, and the Relation it hath to Water; he would be left to die in the Want of Sustenance, just as your *Religion* of Reasoning leaves the Soul to perish in the Want of

Religion. And as such a Man would have no more Benefit from such *Reasoning* about the Relation that Bread had to Water, whether it was the Reasoning of a *Dream*, or the Reasoning of a Man *awake*, because either Way he was kept under the same Want of that which was to preserve his Life; so whether a Man has your Religion of *Reasoning* only when he is *asleep*, or when he is awake, is the same thing; because either Way he is kept under the same Want of that which can alone preserve the Life of the Soul. For the *Good* that is in Religion, or the Good that we want to receive by it, is no more within the *reach* of our *Reason*, or to be *communicated* to us by it, than the Good of Food is in the reach of our Reason, or can be communicated to us by it. And yet as a Man may have the *Good* of Food much assisted and secured to him, by the right Use of his Reason, though Reason has not the Good of Food in it; so a Man may have the *Good* of Religion much assisted and secured to him by the right Use of Reason, though Reason has not the *Good* of Religion in it.

And as a Man ought not to be accused as an Enemy to the true Use of Reasoning about Food, because he declares that Reason is not Food, nor can supply the Place of it; so a Man ought not to be accused as an Enemy to the Use of Reasoning in Religion, because he declares that Reason is not Religion, nor can supply the Place of it.

But to show you the Bottom of this whole Matter, pray consider with me as follows: We have no Want of Religion, but *so far* as we want to *better* our State in God, or so far as we are *unpossessed* of God, or *less* possessed of him than we might be. This is the true Ground of Religion, to alter our *State* of Existence in God, and to have *more* of the Divine Nature or Perfections communicated to us. Nothing therefore is our *Good* in Religion, but that which alters our State of Existence in God for the better, and puts us in Possession of something of God, or makes us Partakers of the Divine Nature in such a Manner and Degree as we wanted it.

Everything that is in Life, has its Degree of Life in and from God, it *lives*, and *moves*, and *has its Being in God.* This is as true of Devils themselves, as of the highest and most perfect Angels. Therefore all the Happiness or Misery of all Creatures consists only in this, as they are *more* or *less* possessed of God, or as they *differently* partake of the Divine Nature, or according to their different State of Existence in God.

But if this be the Truth of the Matter, (and who can deny it?) then we have the Certainty of Demonstration, that nothing can be our *Good* in Religion, but that which *communicates* to us something of God, or the Divine Nature, or that which *betters* our State and Manner of Existence in God.

For if Devils are what they are, because of their State and Manner of Existence in God; if blessed Angels are what they are, because of their State and Manner of Existence in God; then it undeniably follows, that all that is betwixt Angels and Devils, all Beings from the Happiness of the one to the Misery of the other, must and can have no other Happiness or Misery, but according to their *State* and *Manner* of Existence in God, or according as they have more or less of the State of Angels, or the State of Devils in them. Therefore nothing can be our *Good* in Religion, but that which alters our State and Manner of Existence in God, and renders us possessed of him in a different and better Manner.

Now if you were to send to the fallen Spirits of Darkness, all the *Systems* of your Religion of *Reason*, that have been published here, to let them know that they have the Power of their own Restoration and Happiness within themselves, that they need seek to nothing, but their own *natural Reason* and Understanding, and the *Strength* and *Activity* of their own Powers, to raise them to all the Happiness they are capable of; such a Religion would be so far from altering or mending their State of Existence in God, or doing them any good, that it would add Strength to all their Chains; and the more firmly they believed and relied upon it, the more would they be confirmed and fixed in their Separation from God.

And yet, a Religion that must necessarily keep them in Hell, is the only Religion that you will have to carry you to Heaven. May God deliver you from this Error!

On the other hand, if you could infuse into those dark Spirits a Glimpse of that *Light* of the Mind, or *Instinct* of Goodness, which I have said all Mankind have received from Jesus Christ, as their second *Adam*, their Salvation would be so far begun, and Hell would become a State of *Trial* for their Redemption. Therefore that Light of the Mind, or Instinct of Goodness, which I have spoken of, has the utmost Contrariety to your Religion of *Reason*, that can possibly be imagined.

The one is the Beginning of the new Birth in Christ, and the Foundation of Heaven; the other is the Growth of Death, and the very Essence of Hell in the Soul. Now that here is no Aggravation of the Matter, but the plain and naked Truth, you may easily see from a Consideration of the Articles of your Religion of *Reason*. Your Religion of Reason, is a Religion of *natural Strength* and *Power*, that rejects the *Necessity* of a Saviour, that feels no *Want* of him, that rejects the Necessity of *Divine Grace*, the *Guidance* of the Holy Spirit, and feels no *Want* of it; these are the *essential Parts* of your Religion of Reason, which are in Truth and Reality the Religion of Hell, or that *very State* of Mind which reigns and governs there.

For could those miserable Spirits renounce these Articles of your Religion, their Chains of Darkness would break off from them. Could they cast themselves down before God, humbly confessing, that of themselves they are not able to save themselves, or even to think a good Thought: Could they in Humility and Penitence beg of the Mercy of God, to do something *in* them and *for* them, which they cannot do to themselves : Could they acknowledge the *Want* of a Saviour, ask God to *find* one for them: Could they *feel* and *own* the Want of his *Holy Spirit*, and humbly beg of God to be assisted by it, a Door of Salvation would be opened to them. And yet you see that nothing opens this Door, but the plain and full Renunciation of every Part of your Religion of Reason.

And if it be asked, Why they cannot be saved? no other Reason can be given, but because they *will* not; they *cannot* renounce your *Religion of Reason*, that is, they cannot humbly acknowledge their own *Inability* to do themselves good ; they will not admit the Thought of a *Saviour*, they will not be *assisted* by the Spirit of God, or own the *Want* of his Life in them, and therefore they are and must be what they are, Prisoners in Chains of Darkness.

Awake therefore, my dear Friend, and cast away this Religion from you, with more Earnestness than you would cast burning Coals out of your Bosom : For could it only destroy your Body, I should have been less earnest in giving you notice of it. But as I have the fullest Conviction, that it is the *Death* and *Darkness* of your Soul, and is bringing the *Essence* of Hell secretly and invisibly into it ; you must forgive me, if I use all the Expressions and Descriptions I can think of, to prevent your giving into it. Had I a superficial Charity for you, or a slight View of the Hurt you are doing to yourself, I should speak to you accordingly ; but the Depth and Earnestness of my Desire to do you good, must have expressions suitable to it. Study not therefore how to find fault with me, or to dislike the Words, or Manner of my *Style*, for it is the Style of Love and Zeal for your Salvation ; and if you condemn anything but Love in it, you condemn something that is not there.

I have shown you, that the Religion of Reason is the *very State* of hellish Minds, and that they are what they are, because they will *do all* for themselves, place all in their *own Strength*, because they cannot be *humble*, cannot own the *Want* of a Saviour ; and I have only appealed to this Instance of the *Nature* and *Power* of your Religion of Reason, to show you in the most undeniable Manner, that it must, and can have no other Effect upon you, than it has upon them; that it must produce the *same* Hell in your Soul, the same Separation from God, and cannot possibly be any more the Way of Salvation for you, than it is for them.

What is the Reason that the *Faith* of the Devils, or their Belief of a God, does them no good? It is because there is nothing in it but their *own Act*, a mere Product of their own; it is because it is an Act of your *Religion* of *Reason*, that will have no Virtue but by its *own Strength*, and of its own Growth. But if they could have so much of the Religion of the Gospel, as to say in the Language of it, *Lord, help our Unbelief*, their Faith would be changed, and be beneficial to them, only for this Reason, because they had renounced your Religion of doing good to themselves by their *own natural* Powers.

Hence it sufficiently appears, that your Way of natural Reason cannot be the Way of Salvation; 1*st*, Because the *Want* of Salvation is nothing else, but the wanting to have our State, or Manner of Existence in God, altered for the better; or to have *something* of God communicated to us, which we want and are capable of receiving. But if this is the *Nature* of Salvation, then no Religion can *save* us, can do us our *proper Good*, or supply our proper Want, but that which has Power to *alter* our State of Existence in God, or to *communicate* to us that of God which we want, and are capable of. Therefore it follows, that nothing but that same God which created us, which gave us our State and Manner of Existence in him, and communicated to us that which we possess of him; nothing but that same God can *redeem* us, or help us to that State or Manner of Existence in him, which we have lost, or are in want of.

But if God alone can redeem us, and for the same Reason that he alone can *create ;* if Creation and Redemption necessarily require the same Power, and must for the same Reason be necessarily appropriated to God, because each of them equally imply the Communication of *something* of God to us; then I suppose it may be granted, that the Religion of Reason, which is for *saving* ourselves by our own *natural Powers*, is the greatest of all Absurdities; as absurd as to suppose, that we can create by our own natural Powers, because Creation and Redemption both of them equally imply a *Communication* of something of the Divine Nature; and therefore he that cannot do the one, cannot do the other.

And if a Man was to ask himself, why he cannot be the Saviour of other People, as well as of himself? He could say nothing against the one, but what must for the same Reason be said against the other. For if Salvation is a Communication of *something* of God to the Person saved, then it is plain, that a Man can no more do this for himself, than he can do it for another.

There never could have been any Dispute about the *Possibility* of saving ourselves, nor any *Pretence* to save ourselves by our own natural Faculties, had not Men lost all true Knowledge both of God and themselves. For this Dispute cannot happen, till Men suppose that God is some *outward Being*, that our Relation to him is an *outward Relation*, that Religion is an outward Thing that passes between God and us, like Terms of Behaviour between Man and Man ; that Sin hurts and separates us from God, only as a Misdemeanour hurts and separates us from our Prince ; that an offended or angry God either gives or refuses Pardon to us, as an angry Prince does to his Subjects ; and that what he gives us, or forgives us, is something as distinct and different from himself, as when a Prince sitting upon his Throne gives or forgives something to an Offender, that is an hundred Miles from him.

Now all this is the same total Ignorance of God, of what he is, of the *Relation* we have to him, and the Manner of his being *our Good*, as when the old Idolaters took Men to be Gods. And yet nothing is more plain, than that your Religion of Reason is *wholly* founded upon these gross and false Notions of God. You have not an Argument in its Defence, but what supposes all these Errors just mentioned ; that our Relation to God is an *outward Relation*, like that of Subjects to their Prince, and that what we do to, and for God, as our Service to him, is and must be done by our *own Power*, as that which we do to, and for our Prince, must be by our own Power. And here lies the Foundation of all your Religion of Reason and Natural Power, that if it was not *sufficient* to obtain for us all that we want of God, he must be less good than a good earthly Prince, who requires no more of us, than that which we have a *natural* Strength to do, or can do by our own Power.

And yet this Error appears to have all the Grossness of *Idolatry*, as soon as you suppose, that God is no *outward separate* Being, but that we are what we are, have what we have, can do that which we can do, because he has brought us to this State of Life, Power and Existence *in himself*, because he has made us, so far as we are made Partakers or Possessors of his own Nature, and has communicated to us so much of himself ; or, in the Words of Scripture, because *in him we live, move, and have our Being*, and consequently have no Life, Motion or Being out of him. For from this State of our Existence in God, it necessarily follows, first, that by the Nature of our Creation we are only put into a Capacity of *receiving* Good : A Creature as such, can be in no other State ; it is as impossible for him to enrich himself, or communicate more Good to himself, as it was to create himself. 2*dly*, That nothing but God himself can do us any good. 3*dly*, That God cannot do us good, but by the Communication of himself in some manner to us.

For hence it evidently follows, that your Religion of Reason, which supposes that we have natural Powers that can put us in Possession of that, which we want to be possessed of in God, or that we need no more Divine Assistance to recover what we have lost of God, than to obtain a Pardon from a Prince ; or that God need communicate no more of himself to us in our Salvation, than a Prince communicates of himself to his pardoned Subject, has all the *Mistakes*, *Error* and *Ignorance* of God that is in *Idolatry*, when it takes God to be something that he is not ; and has all the *false Devotion* that is in Idolatry, when it puts the same Trust in, and expects the same Help from its *own Powers* and Faculties, which Idolaters did in and from their Idols.

Therefore your Religion of Reason, which you esteem as the modern *Refinement* of an human Mind, and more excellent and *rational* than the Faith and Humility of the Gospel, has all the Dregs of the Heathen *Idolatry* in it, and has changed *nothing* in Idolatry, but the Idol ; but has the same Mistakes of the Nature of God, and of the Manner in which he is *our God*, and *our Good*, as those Idolaters had ; and only differs from them in such a Degree of *Philosophy*, as the Religion of worshipping the *Sun* differs from the Religion of worshipping an *Onion*.

And if you expect that divine Assistance from your *Reason*, which one did from the *Sun,* and another from an *Onion ;* ye are all equally *Idolaters*, though ye may not be equally *Philosophers*.

For as soon as it is known and confessed, that God is all in all, that in him we live, move, and have our Being ; that we can have nothing *separately* or *out* of him, but everything in him ; that we can have no Being, nor any Degree of Being, nor any Degree of Good but in him ; and that he can give us nothing but himself, nor any Degree of Salvation, but in such Degree as he communicates something more of himself ; as soon as this is known, then it is known with the utmost Evidence, that to put our Trust in the *Sun,* an *Onion,* or our *own Reason,* if not equally absurd, is yet equally *idolatrous*, and equally *prejudicial* to our Salvation.

This I think, my dear Friend, may sufficiently show you both the Nature and Danger of your Religion of Reason; and that it can no more supply the Needs and Necessities of your Soul, than an *Idol* can save them that worshipped it; that in this respect it has the *Insignificancy* of an Idol, the *Vanity* of an Idol, and the *Sin* of an Idol; that it is that same Self-confidence, Self-acquiescence, that same Refusal of a Saviour and all divine Assistance, that keeps lost Spirits the Prisoners of Hell. Could they touch the Spirit of the Gospel, their Freedom would be begun; and because they will not, cannot depart in the *smallest Tittle* from your Religion of natural Strength, their Chains are unmovable.

For no Soul can be lost, that can truly humble itself before God, and apply to his *Mercy* to be helped, saved, and redeemed in *such* a Manner as it shall please him. Let it be hid, or buried, or imprisoned where it will, Hell and Earth, Death and Darkness, and everything must give way to the Soul thus converted to God, that has no Confidence in itself, that sees nothing of its own but Sin, and that desires and calls upon God to save it by *some Miracle* of his own Mercy and Goodness. By this *Sensibility* of the *Want* of a Saviour, and by this *humble Conversion* and Application to God for him, all Chains are broken off, all Wounds are healed, and the Soul must infallibly find, if it thus continues to seek, its Salvation in the unknown Depths and Riches of the Divine Mercy.

On the other hand, no Soul, however refined and speculative, however lofty and aspiring in its Imaginations, spiritual in its Conceptions, or deep in its Penetration, can possibly be saved, that trusts in its own Strength and Ability, and will have no *other Saviour* or Redeemer, but its own *natural Reason* and Faculties.

The whole Universe has not two Truths of greater Certainty than these. And yet if they are Truths, and Truths of the utmost Certainty, then the absolute *Necessity* of the Gospel Salvation, and *utter Impossibility* of being saved by your Religion of *Reason*, has its final Decision.

Further, that *Principle* of Life, or *Light* of the Mind, which I have said that every Man receives from Jesus Christ, as the Beginning of his Salvation, is entirely different from your magnified *Light of Reason*, as that signifies a Faculty of viewing the Relations of the Ideas of Things, and drawing Consequences from them. For that Light I speak of, is *Goodness* itself, a *Seed* or *Degree* of so much of the heavenly Life in the Soul; but this Faculty of *Speculating* and *Reasoning* has nothing of the Nature of Goodness or Religion; it has not so much as the *Shadow* of it, and is in its own Nature as foreign from Religion, when it is speculating upon it, as when it is speculating upon anything else. Just as our Faculty of seeing has no more of *Goodness*, or the Nature of an *Angel* in it, when it sees the Picture of an *Angel*, than when it sees the Picture of a Beast.

And as a blind Man has no more Light in him, when he reasons about Light and Colours, than when he discourses about Weights and Measures; so this Ratiocination, or Reasoning of the Mind, has no more of Religion in it, when it speculates its Ideas of God, Goodness and Morality, than when it speculates its Ideas of Trees and Houses.

And the Reason is plain, because this Faculty of speculating and arguing, is only the *Activity* of the Mind upon its own Images and Ideas, and is only the *same bare* Activity, whatever the Images be that exercise it; it has nothing of the Nature of the Images that it views, nor gets the Nature of them, because it views them; as it does not become *dark* when it considers the Nature, Causes, and Effects of Darkness, nor becomes *Light* when it reasons about it; so neither is it *Religion*, nor gets anything of the Nature of Religion, when it is wholly taken up in making Descriptions and Definitions of it.

If the *Needle* touched with the *Loadstone* was an intelligent Being, it could reason and make Definitions of *itself*, of *Attraction*, and of the *Loadstone;* but it would be easy to see, that the *Attraction* in the Needle, or the Virtue of the Loadstone that was left in it, was something in its *whole Nature* really different from this reasoning about it; and that this reasoning and defining had no Relation to this Attraction, nor would ever be the more like it, for its reasoning upon it, though it continued ever so long, or improved ever so much in its Descriptions of it, but would always be at the same Distance from it, and could have nothing of its Nature in it. But now if this reasoning Faculty in the *Needle* should pretend, that the Needle need not be drawn by an inward Attraction, that it need not be *unfixed*, or delivered from any *outward* Impediments of its turning to the Loadstone, because this reasoning Faculty was its *true* and *proper Attraction*, being full of *Ideas* and *Definitions* of it; you would then have a *plain Example* of your Practice, in taking natural Reason to be true Religion, and to have the Nature and Power of *something* that carries the Soul to God.

For this Instance is a clear Explication of the whole Matter; for that which I have called the first *Redemption* of Christ in the Soul, a *Seed* of Life, an *Instinct* of Good, a *Stirring* of Conscience, an *Attraction* to God, is that to the Soul, which *Attraction* is to the *Needle* that is touched, and is as *different* from your Religion of Reason, as a *reasoning* Faculty in the *Needle* would be different from its *Attraction*, and never could be Attraction, or have the Nature of it.

If the Needle loses its Attraction, its Communication with the Loadstone is at an end; and though it reasons never so long about it, it is still at the same Distance from it. So if the Soul loses its *Instinct* of Goodness, its *Seed* of a Divine Life, its *Attraction* to God, all its Reasonings and Definitions about God and Goodness are of no Use to carry it to God, but it must lie in an absolute State of Separation from him, if its Attraction, its inward Tendency to God, is lost.

And let me tell you, my dear Friend, for so I must call you and think of you, that there is much more in this *Instance* than you imagine. For all is *Magnetism*, all is *Sentiment, Instinct*, and *Attraction*, and the *Freedom* of the Will has the Government of it. There is nothing in the Universe but Magnetism, and the Impediments of it. For as all things come from God, and all things have *something* of God and Goodness in them, so all things have *magnetical* Effects and *Instincts* both towards God and one another. This is the *Life*, the *Force*, the *Power*, the *Nature* of everything, and hence everything has all that is really Good or Evil in it; Reason stands only as a Busybody, as an idle Spectator of all this, and has only an *imaginary* Power over it.

We discover this Magnetism in some things, where it breaks out sensibly; but it is everywhere, for the *same Reason* that it is anywhere, though we are too busy with the Fictions of our own Minds to see it, or too much employed in such things as resist and suppress its Force.

But because this Magnetism is a secret Life, that wants to increase its Strength before it can sensibly show its Power; and because we have an *Activity* of *Reason* within us, that is soon in Action, and concerns itself with everything, and takes all upon it, as if it did all; because it can *look* at all, and *dispute* about all, therefore it is, that this Magnetism, or Instinct towards God and Goodness, has much Difficulty to show itself sufficiently, and only stirs now and then within us, or when Sickness, Distress, or some great outward Shock has so dashed in pieces all Images of Reason, and stopped the *Activity* of our Minds, that this secret Power of the Soul has Liberty to awake in it.

This is that Trumpet of God which will raise and separate the Dead, and then all Impediments being removed, everything will take its place, not according to the Images and Ideas it has here played with, but according to the inward Tendency and Attraction of its Nature, and Heaven and Hell will each take its own.

And even whilst we are in this Life, this Magnetism is the *Mark* within us, to what Part we belong; and that which has its Attraction in us, has the Right to us, and Power over us, though for a while Flesh and Blood, and the Nature of our temporal State, hinders this from being visibly and sensibly known.

Nothing however is more plain, than that our Goodness bears no Proportion to our intellectual Abilities of Reason; everyone sees this, and yet no more than this need be seen, to give us the fullest Demonstration, that natural Reason has no Connection with Virtue and Goodness, and therefore surely can have no Connection with our Salvation, or be the proper Cause of it.

Hence we see, that *learned, acute, rational* Philosophers are often *Atheists ;* and those that can demonstrate the Foundation of Virtue, and paint every Office of it, are Rakes and Debauchees, and will sell every Appearance of practical Virtue for a Salary of so much a Year; whilst those that seem to have little of intellectual Accomplishments, are Virtuous and Honest, have a taste and Relish for every practical Virtue.

The natural Love or Affection of Relations, bears no Proportion to our rational Abilities to speak or write of them. A Parent that is of too refined an Understanding to content himself with the Morals of the Gospel, or its low Way of making Men good, and that wants to be entertained with a Virtue of more *Mathematical* Exactness, is often content with the Demonstration, and so remains deficient in the plainest Duties of domestic Affection: when the poor Labourer or Mechanic, that knows not what you mean by a Definition, has all the solid Love and Affection that becomes a good Relation. All this, and much more, which you and everyone may think for himself of the same Kind, is a sufficient Proof, that the *Ground* of Goodness in every Man, is something entirely *distinct* from our natural Faculties of Reason and Speculation.

And therefore, when you place the Power of your Salvation in your *intellectual* Light, or the Strength of your *own Reason*, you place it in your *weakest* Part, in the *poorest*, most *trifling* and *insignificant* Thing that belongs to you, and upon that which has the least Effect in human Life.

The only Good that Reason can do to you, is to remove the Impediments of Virtue, and to give room to that inward *Instinct* or *Attraction* to God and Goodness to display itself; that the inmost Spirit of your Mind may receive its Strength and Assistance from the Spirit of God, from which, as the *Needle* from the Loadstone, it has all its *Instinct* of Goodness and *Tendency* towards God.

For this inward Instinct of Goodness, or Life of God in the Soul, is all the real and living Goodness that is in you, and is as different and distinct from natural Reason, as the *Light*, and *Heat*, and *Power* and *Virtue* of the Sun, is different from a *Picture* of it upon a Piece of *Canvas*, and has as different Effects upon the Mind.

For this Light of bare Reason, or the reasoning Faculty of the Mind, has no Contrariety to the Vices of the Heart, it neither kills them, nor is killed by them. As Pride, Vanity, Hypocrisy, Envy or Malice, don't take away from the Mind its *Geometrical* Skill; so a Man may be most Mathematical in his Demonstrations of the Religion of Reason, when he has extinguished every good Sentiment of his Heart, and be the most zealous for its Excellency and Sufficiency, when he has his Passions in the most disordered State.

But in that *Light* of the *Heart*, or *Attraction* to God, which I have said is common to all Mankind in and through Jesus Christ, all is contrary. As it is a Gift and Grace of God, so it is a *real Life*, a living Thing, a *Sentiment* of the Heart, and so far as it grows and increases in us, so far it destroys all that is bad and corrupt within us. It has the same Contrariety to all Vices of the Heart, that Light has to Darkness, and must either suppress or be suppressed by them.

Now when I speak of this Light, or Instinct of the *Heart*, or Attraction to God, I have not only the Authority of Scripture, but every Man's own Experience on my side; that Distinction between the *Head* and the *Heart*, which everyone knows how to make, plainly declares for all that I have said. It shows that the State, and Manner, and Tendency of our Heart, is all that is good within us; and that the Reasonings and Speculations of the Head, are only an empty Show and Noise that is made in the *Outside* of us.

For that which we mean by the *Heart*, plainly speaks thus much; it is a kind of *Life* and *Motion* within us, which every one knows contains all that is good or bad in us; that we are that which our Hearts are, let us talk, and reason, and dispute what we will about Goodness and Virtue; and that this State of our Heart is as distinct from, and independent of all Speculations of our reasoning Faculties, as it is distinct from, and independent of all the Languages in which a Scholar can reason and speculate upon it. And if a Man should say, that the Excellency and Sufficiency of natural Religion consisted in knowing all the Languages in which Virtue, Goodness and Religion are expressed by different Sounds and Characters, he would have said as much Truth, and as well grounded, as he who places the Excellency and Sufficiency of natural Religion in the many Arguments and Demonstrations which Reason can raise about it. For all Reasoning and Speculation stand on the *Outside* of the Heart, in the same superficial Manner as all Languages do.

For our Heart is our *Manner* of Existence, or the State in which we feel ourselves to be ; it is an inward Life, a vital Sensibility, which contains our Manner of feeling what and how we are ; it is the State of our Desires and Tendencies, of inwardly seeing, hearing, tasting, relishing and feeling that which passes within us: it is that to us inwardly with regard to ourselves, which our Senses of seeing, hearing, feeling, *&c.*, are, with regard to Things that are without, or external to us.

Now as Reason is a poor, superficial, and insignificant Thing with respect to our outward Senses, unable to add anything to our *hearing* and *seeing, &c.*, or to be the true Power and Life of them, by all its Speculations and Reasonings upon them ; so it is much more a poor, and superficial, and insignificant Thing with respect to the inward Sensibility of the Heart, or its seeing, feeling, *&c.*, and much more unable to add to, or amend the State of the Heart, or become the Life and Power of its Motions, by its Arguings about them.

And therefore, to seek for the Religion or Perfection of the Heart in the Power of our Reason, is more groundless and absurd, and against the Nature of Things, than to seek for the Perfection and Strength of our Senses in the Power of our Reason.

Now I appeal to every Man in the World for the Truth of all this ; for every Man has the fullest inward Conviction, that his Heart is not his Reason, nor his Reason his Heart, but that the one is as different from the other in its whole Nature, as Pain, and Joy, and Desire, are different from *Definitions* of them ; and that as a thousand Definitions of Joy and Desire, will not become that Desire and Joy itself ; so a thousand Definitions of Religion will not become Religion itself, but be always in the same State of Distance from it ; and that all Reasoning and Speculations upon Religion, are at the same State of Distance from the Nature and Power of Religion, as Speculations upon our Passions are from the Nature and Power of them.

You know, not by Hearsay, Reasoning, or Books, but by an inward Sentiment, that your Reason can be very nicely religious, very strict in its Descriptions of Goodness, at the same time that the Heart is a mere Libertine, sunk into the very Dregs of Corruption : On the other hand, you know, that when your Reason is debauched with Arguments, is contending for Profaneness, and seems full of Proof that Piety is Superstition, your Heart at the same time has a Virtue in it, that secretly dissents from all that you say.

Now all this Proof that the State of Reason is not the State of your *Heart*, is the same Proof that Reason is not the *Power* or Strength of our Religion, because *what* our Heart is, that is our Religion; what belongs to our Heart, that belongs to our Religion; which never had nor can have any other Nature, Power, or Perfection, than that which is the Nature, Power, and Perfection of our Heart.

You are forced to know and feel, whether you will or no, that God has a certain *secret Power* within you, which is watching every Opportunity of saying something to you, either of yourself, the Vanity of the World, or the Guilt and Consequences of Sin.

This is that Instinct of Goodness, Attraction of God, or Witness of himself in the Soul of every Man, which without Arguments and Reasonings rises up in the Soul, and would be doing some good to it, if not quenched and resisted by the Noise and Hurry either of Pleasures or Business.

And this is everyone's *natural Religion*, or Call to God and Goodness, which is faithful to every Man, and is the only Foundation of all the Virtue and Goodness that shall be brought forth in him. And the least *Stirring* of this inward Principle, or Power of Life, is of more Value than all the *Activity* of our Reason, which is only as it were a Painter of dead Images, which leave the Heart in the same State of Death, and Emptiness of all Goodness in which they find it.

Therefore, my dear Friend, know the Place of your Religion, turn inwards, listen to the Voice of Grace, the Instinct of God that speaks and moves within you; and instead of forming dead and lifeless Images, let your Heart pray to God, that all that is Good and Holy in him, may touch, and stir, and revive all that is capable of Goodness and Holiness in you. Your Heart wants nothing but God, and nothing but your Heart can receive him. This is the only Place and Seat of Religion, and of all Communication between God and you.

We are apt to consider *Conscience* only as some working of our Heart, that checks us, and so we are rather afraid, than fond of it. But if we looked upon it as it really is, so much of *God within* us, revealing himself within us, so much of a heavenly Life, that is striving to raise us from the dead, we should love and adhere to it, as our happy Guide to Heaven.

For this Reason, I have called this *Spark* of Life, or Instinct of Goodness, our *inward Redeemer*; not only because it is the only Thing within, that helps forward our Salvation, but also because it is the first Beginning of Christ's *Redemption* in the Souls of all Men, by his becoming the Atonement for all.

And as it is the first Step of Christ's Redemption in the Soul, and that which became their *Capacity* of Salvation; so the Progress of their Redemption consists in the Increase and Growth of this first seed of Life, till the new Man be wholly raised up by it.

Lastly, Another real Difference between this *Instinct* of Goodness, or Piety of the *Heart*, and your Religion of Reason, is this, that natural Reason in itself is incapable of Jesus Christ; it cannot comprehend him, it is at Enmity with him, and sets itself up against him. For it feels *no Want* of a Saviour, and therefore is *unwilling* to receive one. Or if it were to admit of a Saviour, it must be only such a one as came to increase the Number of its *Images* and *Ideas*, or to help it to be *more active* and artful in the ranging, dividing and distinguishing them. And for this Reason it is, that a Book of *Ideas* and *Distinctions* is more valued by some People, than all the Salvation that is offered in the Gospel.

But this natural Religion or Instinct of Goodness, of which I have spoken, as God's *free Gift* to all Men in Jesus Christ, has that natural Fitness for the receiving of Christ, as the Eye has for receiving the Light; it wants him, it desires him, it is for him, it knows him, it rejoices in him, as the Eye wants, desires, knows, and rejoices in the Light. And of this natural Religion, or Religion of the Heart, does our Saviour plainly speak, when he saith, *He that is of God heareth God's Word*, — and again, *My Sheep hear my Voice*. Therefore this Instinct of Goodness, or Piety of the Heart, though it is God's Gift to Man before his hearing the outward Word, is yet a certain Preparation for it; and if it be brought forth in us, is a never-failing Fitness to receive it. Therefore he that has this *natural* Religion of the *Heart*, of which I have spoken, has the greatest Fitness to receive the Gospel, he is so of *God*, that *he heareth God's Word*, such a Sheep of Christ as knoweth his Voice. And therefore the receiving, or not receiving the Gospel, is the greatest of all Demonstrations, whether a Man hath, or hath not that *right Religion* that is antecedent to it.

Natural Religion, when rightly understood, is a real Thing, and of the same Truth as revealed Religion. But the Mistake lies here, in our taking natural Religion to be the Work or Effect of natural Reason; whereas Reason, or our Faculty of reasoning upon our Ideas, is not a *Part* of natural or revealed Religion, but only a bare Spectator of its own Images of natural and revealed Religion, just as it is not a Part of our *hearing* and *seeing;* nor can come any nearer to them, than as it is a bare Spectator of its own Images of them.

All Men, by virtue of God's first Pardon to *Adam*, are put into a State of Salvation; and as this State, though it is the free Gift of God, is common to all Men, as Men, or born of

Adam; so it may in a good Sense be called their natural State, and the Religion of this State, their natural Religion.

Now the Question is, What is the natural Religion of this State? It is that which his State and Condition speaks to him. Now his Condition and State in the World plainly speaks thus much to him, that he is a *Sinner*, and yet in a State of *Favour* with God, or in a *Possibility* of being accepted of him. Every Man's Nature teaches him thus much, with the same Certainty that it teaches him, that he is weak and mortal. That he is a Sinner, and at the same time an Object of *Divine Mercy*, are things that are made known to him, not by Arguments or Speculation, but by his own being what he is.

Therefore the whole of natural Religion consists in a Man's following this Voice of Nature, and acting conformably to it; in acknowledging the *Sinfulness* of his State, and in *imploring* and *relying* upon the *divine Mercy* to be delivered from it. This is the whole Truth of natural Religion; an humble *penitent Sense* of Sin, and an humble *Faith* and *Trust* in the *Mercy* of God to be delivered from it; though it is not known by what Name to call that Deliverance, or what kind of Saviour is wanted to effect it. But he that thus according to the Direction of his natural State lives before God, in *Penitence,* and in *Faith* in his *Mercy*, is sure of having the Benefit of all the Mercy of God, though he does not know the *Method*, or the *Means*, by which the Mercy of God will save him.

So that *true, natural* Religion and revealed Religion agree in these two great and essential Points, that Man is in a State of *Sin*, and yet in a State of *Acceptance* with God through his *Mercy;* therefore the Piety of the one, is the Piety of the other, viz., a *penitent Sense* of Sin, and a humble *Faith* and *Trust* in God to be delivered from it by *his Mercy.*

And here you may again see, why this Natural Religion is to be considered, not as a Matter of *Reason*, but as an *Instinct* of *Goodness*, or Piety of the *Heart;* because it is nothing else but *so much Goodness,* not in *Idea*, but in the very *inward Essence* of the Soul, as distinguishes and preserves it both from Beasts and fallen Spirits.

Had a Man no *Sense* of Shame for his Sins, he would be in the very State of the *Beasts;* had he no *Faith* and *Hope* in the *Mercy* of God, he would be in the State of the Devils. Therefore that internal *Sentiment* of *Heart*, that *Instinct* of Goodness, is his *only true* Religion of Nature, because it is thus the *Preservation* of his Nature, and the *saving* him from being like to Beasts and fallen Spirits.

Reason therefore, as it is a Faculty of speculating and comparing Ideas, has no more Share in this Religion of Nature, than it has a Share in our natural Powers of *hearing* and *seeing;* and as it can only in a *little Way*, and in certain *Circumstances*, do some outward Service to these *Senses*, so it can only in the same little and low Way help and assist this Religion of Nature by some *outward Services*.

And as this Instinct of Goodness, or inward Sentiment of the Heart, is that alone which *preserves* our Nature, and therefore is alone the *true Religion*, or *Salvation* of Nature; so the whole of all revealed Religion is to *improve* this true Religion of Nature in its *two Essential Parts*, Penitence for Sin, and Faith and Trust in the Mercy of God. For all revealed Religion has only this End, it teaches nothing, intends nothing, but to give us more Reasons for *Penitence*, and more Reasons for *Faith* and *Trust* in the Mercy of God.

And therefore it was that I said, this Instinct of Good, or true Religion of Nature, is the *very Preparation* of the Heart for the Reception of the Gospel. For so much as there is of this *Penitence* and *Faith* living in the Soul, so much it has of Eyes to see, of Ears to hear, and of a Heart to understand all the Truths of Divine Revelation. The Humility and Penitence of the Gospel, the Mercies of God in and through Jesus Christ, are as agreeable to a Man in this State of Heart, as Food and Water to the hungry and thirsty Soul. The Gospel presents everything to him that he wants; and God is thereby become all that to him, which the miserable State of his Soul stood in need of. And so when he finds the Gospel, he finds the Pearl, for which he gladly sells all that he hath.

Therefore a Man can have no greater Proof that the Religion of *Nature* is suppressed in him, that he has not the Religion of *Penitence* and *Faith*, than by his Refusal of the Gospel; for the Gospel as naturally agrees with such a State of Heart, as Light mixes with Light, and Darkness with Darkness.

Lay the Cause of Infidelity where you will, it is a certain Truth, that it lies only in this *Insensibility* of Heart, in this *Extinction* of the Religion of Nature. And if the least *Sentiment* of Penitence arises in your Heart, or a *Sensibility* of the Need of *Divine Mercy*, the Gospel has got so far an Entrance into you, and it cannot lose its hold of you, but by your losing this State of Heart.

Let your Reason pretend what it will, and fancy it has ever so many Objections of *Speculation* and *Argument* against the Gospel, they are all Objections of the Heart. For the Gospel speaks only to the Heart, and nothing but the Heart can either receive or reject it. For this is an eternal Truth, which you cannot too much reflect upon, that *Reason* always *follows* the State of the Heart, and what your Heart is, that is your Reason. If your Heart is full of Sentiments of *Penitence*, and of *Faith* in the divine Mercy, your Reason will take part with your Heart, and will entertain itself with all Arguments, Ideas, and Discourses, that can *exercise* this Religion of the Heart.

But if your Heart is shut up in Death and Dryness, your Reason will be according to it, a *poor Quibbler* in Words, and dead Images, and will delight in nothing but such dry Objections and Speculations as answer to the Deadness and Insensibility of your Heart.

So that what you imagine, of your having a Religion of *pure Reason*, is the merest Fiction of Deceit that can be imposed upon you; for Reason has nothing of *its own*, it acts nothing of *itself*, it barely *reflects* that which comes from the *Heart*, as the *Moon* barely reflects that which comes from the *Sun;* it is the *Servant* of the Heart, and must act or not act in Obedience to it; what the Heart *loves*, that Reason contends for; and what the Heart has no Inclination to, that Reason objects against. Therefore there neither is, nor was, nor ever can be any other Religion but the Religion of the Heart, and Reason is only its Servant, in the same Manner, and in the same Degree, whatever the Religion of the Heart be, whether true or false.

And to imagine that Natural Religion is the Effect of pure Reason and Speculation, is as great an Error against the Nature of Things, and more hurtful to you, than to imagine that *natural hearing* and *seeing* is the Effect of Reason and Speculation.

Natural Religion, if you understand it rightly, is a most excellent Thing, it is a *right Sentiment* of Heart, it is so much Goodness in the Heart, it is its Sensibility both of its Separation from, and its Relation to God; and therefore it shows itself in nothing but in a *penitential Sentiment* of the Weight of its Sins, and in an humble Recourse by *Faith* to the *Mercy* of God. Call but this the Religion of *Nature,* and then the more you esteem it, the better; for you cannot wish well to it, without bringing it to the Gospel State of Perfection.

For the Religion of the Gospel is this Religion of *Penitence*, and *Faith* in the *Mercy* of God, brought forth into its full Perfection. For the Gospel calls you to nothing, but to know, and understand, and practise a full and real *Penitence,* and to know by *Faith*, such Heights and Depths of the divine Mercy towards you, as the Religion of Nature had only some little uncertain Glimmerings of. Therefore there is the same Agreement, and the same Difference between the *true* Religion of Nature, and the Religion of the Gospel, that there is between the *Breaking* of the Day, and the Rising of the Sun to its *meridian* Height; the one is the *Beginning*, and the other is the *Perfection* of the same Thing. And as the Light of the *Daybreak*, and the Light of the *Noon-day*, are both the same Light, and from the same Producer of Light; so the Light of the Religion of Nature, and the Light of the Gospel, are the same Light, and from the same Producer of Light in the Mind.

If you only stood for some time in the first *Break* of Day, sensible of the Misery of Darkness, and only feeling some Hope and Expectation of the Light, yet knowing nothing of that *Globe of Fire* that afterwards was to appear, and bless you with so many unknown and unhoped for Joys and Comforts of the Noon-day Light, you would then resemble one standing for some time in the Day-break of Natural Religion, sensible of the *Weight* of his Sins, and only *hoping* in God for *some kind* of Mercy towards him; yet knowing nothing of that *Globe of Fire*, that *Mystery* of *divine Love* that was by degrees to discover itself, and bless him with so many unknown, unhoped-for Joys and Comforts of the divine Mercy towards him.

The original Instinct of Goodness in the Soul, which I have shown to be the only Religion of Nature, is the Light of *Daybreak* in the Soul, and is that Light which *lighteth every Man that cometh into the World.* The Light of the Gospel is that *Noon-day* Light, which discovers such Joys and Comforts as no one could have thought of, that had only stood in the *Break* of Day.

And as no one, when the Day arises, can reject or dispute the Coming or Goodness of the Rising *Sun*, but because he has *lost* that Sense which was to *distinguish* Light from Darkness; so no one can reject or dislike, or dispute against the Light of the Gospel, but he that has *extinguished* that *Instinct* of Goodness in his Soul, which *alone* can distinguish Good from Evil, and make him love the one, and reject the other.

Don't therefore, my dear Friend, deceive yourself, nor let anyone else deceive you. The Matter is of infinite Consequence that you have before you. You come into the World but once, and have but one Trial, but the Effects of it are to last for ever. The Time of disputing and speculating upon Ideas is short; it can last no longer than whilst the *Sun* of this World can refresh your Flesh and Blood, and so keep the Soul from knowing its own Depth, or what has been growing in it. But when this is over, then you must know and feel what it is to have a Nature as *deep*, and *strong*, and *large* as Eternity.

If you have lived upon the Amusements of *Reason* and Speculation, your Life has been worse than a *Dream*, and your

Soul will, at the End of such a Life, be left to itself in its own *Darkness, Hunger, Thirst,* and *Anxiety,* to be for ever devoured by its *own Fire.* But if you have watched over that *Instinct of Goodness* which God planted in your Soul, and have exercised yourself in that *Penitence* for your Sins, and humble *Faith* in the *Mercy* of God, that the Gospel proposes to you; then when your Body falls off from you, you will feel and know what a Kingdom of God lay hid in your Soul, you will see that you have a *Life* and *Strength* like that of Eternity, and the Fulness of God himself will be your everlasting Enjoyment.

For Heaven and Hell stand ready to awake and be revealed in you, and can no longer be hid from you, than whilst you are under the Cover of Flesh and Blood. And then will be fully verified in you that Saying of Scripture, *he that seeketh findeth:* For you will find that which you have sought, and according to your Faith, so will it eternally be done unto you. Your Soul will have nothing taken from it, but it will have all *that Good* which you sought after, and provided for it. You chose to be *saved* only by the Powers of your *own Reason,* and refused the *Mercy* of God that was to have saved you, and therefore you will have that *very Salvation* you have chosen, you will be entirely *without* the *Mercy* of God, and left wholly to your *own Nature:* And that Salvation is the Misery of Hell.

You are now your own *Carver,* and must be *that* which you shall have made of yourself. If the Depth of your Heart has not in this Lifetime its proper Cure; if it has not something done to it, which your *Reason* can no more do, than it can create the Light, your Heart will become your Hell. And if you let the Light of the Gospel shine into it, and revive the *good* Seed of Life in it, then it will become the Seat and Habitation of your Heaven.

You may perhaps imagine, that because you practise Sobriety and Justice, and are a Friend to moral Behaviour, both in yourself and other People, that therefore your *Disbelief* of the Gospel cannot proceed from the *Disorder* of your Heart, or a *Want* of Piety. But this, Sir, is all Mistake. For you may have all this moral Behaviour, and yet have *nothing* at all of that *Sentiment* of *Penitence,* and *Faith* in the divine *Mercy,* which I have shown to be the *only true* Religion of Nature. It is as easy to have all this kind of Goodness which you appeal to, as it is to be *civil, well-bred,* and a Friend to the *Peace* and *Order* of that Society of which one is a Member. Even an *Atheist* may find his Ends, and act suitably to his own Principles of Self-love, Ease and Reputation, by this moral Behaviour.

But the Preaching of the Gospel discovers all, and shows

the Errors of a late Book. 101

from what Principle all this Morality proceeds. If there was this *Sentiment* of *Penitence* and *Faith* in the Mercy of God at the Bottom, then this Morality would want and rejoice at the Precepts and Doctrines of the Gospel, because they raise a Morality upon the Foundation of *Penitence* and *Faith*. But when this Morality is only a *worldly* Wisdom, a *Convenience* of Life, a *political* Conformity, and as mere a *Gratification* of *Selfishness*, as any other worldly Accomplishments are, then this Morality is in the greatest Enmity with the Gospel, because the Gospel takes away its Worth, and all the Self-accomplishment that was placed in it.

Therefore it is not the mere moral Man that has that *Goodness* of the Heart, that is a Qualification to receive the Gospel: For an *Atheist* may be such a *moral* Man; but it is he, whose Heart is in a *State* of *Penitence* for his Sins, and *humbly* looking to the *Mercy* of God to be *some way* or other delivered from them.

This is the *only* Foundation of a religious Morality, and this is that *State* of *Heart* which must be wanting in *every* Moralist that *refuses* the Gospel.

Hence therefore it is plain, that you may have a great deal of Morality in your Behaviour, and yet nothing of the *Religion of Nature* in your Heart, and so be entirely unqualified to receive the Gospel, because of the *Disorder* of your Heart. For the Morality of an *unreformed* Heart, adds no more Goodness to it, than *whited Sepulchres* do to the *Rottenness* of dead Men's Bones.

What I say I say not to reproach you, but from a sincere Desire of doing you all the good that I can. For I have too much Experience myself of the Weakness and Mistakes of human Nature, to reproach any Degree of them in other People. But if you will take in good Part what is well meant, I hope you will find that I have been your Friend in discovering the Bottom of your Disorder.

But it may be you will say, you would believe the Gospel if you could, but that its Evidence cannot have that Effect upon your Mind. You may say also, the Gospel is a Matter of Fact; you must examine into the Truth of it, as you do into the Truth of other Matters of History; and as both the internal and external Evidence of the Gospel is much defended and opposed by learned Men, its Evidence is so perplexed, and made a Matter of such laborious and intricate Enquiry, that your Mind cannot come at any Certainty of what you ought to believe concerning the Truth of it.

I will therefore propose to you the *shortest*, and at the same time the *surest* of all Methods, and such as you shall either be obliged to acquiesce in as sufficient, or to own that you have suppressed that *Instinct* of Goodness within you, which I have shown to be the original Birthright of all Mankind, and to be the *only* State of Heart that *saves* us from being a mere Mixture of the Beasts and the Devils.

I don't recommend to you to lay aside Prejudice, and begin again the Controversy from the Bottom, and read all on both Sides with all the Impartiality that you can. I would as soon send you on a *Pilgrimage*, to be a *Penitent*, as propose to you this Travel to be a Christian. The Truth of the Gospel lies much nearer to us than we imagine, and we only dispute and wrangle ourselves into a Distance from it.

Do you think that you need many Books to show you that you are a *Sinner*, that you have the Disorder of almost all the *Beasts* within you; that you have besides this, such Passions and Tempers of Pride, Envy, Selfishness and Malice, as would make you shun the Sight of other People, if they could see all that passes within you? Need any Learning instruct you, that at the same time that you have all these Disorders, both of the Beasts and evil Spirits within you, you have a great Desire to seem to be without them, and are affecting continually to have, and appear in those very Virtues which you feel the Want of? When you are full of Hatred and Envy, you affect to be thought good and good-natured, when proud, to appear as humble.

Now I desire you to know no Books, but *this Book* of your own Heart, nor to be well read in any Controversy but in that which passes *within you*, in order to know the Gospel to be the greatest of all Truths, and the infallible Voice of God speaking the Way of Salvation to you. No *Echo* answers to the Voice that raises it, so certainly and agreeably as the Voice of Nature, or the State of your own Heart answers to that which the Gospel preaches unto you. And this I will show you to be the shortest and surest of all Methods to discover the Truth of the Gospel.

The Gospel is built on these *two Pillars, First*, That you are a *fallen: Secondly*, That you are a *redeemed* Creature. Now every Man's own Soul, and what daily passes within him, speaks these two great Truths to him, with a Conviction and *Sensibility* that cannot be avoided.

You have seen, and you feel, and know that you are a Sinner, that you have the Disorders of the Beasts, and the Depravity of evil Spirits within you. Is not this saying to you, not in the Sound of Words, but by the *Frame* and Voice of your Nature that you are a *fallen* Creature, and not in that State in which a good Being must have created you? For I appeal to yourself, in your own Degree of Goodness, if you could create your own Children, whether you would not create them in a better State, and with less Evil, both of the Beast and the Devil, in them, than that in which you were born yourself?

Therefore, only supposing God to have your Degree of Goodness, he could not have created the first Man, from whom your Nature is derived, in the State that you are; and therefore supposing him only to be good, you have a sufficient Proof; but supposing him to be infinitely good, or Goodness itself, you have an infallible Demonstration written in the Frame of your Nature, that you are a *fallen* Creature, or not in that State in which God created you.

Again, Do you want any Learning, or Books, or Reasoning, to show you, that every Man, as well as yourself, affects to appear virtuous, to have good Qualities, and is ashamed of every beastly and diabolical Disorder; and would seem to have Virtues and Goodness that he has not, because of an innate Love that he has for them, and from a Sense of their being proper for him? And is not this saying again with the same Fulness of Certainty, that you are a *redeemed* Creature, that there is in you an *inward* Redeemer, a *Light* of the Mind, a *Seed* of Goodness, an *Instinct* to Virtue, given you by God, though without Revelation you don't know *when* nor *how*?

And is not this such an Evidence of the *Truth* of the Christian Religion, and of its *Fitness* to *save* your Soul, as not only needs not the Assistance of foreign Books and Learning, but is also sufficient to support itself against all the Books and Learning in the World that should oppose it? Can any Echo answer better to the Voice that raises it, than the Voice of your Nature answers to the Sound of the Gospel? And do you not hereby plainly see, that you stand nearer to the Truth of the Christian Religion, than you do to anything else? It is only the Description of that which passes within you. It is the Book of yourself, it talks of nothing *out* of you, it speaks but that which is written *within* you, and therefore you have a sufficient Help to understand it. To look for *outward* Testimonies, is like looking for yourself *abroad;* turn but your Eyes inward, and you have no need of Miracles to show you, that Jesus Christ came from that God that made you, and that he teaches you the only Way to find that Perfection and Happiness for which he made you.

What can the Gospel say to you of the Fall of Man, that your Heart does not feel to be true? What can it say to you of your Redemption, that is not at the same time said to you by the State of your own Soul?

For if you were not fallen, how could you labour under so much Corruption? A sinful Creature cannot come from God in its sinful State. And, on the other hand, if you were not redeemed, how could you feel a Dislike of Sin, an Inclination to Goodness, and a Desire of appearing virtuous? For what else is this Desire of Goodness, but a certain *inward Principle* that has begun your *Redemption*, and is trying to carry it on?

Now the Christian Religion says nothing to you; it has not one Doctrine, or Practice, or Institution, but what has its immediate Relation to these two great Truths, and is, for the sake of them, either to convince you of your Fall, or to assist your Redemption.

Now if a Revelation from God had only told you, that you had a Mixture of *Evil* and *Good* in you, could you have any doubt about the Truth of such a Revelation? Or if it told you that the Evil came from the Fault of your first Parents, and the Good was God's free Gift to you at their Fall, that the Evil might be resisted and suppressed; if it told you, that God had a Desire, and a Design in the Depths of his Mercy, to assist the *Good* that was in you, that it might conquer and put an entire End to all the Evil of your Nature, would you ask for Proofs of the Goodness of such a Revelation, or of its being worthy of God, and suitable to your own Needs?

Now the Christian Religion is this Revelation. It tells you only this great Truth, that you are *fallen* and *redeemed*, that is, that you have a Mixture of *Evil* and *Good* in you; it tells you that God, as early as the *Fall*, redeemed you, when the *Seed* of the Woman became the Enemy of the *Serpent;* that is, as soon as the Evil came into you, he of his *free Gift* put a good *Power* into you to withstand it; it tells you, that from the Beginning of the World, it has been God's gracious Desire and Design in and by Jesus Christ to render your Redemption effectual, that is, to make the *Good* that is in you perfectly overcome all your *Evil*.

Complain therefore no more of want of Evidence; neither *Books*, nor *Study*, nor *Learning* is wanted; the Gospel is *within* you, and you are its *Evidence;* it is preached unto you in your own Bosom, and everything within you is a *Proof* of the Truth of it.

Ask how you shall know there is such a thing as Day and Night; for the Fall and Redemption are as manifest *within* you, as Day and Night are Manifest *without* you.

Here, Sir, in this intimate and true Knowledge of yourself lies the most precious Evidence of the Gospel, and is as near to you, as you are to yourself; because all that is said and declared, and recorded in the Gospel, is only a plain Record of that which is said and done, and doing in yourself.

And when you once feel it thus proved to you, by its Agreement with the State of your own Nature, then it becomes a Pearl that is dearer to you than your Life ; and what is best, it is then a Pearl which no one can rob you of. You are then in such Assurance and Possession of the Power and Goodness of Christ, as those blind Men were, whose Eyes he had opened to see the Light.

Then all the Wrangle and Dispute of Learned Men against the Truth of the Gospel, will signify no more to you, nor raise any more Doubt in you, than if by *History* and *Criticism* they would prove, that you never had any Benefit from the Light of the Sun.

If you go *only* outwardly to work, and seek only for an outward Proof of the Truth of the Gospel, you can only know it by such Labours, and in such Uncertainty as you know other Matters of History, and must be always balancing what is said for, and against it. And if you come to believe it this way, your Faith will be held by an uncertain Tenure, you will be alarmed at every new Attack, and frightened at every new Enemy that pretends to lessen the Evidence of the Gospel.

But these, Sir, are Difficulties that we make to ourselves, by neglecting the proper Evidence of the Gospel, and choosing only to know it, as we know other Histories that have no *Relation* to us, or *Connection* with our own State.

The Gospel is not a History of something that was done and past 1700 Years ago, or of a Redemption that was then *present*, and only to be transmitted to Posterity as a Matter of *History ;* but it is the Declaration of a Redeemer, and a redeeming Power that is always in its *redeeming State*, and equally *present* to every Man.

We all stand as near to the Reasons and Motives for receiving the Gospel, as they did to whom it was first preached. No one then did, or could receive Jesus Christ when he was on Earth, but for the same Reasons, that the *Sick*, the *Lame*, and the *Blind*, sought to him to be cured, namely, because they felt their *Infirmities*, and wanted to be *relieved* from them. But if this State of Heart, or their Sensibility of their Condition, of what they were, and what they wanted, was then the *only possible* Reason they could have for receiving Christ ; then it follows, that every Man of every Age, has all the Reasons for receiving or not receiving the Gospel within himself, and stands just as near to and just as far from the Evidence of it, as those did who first heard it.

If you know of no Burden or *Weight* of Sin, nor *want* any *Assistance* to overcome it, the Gospel has *no Evidence* for you; and though you had stood by our Saviour, you had been never the nearer to it. But if you know your State, as the *Sick*, the *Lame*, and the *Blind* knew their State; if you groan under the Power of Sin, and are looking towards God for some Assistance to overcome it, then you have *all* the *Reasons* for receiving the Gospel written in your Heart, and you stand as *near* all its *proper* Evidence, whether you were born the last Age, or 1700 Years ago.

Now if you don't *know* and *feel*, that the Gospel has this Foundation in you, that you have that *Fall* and *Redemption* in you that it teaches, then all external Evidence of it can be of no use to you, because you are not the *Person* that wants *such* a Salvation.

But if you know that these two things are written in the Frame of your Nature, that Evil and Good, or the *Fall* and the *Redemption*, are at Strife within you, and that you want some Divine Assistance to help you to overcome the Evil that is in you; then the Gospel needs no external Evidence, because your Heart is a Witness of all the Truth of it. For you are then only doing that in a lower Degree, which the Gospel teaches and enables you to do in a more perfect and prevailing Manner.

Further, if you have only that *Instinct* of Goodness in you, which I have shown to be the *only Religion* of *Nature;* if you have a Desire to act suitably to this State of your Heart, this Struggle of Evil and Good that is in you, and are weary of your Sins, and desirous to be delivered from them, then you are fully prepared to love, admire, and receive all the Precepts of the Gospel, because they have no End, but to do that which you want and desire to have done in you; that is, to suppress the Power of Evil in you, to destroy the old Man, or the first Life of your corrupt Nature, and to raise the new Man, or Principle of Goodness that is in you, to its full State of Strength and Perfection.

And here you have the shortest and surest of all Methods, to find both the Truth and Excellency, and Necessity of the Gospel Method of Salvation.

I put no Labour or deep Enquiry upon your Hands: I desire you only to know, what you cannot help knowing, that you have *Good* and *Evil* alive, and at work in you. For this is the whole of the Fall of *Adam*, and of the Redemption of Jesus Christ. Say that you have no Evil in you, and I will not desire you to believe the Fall of *Adam*. Say that you have no Sense of Goodness in you, and I will not desire you to acknowledge the

Redemption through Jesus Christ. But if neither of these can be denied to be in you, if your own Heart confesses these two things; how can you want a Proof of the Truth of that Religion, which only tells you that which your own Heart is a Witness of?

Again, Say that you have no *Instinct* of Goodness in you, that you have no *Dislike* of the Corruption of your Nature, nor the *smallest* Desire to be free from it, and then I will excuse your Ignorance of the Truth and Fitness of the Precepts of the Gospel.

But if you will but own *so much* of natural Religion, as to be *at all* troubled at your Sins, or but *secretly wish* that God would *some way* or other help you to get the better of them; then you are under a Necessity of seeing and knowing that the Precepts of the Gospel are highly suited to the State of your Soul, to assist *this Degree* of natural Religion in you, and to help you to *that Conquest* over Sin which you want.

So that from this plain and easy Knowledge of yourself, you are absolutely obliged either to deny the *most known* State of your Heart, and to deny that you have *any Degree*, or *Desire* of Goodness in you; or to own the Gospel to have *everything* in it, both as to Doctrine and Precept, that strictly answers to the *State* and *Necessities*, and good Inclinations of your Heart.

And therefore the Proof of the Gospel is at *no Distance* from you, requires no Labour of Learning, or Search of History, but arises from the most obvious Knowledge of yourself, what you are, and what you want. And you may have the utmost assurance, that you cannot hurt or deceive yourself in this short Method that I have recommended. For if you cannot be hurt or deceived in believing yourself to be a *Sinner*, and yet to be in a State that *admits* of the divine *Mercy* to you, then you are sure that you cannot have any Hurt or Deceit put upon you by the Gospel; because it is to do nothing to you, you are to receive nothing from it, but a *Confirmation* of your *Penitence*, and a *Strengthening* your *Faith* in the Mercy of God.

Understand all the Gospel in this Manner, and then you understand it according to the Truth, as it is in itself. For there is not a Doctrine or Precept of the Gospel, but is given you for this End; to perfect your Penitence, to show you all the Grounds, and Reasons, and Extent of it, and to confirm, increase, and exercise your Faith in the Mercy of God, by such a Discovery of God, and his Goodness towards you, as without the Gospel could not have been known.

So then, if you know the Religion of *Nature*, the Religion of *Penitence* and *Faith*, to be a true and good Religion; if the Proof of the Truth and Goodness of this Religion lies *within you*, then the Proof of the Truth and Goodness of the Gospel is in the *same Degree* of Nearness to you, and you cannot but know it in the same Manner and Degree as you know yourself, what you are, and what you want.

Thus much may serve to convince my unbelieving Reader, if I have such a one, whom I would fain lead to God, that I have said nothing in favour of a modern Religion of Reason; which I have shown to have the *Vanity, Insignificancy,* and *Sin* of the ancient Idolatry in it, and to be that *very Confidence* in natural Strength, and *Hardness of Heart,* which keeps fallen Angels Prisoners of Darkness.

I must now say a word to the zealous Christian, who may perhaps imagine, from what I have said of that inward Light, which is the *Gift of God* to all Men in Jesus Christ, that I have brought this Light too near to the advantageous State of revealed Religion, whether Jewish or Christian.

To such a one I say, first, that what I have said of this *Light* of the Mind, or *Instinct* of Goodness common to all Men, is so much said of the *Light* and of the *Benefit* of Divine Revelation. Because this *Light* of the Mind, or *Instinct* of Goodness, is not something *independent* of, and *antecedent* to all divine Revelation, but was the *Effect* of God's revealing himself as *reconciled* to *Adam* through the *Seed of the Woman*. God's pardoning *Adam* as the *Head* and *Representative* of all Mankind, and giving him a Mediator and *Redeemer*, was putting him into a State and Capacity of being *renewed* in his Mind; and this *renewing Power*, which God then by pardoning him bestowed upon him, is that *Instinct* of Goodness, or *Light* of the Mind, of which I have spoken. And therefore all the *Possibility* of Religion, and all that is *good* in it, is to be ascribed to divine Revelation.

Secondly, What I have said of this common Light, or Piety of the Heart, is only to signify, that they have a *Possibility* of such good Dispositions as belong to those, of whom it is said, 'He that is of God, heareth God's Word'; and of such as Christ spoke, when he said, 'My Sheep hear my Voice.'

Now if there were not a *Possibility* or *Capacity* of this Degree of Goodness in Men, distinct from all outward Revelation, How could Mankind be fit for God to make a Revelation to? For if Men could not be in *this State* of Goodness, so as to be *prepared* or *qualified* Hearers of the Word of God, why should God speak to them? Or why should the Voice of Christ be sounded, if there were *no Sheep* that could know it? Therefore what I have said of this Light of Men, is only so much said of their *Capacity* to receive divine Revelation; it is only a *Glimmering* of Light, a *Seed* of Goodness, a *Possibility* of Piety, which lies only in the

the Errors of a late Book. 109

Soul, as the *Beginning* of its Salvation, and therefore is in great want of, and must be much benefited by further Revelations from God.

I have not considered it as a *Species* of Religion that may *trust* in *itself*, or set up *itself* against Divine Revelation, as having no Need of it. When it is thus, it is not the Religion that I speak of, it is so far from being then the *Light* of Christ in the Soul, or the *Instinct* of Goodness that it had from him, that it is the *Darkness* and *Depravity* of the Heart, and the *Foundation* of that Hell which will be at last manifested in it.

Lastly, If my zealous Christian should find it a disagreeable Thought to him, to think that *all Mankind* have had some *Benefit* from Christ, and that the *Seed of the Woman* from the Beginning has helped, and will to the End of the World help and call *every Man* to resist and make War against the Serpent; I must tell him, he need have no greater Proof than this, that his own Heart is not yet truly Christian, that he is not a true Disciple of that Lord who *would have all Men to be saved*.

Having said this much to guard against all Misapprehension, either by the Unbeliever, or the Christian, I now return to my Subject, concerning the Benefits of Christ, as he is the Saviour of Mankind.

Now this great Truth that I have already declared, namely, that all Mankind were pardoned and redeemed in *Adam's* Pardon and Redemption; that at the Fall, Jesus Christ became the *second Adam*, or Parent of all Mankind, who from him received a Principle or Seed of Life, an Instinct of Goodness, which was to be in every Man a *Beginning* of a new Birth, a *Possibility* of his Salvation, or receiving a new Man from this second *Adam*, in the same Reality as he received a *natural* Life from the first *Adam;* this great and glorious Truth is of great Importance when rightly known, and is the Key to all the Mysteries of Scripture; it leads you into the Fulness of the greatest Truths, and disperses all Difficulties.

This *free Gift* of God to all Men, in thus making all Men *Partakers* of Christ's Redemption, by a Seed of Life, which all Men, as Men, receive from Christ, is the true and solid Meaning of that which is called *Preventing Grace*, and which, when rightly spoken of, is said to be common to all Men. It is *Grace*, because it is God's *free Gift;* we could not lay hold of it by any Power of our own, nor had any Right to claim it. It is *Preventing* Grace, because it prevents, or goes before, and is not given us for anything that we have done. And therefore it has its plain Distinction from God's *assisting* Grace, which always is in *Proportion* to the Nature of our Actions, and only works as they work. Hence there is a full End of all the wretched Disputes of an abominable *Election* and *Reprobation*, and of other Disputes concerning the Grace of God.

For if all Men, as Sons of *Adam*, are by the *free Gift* of God made Sons of the *second Adam*, and, as such, have a *Principle* or *Seed* of Life in them from him, in order to be raised up to a Perfection of the new Man in Jesus Christ; and if this *Seed* of Life, or *Instinct* of Goodness, or Light of the Mind, is the *General Preventing* Grace of all Men, that enables them so to act as to obtain God's *assisting* Grace in the Renewal of their Minds; then you must easily see, that all Men have a *general Call* and a general *Capacity* to obtain their Salvation, and that the Doctrine of *particular absolute* Election and Reprobation is plucked up by the Roots, and most of the Difficulties of God's Dispensations fairly solved. But this by the by.

Now you must have observed that this *general* Grace, or *Redemption*, or *Life* given to all Men in Christ as their *second Adam*, is not done only by an *outward teaching*, as when one teaches another the Way of a new Life, or by an *outward Adoption*, as when a Person takes a Stranger to be his Son; but by the *Communication* of an essential *Seed* or *Principle* of Life from the second *Adam* to all the Sons of the first *Adam*. From which Seed or Principle of Life, every Son of *Adam* has Christ for his spiritual Father and Parent in the *same Reality*, as he had the first *Adam* for his natural Parent.

For this Reason, the *Change* that Religion aims at, is constantly represented as a *New Birth*, and our Progress in Religion as our Progress in *Regeneration*, or being born again. We are not called upon only to change our *Notions*, or to receive such an *Alteration*, as *Scholars* may receive from their *Teachers*, but to die to ourselves, that a new Life may be raised up in us; or to suffer something to be revived in us that is not of our own Growth, or any Change that we can make upon ourselves.

Thus says our Lord, 'Except a Man be born of Water and of 'the Spirit, he cannot enter into the Kingdom of God.'* And to show that this new Birth is to be understood according to the *literal Truth* of the Expression, there is added, 'That which is 'born of the Flesh is Flesh, and that which is born of the Spirit 'is Spirit.' Therefore the Birth of the Spirit is as *real* as the Birth of the Flesh, and Christ is a Principle of Life to us, as surely as we derive our Flesh from *Adam*.

Again, 'The first Adam was made a living Soul, the last Adam 'was made a quickening Spirit.'† That is, the first *Adam* was

---

* John iii. 5.   † 1 Cor. xv. 45.

made to be a Fountain, or Original, of a *natural Life* to Men, the second *Adam* was made a Reviver or Parent of a *spiritual Life* in Men. Therefore the spiritual Life derived from the second *Adam*, is in the same *Degree of Reality*, as the natural Life derived from the first *Adam*. The Apostle adds, ' The first ' is of the Earth, earthy : the second is the Lord from Heaven. ' And as is the earthy, such are they also that are earthy : And ' as is the heavenly, such are they also that are heavenly.'

Therefore those that are related to Christ, have his heavenly *Life* and *Nature* in them, in the same *Reality* as those that are related to *Adam* have his earthy Nature in them. 'And as we ' have borne the Image of the earthy, so we shall also bear the ' Image of the heavenly.' Therefore, as we bear the Image of the first *Adam*, by having *his Nature and Life* in us, *derived*, from him ; so we can only bear the Image of the second, by having his *Nature and Life* in us, *derived* from him.

So that it is an undoubted Truth, that Christ is our second *Adam*, or a Raiser of a *new Birth* and *Life* in us, in the same Reality as we have our natural Birth and Life from *Adam*. Hence it is that you see so much mention in Scripture of Christ's being *in us, formed* in us, *revealed* in us, of our *putting* on Christ, of our receiving Life from him, as the Branches from the Vine. Hence also so much mention of a *new* and *old* Man that is in us, and the whole of Religion represented as a Contest betwixt this twofold Man that is in us, the one from the first, the other from the second *Adam*.

The Knowledge of this great Truth, that Christ is our second *Adam*, as mentioned above, renders all the most mysterious, and seemingly hard Passages of Scripture, not only plainly intelligible, but full of a most affecting Sense. Thus when it is said, that Christ must be *formed* in us, and that 'we are Members of ' his Body, of his Flesh, and of his Bones,' &c.* All this, and the like, is highly intelligible, as soon as it is known, that Christ is the *Parent* of a spiritual *Man* in us, in the same *Reality*, as *Adam* is the Parent of our natural Life.

Thus also when Christ saith, 'Except ye eat the Flesh of the ' Son of Man, and drink his Blood, ye have no Life in you.' And again, ' I am the Bread of Life, he that cometh to me shall never ' hunger, and he that believeth on me shall never thirst.'† And again, ' Whosoever shall drink the Water that I shall give him, ' shall never thirst : But the Water that I shall give him, shall be ' in him a Well of Water springing up into everlasting Life.'‡ And again, ' I am the Resurrection and the Life.—Whosoever ' liveth and believeth in me, shall never die.' §

---

* Eph. v. 30.   † John vi. 35.   ‡ John iv. 14.   § John xi. 25.

Now if Jesus Christ had been only a Teacher of *Morality*, how unaccountable must all this Language have been? But as soon as it is known that he is a spiritual *Parent*, or *Principle* of Life to us, in the same Reality as we derive our Flesh and Blood from *Adam*, and that this *Life* lieth in us as a *Seed*, which is to be brought forth to the Fulness of its Stature by *Faith* in Christ, then all these Passages have a Meaning that is plainly intelligible, yet never to be exhausted, but is always suited to the State and Progress of the Reader.

For if Christ is a Principle of Life to us, and this Life is *drawn* into, or *formed* in us by means of our *Faith*; then how justly are we said to eat Christ as the *Bread of Life*, to *eat his Flesh, and drink his Blood, &c.*, when by Faith we draw him into us, as our Principle of Life? For what can express the Nature of this *Faith*, so well as *Hunger* and *Thirst*? Or how can it be a *real* Faith, unless it have much of the Nature of *Hunger*, of a strong *Desire*, and ardent *Thirst*?

Therefore all these Expressions are as *literally* suited to the Nature of the Thing, to *that* which Christ is to us, as human Words can be, and are not a Language adapted to our *Reason*, to increase its Ideas; but are the Language of Heaven to the heavenly Part of us, and are *only* to excite, direct, and confirm our *Faith* in Christ, or to raise, increase, and exercise our *Hunger*, *Thirst*, and *Desire* of the new Birth of Christ in our Soul.

But this Author knowing nothing of this Doctrine, is forced to deny the most precious Truths of Scripture. Thus all that our Saviour says of himself in the sixth of St. *John*, of his *Flesh* being 'Meat indeed, and his Blood Drink indeed,' and of the *Necessity of eating and drinking it, to have eternal Life in us;* all this, says this Author, ' was only a very high figurative Represen-
' tation to the Jews then about him, of their Duty and Obliga-
' tion to receive into their Hearts, and Digest his whole Doctrine,
' as the Food and Life of their Souls.'*

Therefore, according to this Author, Christ is our Life, in no other Meaning or Sense, than any other Person who teaches us any Doctrine that may do us good, and we have no Life from him any other way, than we may have from any Teacher of useful Truths. And therefore what he says of himself, of his being the *Life* of the World, has just as much Truth in it, as if any of the Apostles had said the same things of themselves. Nay, had *Socrates* or *Plato*, or anybody else, preached the same Gospel that our Saviour has done, there had been just the same Meaning, and neither more nor less in it than in the Gospel of Jesus Christ.

* Page 100.

St. John saith, 'Who is a Liar, but he that denieth that Jesus 'is the Christ? He is Antichrist that denieth the Father and 'the Son.'*

Now surely the Son could not be mentioned with the Father, as an equal Object of our Faith and Acknowledgment, if he could not in *Reality* be said to be our *Life* in such a Sense, as the *Father* may be said to be *our God*, not by a *very high* or *strong Figure of Speech*, but in Truth and Reality.

The Scriptures tell us, that Jesus Christ is the 'Word that was 'with God,' and 'was that God by whom all things were made.'† 'That by him all things were created that are in Heaven and in 'Earth, visible and invisible,—and that in him all things con- 'sist.'‡

Must not this Author be here obliged to have recourse to much *higher and stronger Figures of Speech,* to account for the Meaning of these Expressions? For if there is anything in the Nature of our Saviour, to support the *literal* Meaning and Truth of these Expressions, then it must not only be *groundless*, but absolutely *false*, to say, that we can only be said *to dwell in him*, or have *our Life* from him, by a very high or *strong Figure* of Speech.

For surely, if all things both in Heaven and Earth are created by him, if 'in him all things consist,' then it may be said without any strong Figure, that he is *our Life*, and that we 'dwell in 'him, and he in us,' in the same Reality, as we are said to 'live, 'and move, and have our Being in God.' For if this Creator becomes our Redeemer, we may be said to receive Life from him, to be new-born, or created again by him, in the same Reality and Fulness of Truth, as we can be said to be created by him at first.

When therefore this Author saith, 'We may be said (by a 'strong Figure of Speech) to dwell in him, and he in us; to be 'one with Christ, and Christ with us,' that is, that 'Christ and 'we, to all the Intents and Purposes of true Religion, shall be 'in perfect Friendship and Union together'§: It is the same barefaced Denial of the Gospel, the same direct Blasphemy against God, as to affirm, that God can only by a *strong Figure of Speech*, be said to be our *Life*, our 'Creator, in whom we live, 'and move, and have our Being.' It is the same Blasphemy as to affirm, that we have no Relation to, or Dependence upon God, or Existence in him, but such as any *Party* of People, whether at *Court*, or the *Exchange*, have with one another, when they are to all the *Intents* and *Purposes of their Party* Interest, in *perfect Friendship* and *Union* together.

---

* 1 John ii. 22. † John i. 3. ‡ Col. i. 16. § Page 111.

But to return: From this Doctrine of Christ's being a *Principle* of Life, or *Parent* of a new Birth in us, we may see the plain Reason, why the Scripture describes a Christian as a Creature or Instrument of the Holy Spirit, and entirely animated by it, so far as he is truly Christian. Because as Christianity consists in the Birth of a new Man within us, it must needs have a Spirit and Breath as suitable to it, as the Spirit and Air of this World is suitable to a Life of Flesh and Blood. And as every Thought and Motion of our outward Man must be in, and by the Assistance of the Spirit, and Air of this outward World: so every Thought, and Motion, and Desire of our inward spiritual Man, must be in, and by the Assistance of the Spirit, and Air of that World, whose Creature it is.

Now, was there not as really this new spiritual Man within us, in the same Reality of Existence, as our outward rational Nature, there could be no Foundation for this Doctrine of the Necessity of God's Holy Spirit. Nor could the Scripture Account of the Guidance of that Holy Spirit be at all intelligible, upon this Supposition, that we had nothing more in us, but our *outward rational* Nature.

Thus when it is said, *No one can call Jesus the Lord, but by the Holy Spirit:* How could this be intelligible, or have any Truth in it, if there were not a Principle in us, a spiritual Man, distinct from our rational Nature? For our rational Nature can as well call Jesus Lord, as it can call anyone else Lord, or as *Judas* said, ' Hail Master.'

Therefore since Man in his natural State, and by his Powers as a rational Man, cannot truly call Jesus Lord, it follows, that he has a spiritual Nature or Principle in him, entirely distinct from his rational Nature, and which receiving its Life and Power from the Spirit of God, has alone the *Power* of owning, knowing, and receiving Jesus Christ as Lord.

St. Paul saith, ' Ye are not in the Flesh, but in the Spirit, if ' so be the Spirit of God dwelleth in you. Now if any Man hath ' not the Spirit of Christ, he is none of his.'* And again; ' Now ' we have received not the Spirit of this World, but the Spirit ' which is of God, that we might know the things that are freely ' given to us of God. But the natural Man receiveth not the ' things of the Spirit of God; for they are Foolishness unto him, ' neither can he know them, because they are spiritually dis- ' cerned.'†

Therefore there is a *spiritual Life*, or *Man* within us, by which alone we have our *Communication* with God, and which is so

---

* Rom. viii. 9. † 1 Cor. ii. 12.

distinct and different from our *natural, rational* Man, that they are of a Nature contrary to each other. The one is by Nature fitted to receive, and know the things of the Spirit of God; the other has a Nature that cannot know, nor receive them.

This is not to be understood, as if the natural Man could not understand the Words of Scripture, as other Words are to be understood, for he can reason and discourse as well upon Scripture, and the things of the Spirit of God, as upon other Matters.

Neither are we to take him that is able to *discern* things spiritually, to be only such a one whose Faculty of *Reasoning* is assisted by the Holy Spirit. For this does not make the spiritual Man here spoken of. No, the Subject of the Holy Spirit, or that which operates upon in us, is not our *reasoning Faculty*, it no more assists our Reason in this manner, than it assists our Eyes to read a difficult Print, or our Ears to hear Sounds more distinctly.

For as the Holy Spirit is *Holiness* itself, or the *Life* and *Power* of Holiness, so it operates only in the manner of itself, and only upon that Part of us, which has its own Nature, or a real Agreement with it. Therefore the spiritual Man that is animated, enlightened and guided by the Holy Spirit, is that *vital Instinct* of Goodness, that *Spark* of Life, of which I have spoken so much, and which shows itself in an inward *Sentiment* of the *Weight* of Sin, and in an inward *Sentiment* of *Hope* and Conversion to the *Mercy* of God.

This is the Beginning, or Foundation, or Seed of that spiritual Man, for whom the Scriptures are written, to whom they speak, and who alone has a Capacity to hear and receive them, because he alone has a Capacity to be animated, moved, and governed by the Holy Spirit.

And therefore it is, that our Saviour saith so often, 'He that 'hath ears to hear, let him hear.' Meaning only this inward State of Sensibility of the Heart. He is so far from saying, according to modern Learning, he that hath *clear Ideas*, that has accustomed himself to *Reason*, and distinguish about them; he that can speculate impartially, and search into the Nature of Things, Actions and Persons, by comparing the Ideas of them; let such a one so prepared, draw near to the Kingdom of Heaven; he is so far from saying anything like this, that he rejects it all as the *Burden* and *Darkness* of the Heart, and says, 'Except ye 'be converted, and become as little Children, ye cannot enter 'into the Kingdom of God.'

But you will perhaps say, If the Scriptures are not proposed to our *Reason*, if Reason is not the *Subject* or *Faculty* of Religion in us; is not this the same as to say, that the Scriptures and Religion are proposed to the *unreasonable* Part of us; Is it not saying, that we must neglect or suppress that which is most excellent in us, in order to be religious?

You shall see Reason possessed of all that belongs to it, and yet Religion set up in a better Place.

I will grant you much more than you imagine in respect of Reason; I will grant it to have as great a Share in the good Things of Religion, as it has in the good Things of this Life; that it can assist the Soul, just as it can assist the Body; that it has the same Power and Virtue in the *spiritual* World that it has in the *natural* World; that it can communicate to us as much of the one as of the other, and is of the same Use and Importance in the one as in the other. Can you ask more?

Now Man considered as a Member of this World, that is to have his Share in the Good that is in it, is a *sensible* and a *rational* Creature; that is, he has a certain Number of *Senses*, as Seeing, Hearing, Tasting, Smelling and Touching, by which he is *sensible* of that which the outward World, in which he is placed, can do to him, or communicate to him, he is sensible of what Kind and Degree of Happiness he can have from it; besides these *Organs* of Sense, he has a *Power* or Faculty of *reasoning* upon the Ideas which he has received by these Senses.

Now how is it, that this World, or the good things of this World are communicated to Man? How is he put in Possession of them? To what *Part* of him are they proposed? Are his *Senses* or his *Reason* the Means of his having so much as he has, or can have from this World?

Now here you must degrade Reason, just as much as it is degraded by Religion. And as we say, that the good Things of Scripture and Religion are not proposed to our Reason; so you must say, that the good Things of this World are not proposed to our Reason. And as St. *Paul* says, the *natural* Man cannot receive the Things of the Spirit of God, because they are *spiritually* discerned; so you must also say, the *rational* Man cannot receive the Things of this World, because they are to be *sensibly* received, that is, by the Organs of Sense.

Thus must you necessarily set Reason as low, with respect to the Things of this World, as it is set with respect to the Things of the spiritual World. It is no more the Means of communicating the good Things of the one, than of communicating the good Things of the other.

It stands in the same Incapacity in one World, as in the other.

For everyone knows, that we know no more, can receive no more, can possess no more of anything that is communicable to us from this World, than what we know, receive and possess by our *Senses*, or that *sensible Capacity* that is in us, of having something communicated to us by the World. *Sounds* are only proposed to our *Ears*, Light to our *Eyes;* nothing is communicated to our *Reason;* no Part of the World hath any Communication with it. Reason therefore has no *higher* Office or Power in the Things of this World, than in the Things of Religion. The World is only so far known, received and possessed, as we receive and possess it by our Senses. And Reason stands by, as an impotent Spectator, only beholding and speculating upon its *own Ideas* and *Notions* of what has passed between the World and the *sensible* Part of the Soul.

And as this is the State of Man in this World, where he receives all the Good he can receive from it, by a *Sensibility* of his Nature, entirely distinct from his Faculty of reasoning; so is it his State with regard to the spiritual World, where he stands only capable of receiving the invisible good Things of it, by a *Sensibility* of his Nature, or such a Capacity as *lets* the spiritual World into him, in the manner as the natural is let into him in this Life. Religion therefore does no more violence to your Reason, or rejects it in any *other way*, than as all the good Things of this Life reject it. It is not *Seeing*, it is not *Hearing*, it is not *Tasting* and Feeling the Things of this Life, it can supply the Place of no one of these Senses. Now it is only thus *helpless* and *useless* in Religion; it is neither Seeing, nor Hearing, Tasting nor Feeling of spiritual Things; therefore in the Things of Religion, and in the Things of this World, it has *one* and the *same* Insignificancy. So that the Things of the Spirit of God belong not to Reason, cannot be known and received by it, for the same Reason, that the good Things of this World belong not to Reason, and cannot be known and received by it.

It is the *Sensibility* of the Soul that must receive what this World can communicate to it; it is the *Sensibility* of the Soul that must receive what God can communicate to it. Reason may follow after in either Case, and view through its own Glass what is done, but it can do no more.

Now the *Sensibility* of the Soul, which is its Capacity for Divine Communications, or for the Operation of God's Holy Spirit upon it, consists in an *inward Sentiment* of the *Weight* and Disorder of *Sin*, and in an inward *Sentiment* of *Hope* and *Conversion* to the Mercy of God. This is the first *Seed* of Life, sown into the Soul when *Adam* was redeemed; and it is this *Seed* of Life, or *Sensibility*, that the Holy Spirit of God acts upon, moves and quickens, and enlightens; and to this it is, that all that is said in the Scripture is addressed. Nothing but this *Sensibility*, or State of Heart, has Eyes to see, or Ears to hear the *Things* of the Spirit of God.

Reason may be here of the same Service to us, as it may be when we want any of the Enjoyments of this Life. It may take away a *Cover* from our Eyes, or open our Window-shutters, when we want the Light, but it can do no more towards seeing, than to make way for the Light to act upon our Eyes. This is all its *Office* and *Ability* in the good Things of Religion, it may remove that which hinders the *Sensibility* of the Soul, or prevents the Divine Light's acting upon it, but it can do no more.

Hence you may judge of the following Passage of the *Plain Account*, ' We may be sure we are pleasing God, whilst we are ' obeying the Command of his Son.'—' *But in this particular Instance of our Duty*, we can with *Reason go further, I say* with ' Reason ; *because the Benefits received from all such Performances* ' *by reasonable* Creatures, *cannot possibly be received but in* a ' reasonable *way. These duties, how well soever performed, cannot* ' *be supposed to operate* as Charms ; *nor to influence us, as if we were* ' *only* Clock-Work, or Machines, *to be acted upon by the arbitrary* ' *Force of a superior Being.*'*

Now all this is in direct Contradiction to the Nature and State of Man in this World. For no good thing of this World, no Power or Virtue in the whole System of Beings that surround us, can possibly be communicated to our *Reason*, or by the *Way* of our Reason. Whatever the World communicates to us of its Power and Virtue must be communicated to the *Sensibility* of our Nature, to that Part of us which is as distinct from our reasoning Faculty, as *seeing* the Light is distinct from a *Conjecture* about the Nature of it.

Now let us suppose a Man to stand in this World, only with his *rational* Nature, or Faculty of *reasoning*, but destitute of the *Sensibility* of his Nature, or the *Organs* of Sense ; What would all this World, or all the Good of it signify to him ? If he was to receive nothing but by the *way* of *Reason*, would it not be the same thing as to say, that he was to receive nothing from it ?

Now this is the State that this Author would have you be in, with relation to God, and the spiritual World. No Power, or Virtue, or Influence of God, or the spiritual World, is to be communicated to you, but by the *way of Reason*, and you are to stand with relation to all the Riches and Powers, and Virtues of God, and the spiritual World, in the same State as he stands in this World, who is to know and feel, and possess no more of it, than he can know, and feel, and possess by the way of Reason, without any *one Sense*. Therefore it is plain, that this Author

---

* Page 154.

desires all Communication from God to you, to be as much at an end, as all Communication from this World must be at an end, if you had not *one Sense* left.

I have just supposed a Man to stand in this World, *without* all Sensibility of Nature, endued only with a Faculty of *reasoning;* let it now be supposed, that you had a Power to awaken a Sensibility of Nature in him, and to help him to all those Senses that are common to Man. Would you say, this must by no means be done? Would you say, that you must keep off this Sensibility of Nature, that you might preserve him a free Agent? And that if the Light and Heat of the Sun, the Virtues and Powers of the World, should operate upon him in any other manner than by the way of Reason, he would be turned from a rational Creature, into a mere Machine and Clock-work.

Now this is the Way that this Author would preserve you a *Free Agent*, with relation to God, and the spiritual World: He will not allow you to have any Senses, that he may preserve your Reason. For if God, or the spiritual World, could do that to you, which this outward World can do to a Man that has his Senses; if God should communicate any Good to you, as the *Sun* communicates its Light and good Influence without the Assistance of your Reason, and only by making you *sensible* of them, you are undone, the *Freedom* and *Rationality* of your Nature is lost, and you are turned into *Clock-work*.

Let me ask this rational Man, who is so great an Enemy to all that is not done in a *rational Way*, whether he feels no Attachment to the World, and his Interest in it; whether he pursues it *no further*, and has no *Sensibility* of its Power over him, but just so much as *pure Reason* and the Light of the Gospel raise in him; whether he has no *Self-love*, no *Family-love*, no *Party-love*, no *Ambition*, no *Pride*, no *Sensuality*, but what is weighed out to him by Arguments and Motives of pure Reason, enlightened by the Letter of the Gospel? Now if there is something of those Tempers in him, arising from some *secret Power* that is working in him, that has not all its *Life* and *Working* from pure *Reason*, will he therefore say, that he is a mere *Machine*, that he has no Liberty left, that he is no longer a rational Creature; Now if a Degree of Goodness should steal upon him this way, without consulting his Reason, if he should find a *heavenly* Love, a *Purity* of Heart, an *Attraction* to God, a Desire of *Holiness*, a *Poverty* of *Spirit*, a *Contempt* of the World, a *Sensibility* of the Greatness of eternal Things, *stirring* and *awakened* in him in a greater degree than ever he intended to have them by his *own Reason*, would he be obliged to cry out, that his *reasonable Soul* was undone, that he had lost the *Rationality* of his Nature, was become a *Machine*, because such a Sense of God and Goodness had got Entrance into him without consulting his Reason?

And if God is as ready to operate upon our Souls, and to manifest his Power and Presence in them, when we give way to it, as the World and the Devil are when we leave an entrance for them, has a Preacher of the Gospel any Authority from thence, to reproach this divine Assistance, as 'Communications 'and Impressions from above, which leave the Mind in a State 'satisfied with what carries no rational Satisfaction in it?'*

For however this Author may please himself with thinking that his Mind is free from *Communications and Impressions from above, and satisfied only with such Things as carry a rational Satisfaction in them;* yet it is an eternal immutable Truth, founded in the Nature of Things, that no Soul can enjoy any Degree of Good whatever, but by a *Communication* or *Impression* of something upon it.

Every Creature, as such, is by the Necessity of its Nature, in a State of *Poverty* and *Want,* and may be defined to be only a *Capacity* to receive so much Good as shall be communicated to it, or impressed upon it. Were not this the State of our Souls, it would not be the State of our Bodies; and as the Body stands in this World in Poverty and Want, only *capable* of being fed, nourished, comforted and blessed by Communications and Impressions from the Things that surround it, so the Soul stands in the same Poverty and Want in the spiritual World, and *only capable* of being nourished, comforted, and blessed by Communications and Impressions from God.

So that this Author's Satisfaction which he has chosen for himself, a Satisfaction purely *rational,* or by *way* of his Reason, instead of divine Impressions, is the Choice of a Man in a *Dream*, that knows nothing of the Nature of God, or of his Soul, or of the State and Nature of Things. For the Satisfaction of every Being, from the highest Angel to the lowest of human Creatures, is all *sensible,* and wholly seated in the *Sensibility* of their Nature.

This is as certain, as that a Child has no *rational* Satisfaction; for no Man ever was satisfied or dissatisfied for any other Reason, or upon any other Account, than as a Child is satisfied or dissatisfied, namely, according as its *Senses*, or the *Sensibility* of its Nature, has or has not that which is agreeable to it. For Nature shows what it is in a Child, and does not become *another* thing in a grown Man. The Child has no Cunning or Fraud, and therefore he plainly owns what he wants and cries for it.

---

* Page 156.

Grown Men are under the same *Sensibility* of Nature, want only what the Child wanted, *viz.*, to have their Senses gratified, but they have the Cunning not to *own* it, and the Fraud to *pretend* something else.

And thus it must be with every human Creature. He must be governed by *this Sensibility* of his Nature, must be happy or unhappy, according as his Senses are gratified, till *such time* as he is born again from above, till the *new Birth* has awakened *another Sensibility* in him, and opened a way for divine *Communications* and *Impressions* to have more Effect upon him, than the Things of this World have upon his natural Senses. For no created Being whatever, can any Moment of Time be free from Communications and Impressions of some kind or other; if it is not governed by Communications and Impressions from *above*, it is certainly governed by Communications and Impressions from *below*.

The *Needle* that is touched with the *Loadstone*, does not *then begin* to be under the *Power* of Attraction, for it was under the Power of Attraction from the Earth before. And if it loses the Attraction of the Loadstone, it does not cease to be attracted by something else.

The Soul that is touched with an Impression from God, does not *then begin* to be under the *Power* of something that acts upon it, for the World and the Devil, or the Nature of those Things that surround it, attract it, and act upon it. For as it has something of the Nature of everything in it, so the whole Nature of Things as continually act upon it by Impressions, as the *Sun* acts upon everything that has anything of the *Nature* of the Sun in it.

Now the *Freedom* of the Will, is not a Freedom *from* Communications and Impressions, but is only a Liberty of *choosing* to be made happy, either by yielding ourselves up to the *Attraction* or *Operation* of God upon us, or to be miserable, by yielding ourselves up to the *Impressions* of the World, and sensible Things.

There is no *middle* way; if we *reject* or make ourselves *incapable* of Impressions from God, we are the Machines and Clockwork of this sensible World.

Two Men born blind may talk and dispute about receiving Light in a *rational way*, and think it ought only to be received by their *Reason*, or in Conformity to its Power of speculating; as soon as their Eyes are opened, they both see that *Reason* was a *Fool*, and that Light can only act upon them by way of *Impression* upon the Sensibility of their Nature.

It is so far therefore from being a dangerous Delusion to

expect, *desire*, *believe*, and *pray* for Communications and Impressions from above, by means of the holy Sacrament, that it is as right and sound a Faith, and as beneficial to the Soul, as to believe that the Goodness of God's Providence is in everything, and that everything is blessed by his Power and Presence in it to the faithful Receiver.

All the Perfections of God have some kind of Similitude or Resemblance of their Power in the Perfections of the *Sun*, which refresh our animal and rational Nature by continual Communications and Impressions upon it, as the Perfections of God communicate and impress themselves upon the inmost Spirit of our Souls.

And he that would have his animal rational Nature comforted and refreshed only in a *rational* way, without Communications and Impressions from the Sun, would be just such a *Pleader* for *Reason*, as he that would have religious Satisfaction only in a rational way, without Communications and Impressions from above.

For the Impressions from God are more necessary and essential to the pious Life of the Soul, than the Impressions of the Sun are to the comfortable Life of our outward rational Man.

And he that prays for nothing else but these divine Communications and Impressions, who thinks of nothing else, desires nothing else, trusts in nothing else, as able to comfort, strengthen, and enrich his Soul: He that is thus, all *Prayer*, all *Love*, all *Desire*, and all *Faith*, in these *Communications* and *Impressions* from above, is just in the same State of *Sobriety*, as he that only prays that God *would not leave him to himself*.

For he that is without anything of these Communications and Impressions of God upon him, is in the same State of *Death* and *Separation* from God as the Devils are. And to turn Men from the *Faith* and *Love*, and *Desire* of these divine Impressions, is to lay the *Axe* to the Root of Religion, and is as *direct* a way to *Atheism*, as to teach them, as *Epicurus* did, that God is *afar off*. For a God *without* any Communications and Impressions upon us, and a God *afar off*, are equally atheistical Tenets, equally destructive of all Piety.

The one Opinion is the same Denial of God as the other.

And when Men have once lost *all Sense* of the Necessity of being inwardly, invisibly, and secretly supported, assisted, guided, and blessed by Communications and Impressions of God upon their Souls, it signifies not much what Religion they profess, or for what Reason they profess it, whether they have the Reason of *Epicurus*, or *Hobbs*, or this *Author*. For a Religion has no good of Religion in it, but so far as it introduces the *Life*, *Power*, and *Presence* of God into the Soul.

For there is nothing good even in Heaven itself, but the *Fulness* of divine Communications and Impressions; no Wretchedness in Hell, but what arises from an entire Cessation of them; and this Life has no *Possibility* of being changed into a heavenly Life, but so far as it is capable of divine Communications and Impressions.

For as the *Sun* is the Light of this World, only by Communications and Impressions of his Light upon all Objects, according to their Capacity to receive it; so God is the God of all his Creatures, only by Communications and Impressions of his Life, and Power, and Presence upon all his Creatures, according to their Capacity to receive them. And therefore to discredit and ridicule the *Desire, Hunger, Faith,* and *Expectation* of divine Communications and Impressions in all Acts and Parts of Religion, is to teach Men to *unite* Religion with *Atheism*, and to make their very Acts of Religion, a *Renunciation* of, and *Departure* from God.

Had this Author openly and plainly said with *Epicurus*, God is *afar off*, the *Atheism* had been plain and apparent, and confessed by all; and yet he has said more than this; for to say that we are without all Communications and Impressions of God upon us, for this Reason, because they would make us *Machines* and *Clock-work*, and could give us no *rational* Satisfaction, is not only saying that God is *afar off*, but that he *ought* and *must* continue to be so, if we are not to be Machines, and lose the Rationality of our Nature. So that according to this Author's Doctrine, rational and free Agents are not only to believe with *Epicurus*, but also ought to rejoice that God is *afar off*, and to desire, for the sake of the Rationality of their Nature, that he may always be at the same Distance from them.

Hence it is, that this Author is, as *Epicurus* was, forced to invent a *summum bonum*, or chief *Good* for Man, exclusive of the Enjoyment of God. Thus says he, ' The highest Good of mortal ' Man, is the uniform Practice of Morality, chosen by ourselves, ' as our Happiness here, and our unspeakable Reward here-' after.'*

For as *Epicurus* was forced to place the *highest Good* of Man in his *Philosophical Garden*, because he had separated the Gods from Men, and placed them apart by themselves; so this Author having rejected all divine Communications and Impressions upon us, as having no rational Satisfaction in them, as making us Machines and Clock-work, was forced to invent a *highest*

---

* Page 157.

Good for mortal Man, both here and hereafter, that has nothing of Good in it.

Epicurus therefore and this *Parochial Minister* of the Gospel agree in this; First, that they place the *highest Good*, or *Happiness* of Man, in something that is *exclusive* of God. Secondly, that they place it in something that they *can do* for themselves.

The *Church*, of which this Author says he is a *Minister*, sings every Day, 'Holy, Holy, Holy, Lord God, Heaven and Earth 'are full of thy Majesty and Glory;' but according to him, it sings of something that is no Part of its Happiness, either here or hereafter.

The Gospel, of which he pretends to be a Preacher, brings the glad Tidings of a Saviour, and Salvation to all Mankind; but he preaches a *highest Good* of mortal Man, that has nothing of this Saviour or Salvation in it.

Jesus Christ says, 'Except a Man be born again of the Water 'and the Spirit, he cannot enter into the Kingdom of God.' That 'as the Father raises up the dead, and quickeneth them, 'even so the Son quickeneth whom he will.'[*] And 'that to as 'many as received him, to them gave he Power to become the 'Sons of God.' Who 'were born, not of Blood, nor of the Will 'of the Flesh, nor of the Will of Man, but of God.'[†] Again, 'If 'ye abide in me, and my Words abide in you, ye shall ask what 'ye will, and it shall be done unto you. Ask and ye shall 'receive, that your Joy may be full. If any Man love me, my 'Father will love him, and we will come unto him, and make 'our abode with him.' The Apostle saith, 'Giving thanks unto 'the Father, who hath delivered us from the Power of Darkness, 'and hath translated us into the Kingdom of his dear Son, in 'whom we have Redemption through his Blood.'

Now had a *Celsus*, or a *Porphyry*, or any *modern* Adversary of the Gospel, a mind to show their utmost *Detestation* and *Abhorrence* of these Doctrines, of a Birth of the *Spirit*, a *Birth* of God, a *quickening Saviour*, a Life *in him* and through him, a Redemption *through his Blood*, a *Translation into his Kingdom*, of our *asking and receiving all* through him, of his Father's and his *Abode* in us, had they the greatest Desire to persuade all People that all this was a *groundless Fiction*, without the least Truth or Reasonableness in it, need they declare any more, or desire any more to be believed than this, 'That the highest Good of Man, 'is the uniform Practice of Morality, chosen by ourselves, as our 'Happiness here, and our unspeakable Reward hereafter?' For

---

[*] John v. 21.   [†] John i. 12.

is not this the same thing as to say, all the Doctrines of the Gospel *Saviour* and Salvation, of a *new Birth*, of the Spirit of God, of *Redemption through Christ*, of *Righteousness* in him of entering into *his Kingdom*, are absolutely false? For it is the same total Denial of all the Christian Method of Salvation, as to say, that we have our Happiness or highest Good both here and hereafter from *Epicurus*. For the Salvation, and Happiness, and eternal Life which we receive through Jesus Christ, is equally denied and rejected as false, whether you place our *highest Good* in what we can do for ourselves, or in what *Epicurus* can do for us.

The Scripture saith, 'The Gift of God is eternal Life, through 'Jesus Christ our Lord.'* And again, 'He that hath the Son, 'hath Life; and he who hath not the Son, hath not Life.'† Again, 'By Grace ye are saved through Faith; and that not of 'yourselves, it is the Gift of God.'‡ And again, 'If Christ be 'not raised, ye are yet in your Sins:' And, 'as in Adam all died, 'so in Christ shall all be made alive.' And again, 'Your Life is 'hid with Christ in God. When Christ who is our Life shall 'appear, then shall ye also appear with him in Glory.'§

Now this Author does not expressly say all this is absolutely false, and not fit to be believed, but he only desires you to believe something, that will show it to be *impossible* to be true.

For if our *own Morality, chosen by ourselves, is our highest Good and Reward both here and hereafter*, it is impossible to be true, *that* we have *no Life* but in the *Son of God*, or that eternal Life is the *Gift of God* to us through Jesus Christ, or that we are *saved by Grace*, through Faith, *and not of ourselves*.

So that this Author is not to be considered as one that has barely mistaken something in the Nature of the Sacrament, but as one that rejects the *whole Method* of Salvation through Jesus Christ, and will have no Happiness or Redemption from him here, or eternal Life hereafter.

When therefore he saith, 'Do we not partake of the Benefit of 'Remission of our Sins, by partaking of the Lord's Supper 'worthily? I must answer, No; if the Gospel be true.' ‖

This ought to have no more Weight with you, than if *Celsus* or *Porphyry*, or *Hobbs*, had said the same thing. For since he makes our *own Morality*, chosen by ourselves, to be our *highest Good, both here and hereafter*, he as absolutely rejects our Salvation through Jesus Christ, and denies the Love and Goodness of God towards us in Christ Jesus, to be our *highest Good, both here* and *hereafter*, as ever *Celsus* or *Porphyry* did: And therefore can

---

* Rom. vi. 23. † 1 John v. 12. ‡ Eph. ii. 8. § Col. iii. 3. ‖ Page 144.

have no more Right or Pretence to explain any Part of that Salvation, which he has so totally denied, than they had. In the Gospel, says he, *No Pardon of past Sins is promised or given,* unless to those just *converted, renouncing their Sins, and baptized into the Christian Faith; or to those, who having sinned after Baptism, actually amend their Lives.* This is to show you, that there is no Remission of Sins obtained by the worthy partaking of the Sacrament, *if the Gospel be true.*

Now in the Gospel, our Blessed Lord seeing their Faith, 'saith 'to the Sick of the Palsy, Son, be of good cheer, thy Sins are 'forgiven thee.'

Now here Pardon of Sins is given, directly contrary to this Author's Assertion, to one not converted and baptized into the Christian Faith, but because of his and their *Faith* that brought him on a Bed.

Again, of *Magdalen,* our Lord saith, ' Her Sins, which are 'many, are forgiven ; for she loved much. But to whom little is 'forgiven, the same loveth little.'

Here you see again a plain Confutation of this Author's Doctrine; for here Remission of Sins is actually given and declared to be due to *Love,* and Love is affirmed to be the *Measure* of it.

Therefore it is an undeniable Doctrine of the Gospel, that *Faith* and *Love* are *certain* Means of obtaining Remission of our Sins; if therefore the Sacrament is an *Exercise* of our *Faith* and *Love,* then we have the utmost Assurance from our Saviour's own Words, that we thereby obtain Remission of our Sins.

But this Author has another Argument against it, taken from our *Liturgy.* In our Public *Office,* says he, ' it is not supposed 'that the worthy partaking of the Lord's Supper does itself 'operate this Forgiveness; but it is made part of a Prayer to God, 'that they who have partaken of it, may obtain Remission of their 'Sins, &c. They are taught to pray thus, after the Act of Com- 'munion is over, which supposes that it is not already obtained.'*

Now if there was any Truth or Reason in this Argument, it would follow, that our Saviour's Apostles had obtained *no Remission* of Sins from him; and though he had *chosen* them out of the World, called them his *Friends,* and declared his *extraordinary Love* for them, and though they *left all and followed* him, yet he had not done that for them, which he had done for the sick of the Palsy, and many others ; for this Reason, because he had taught and enjoined them a Form of Prayer, in which they were to *pray for the Forgiveness of their Sins.*

* Page 145.

For if it is rightly argued, that there is *no Remission* of Sins obtained by the Use of the Sacrament, because *afterwards* there is *Prayer* made for the Forgiveness of Sins; then it must follow, that our Saviour's Apostles could not have received any Remission of Sins, when he taught them to pray for it. It must follow also, that he never intended that they should be in the *State* of new Converts, *baptized* for the Remission of their Sins, because then they could not without great Absurdity have used that Form of Prayer which he gave them.

It follows also, that the Apostles could not have taught this Form of Prayer, or enjoined the Use of it to their new baptized Converts, because it would have been, according to this Author, a proving to them, that they had not received the Pardon of their Sins by Baptism.

Now the Inconsistency which this Author finds in praying for the Forgiveness of Sins, and all other Benefits of Christ's Passion, after the Reception of the Sacrament, if the Sacrament itself was a means of obtaining them, all this Inconsistency and Difficulty had been removed, if he had only known or acknowledged, that the Christian Life is a *progressive* State, and that Forgiveness of Sins is a Grace and Benefit of Jesus Christ, bestowed upon us in the same manner as every other Grace or degree of Holiness, as a *Talent* to be improved, as a *Seed* to be nourished up by us to its full Growth. And for this Reason it is, that we are obliged to pray for every Grace, and every Virtue, that we have *already* received, because we had received it to grow up in us, and *Prayer* or *Desire* of it is the only Soil in which it can grow.

Thus he to whom God has *already* given the Grace of *Penitence*, for that reason *prays* for Penitence; he that has already received of God the Gift of *Faith*, for that reason prays, *Lord, help thou my Unbelief;* and he that is the *fullest* of Righteousness, feels the greatest *Hunger* and *Thirst* after it.

But according to this Author's Religion, he that has received the Spirit of God, cannot be supposed to pray for it; and yet according to the Religion of the *Gospel*, no one can pray for it, but because he has received it.

I shall now only add a word or two on what this Author says in Defence of the *Safety* of his Doctrine of the Sacrament; though it should be erroneous.

It ought certainly,' says he, 'to be far from the Thoughts of 'every Christian to lessen any Privileges, or undervalue any 'Promises, annexed by Christ to any Duty or Institution of his 'Religion. It is an inexcusable Carelessness to do it for want of 'due Consideration.—But this, I think, may with Truth be said,

'that an Error of this sort (should it be supposed) does not really
'hurt any Christian, nor alter the Effect of the Duty at all.'*

The Safety therefore of his Doctrine of the Sacrament, supposing it to lessen and undervalue the Benefits of it, is grounded upon this general Proposition, which he takes to be a great Truth, *viz.*, ' That to lessen or undervalue the Privileges and Promises 'annexed *to any Duty or Institution by* Jesus Christ, does not ' *really hurt* any Christian, or *alter the Effect* of the Duty at all.'

Now this Doctrine directly leads to *Infidelity*, for Infidelity is nothing else but a *lessening* and *undervaluing* the Privileges and Promises annexed to *Faith* in Christ.

The Scripture saith, ' In this was manifested the Love of God 'toward us, because that God sent his only begotten Son into ' the World, that we might live through him ;' and again, *He sent his Son to be the* Propitiation *for our Sins.*† ' God so loved 'the World, that he gave his only begotten Son, that whosoever 'believeth in him should not perish, but have eternal Life.' Here the Privilege and Promise of *Life*, and *Atonement* for our Sins, is annexed to *Faith* in Christ ; but according to this Author, it does you no *real Hurt*, nor *alters* the *Effect* of your Faith at all, though you *lessen* and *undervalue* this Privilege and Promise of Life, and Atonement for your Sins, offered to your Faith in Christ Jesus.

Is not this directly saying, that Infidelity is as safe and beneficial to you, as a Belief of the Privileges and Promises of the Gospel ? Is it not saying, that it is as beneficial to you to esteem Christ only as a Carpenter's Son, as to expect *Atonement* and *Life* from him, as the only begotten Son of God ?

It is said of our blessed Lord, that among those of his own Country *he did no mighty Works, because of their Unbelief.* Now what was their *Unbelief?* It was nothing but the *Infidelity* which this Author would prove to be *harmless ;* it was only a *lessening* and *undervaluing* all those Privileges and Promises which our Saviour offered to those that would have a just Sense of the Value of them. Now if we lessen or undervalue any Privileges and Promises annexed to Faith in Christ, or any other Duty, such *Unbelief* will certainly have the same Effect upon us that it had upon those amongst whom Christ lived, it will hinder him from doing any mighty Works among us, or in other Words, render our Knowledge and Profession of him ineffectual to our Salvation.

Prayer and *Faith* are amongst the greatest Duties of the Christian Life, and are the most powerful Means of obtaining

---

* Pref., p. 5. † 1 John iv. 9.

all the Blessings of our Salvation. Now to these two Duties the greatest *Privileges* and *Promises* are annexed by Christ. The Promise of the Holy Spirit is made to Prayer. Now, according to this Author, if you lessen and undervalue this Privilege and Promise annexed to Prayer, if you grow indifferent about the Necessity or Benefit of the Holy Spirit, and fancy that you are sufficient of yourself for all the Virtue that you want, all this does you no *real Hurt*, nor *alters* at all the *Effect* of your Prayer.

Again, another Privilege annexed to Prayer, is that of being heard in and through the *Name* of *Christ*.

'Hitherto,' says our blessed Lord, 'ye have asked nothing in 'my Name; ask and ye shall receive, that your Joy may be full.'— 'Whatsoever ye shall ask the Father in my Name, he will give 'it you.'*

Now if any Infidel, to abate your Zeal for, and Confidence in this kind of Prayer, should teach you, that no one can suffer any *real Hurt* by *lessening* and undervaluing Prayer in the *Name of Christ*, and that it would have the same Effect upon you, though you expected little or no Good from it, the Gospel would be preached to you, just as it is by this Author.

Again, ' All things whatsoever ye shall ask in Prayer, believing, 'ye shall receive.' Now what is this *believing*, but an entire Faith in the Privileges and Promises annexed to Prayer?

But if Prayer is effectual because of this Faith in the Promises made to Prayer, then everyone suffers a *real Hurt*, and the *Effect* of his Prayer is altogether hindered by this want of Faith, or by a lessening and undervaluing the Privileges and Promises annexed to it.

But if this Author's Doctrine was true, it might then be said, in Contradiction to the Gospel, Prayer does you as much real good when you have little or no Faith in it, as when you have ever so much, and your believing is no help to your receiving.

The Scriptures attribute a kind of Omnipotency to Faith; thus, ' All things are possible to him that believeth.' Again, ' According to thy Faith, so be it done unto thee.—Thy Faith 'hath saved thee.—Thy Faith hath made thee whole.' But according to this Author, it must be said, that the Want of Faith does you no *real Hurt*, that you will be *healed* and *saved*, *and have all things done to you*, in the same manner, whether you be faithless or believing.

And on this Foundation it is that he grounds your *Safety* in receiving his Doctrine of the Sacrament, though he should have lessened and undervalued the Benefits annexed to it. But you

---

* John xvi. 24.

ought to observe, that you can have no Safety in receiving his Doctrine of the Sacrament, unless it be safe for you to receive another Gospel.

Had the *Sick*, the *Lame*, the *Blind*, and the *Deaf* believed that which this Author would have you believe, as safe Doctrine, *viz.*, that to lessen and undervalue the Promises and Privileges made to Faith, could do them no *real Hurt*, they had continued in their Infirmities, merely for knowing Jesus Christ and the Gospel as this Author would have you know them.

When two *blind* Men ran crying after our Saviour to have Mercy on them, 'He saith unto them, Believe ye that I am able 'to do this? They said unto him, yea, Lord. Then touched he 'their Eyes, saying, according to your Faith be it unto you. And 'their Eyes were opened.'* The poor Woman that wanted to be healed of her Infirmity, said, 'If I may but touch his Clothes 'I shall be whole:' Upon this Faith of the Woman, our Saviour said, 'I perceive that Virtue is gone out of me;' and turning him about, and seeing the Woman, 'he said unto her, Daughter, be 'of good comfort, thy Faith hath made thee whole.'†

Now, had the blind Men answered to our Saviour's Question, No, Lord, we do not believe that thou canst give us Sight; had the diseased Woman said, I am so far from expecting to be healed by touching his Clothes, that I don't believe he has the Power of healing in himself; according to this Author, their *Infidelity* must have helped them to just the same Benefit from Christ, as their *Faith* did, notwithstanding that Christ himself ascribes it to their Faith. For unless it be true, that their want of Faith had helped them to the same Benefit from Christ that their Faith did, it cannot be true, that to *lessen and undervalue the Privileges and Promises annexed to any Duty, does you no real Hurt, nor alters the Effect of it at all.*

And therefore the Safety which this Author proposes to you, in lessening and undervaluing the Privileges and Promises annexed to the Sacrament, is only the Safety of Infidelity, and such a Safety as they are in, who lessen and undervalue the Privileges and Promises annexed to Faith in Jesus Christ.

And indeed herein he is, though inconsistent with the Gospel, very consistent with himself. For if, as he has said, *an uniform Morality chosen by ourselves, is our highest Good both here and hereafter;* our highest Good makes Christ as needless to us as the Sacrament; for if this is true, you can no more need the Benefits of a Saviour, than the Benefits of a Sacrament, and it can signify nothing to your Happiness, whatever Privileges and

---

* Matt. ix. 30.   † Matt. ix. 22.

Promises are offered to you in the Gospel, because you want none, can receive none as a Part of your Happiness, because you have it all from yourself, both here and hereafter.

So that if this Minister of the Gospel carries his Point with you, if you believe his Doctrine of the Sacrament, upon the *Principles* on which he teaches it, you may indeed retain something of the *outward Form* of the Sacrament, but must reject the *whole Salvation* of the Gospel.

FINIS.

The Introduction.

I SHOULD reckon it a Matter of great Importance, if I knew how to bespeak the *serious Attention* of the Reader to one of the greatest Articles of the Christian Religion, and of the greatest Concern to himself.

And though the Subject is *particular*, and seems only to relate to *one Point*, yet the Things which will here come under Consideration, will extend to Matters of the most general Moment, and contain the most affecting Reasons to awaken and convert the Heart both of the *Deist*, and the Christian.

For it is my Intent so to search and lay open the true Grounds and Reasons of the Christian *New-Birth*, that the Things said, may equally reach both these sorts of Readers.

For the Deists, and Unbelievers, have a great Share of my compassionate Affections, and I never can think, or write of the infinite Blessings of the Christian Redemption, without feeling in my Heart, an impatient Longing to see them the happy Partakers of them. And as one naturally believes, what one strongly wishes; so I cannot help hoping, that both Christians and *Deists* will here find Truths of such a Nature, as must in some Degree touch their Hearts, if not read with *Prejudice and Aversion*.

THE
GROUNDS AND REASONS
OF CHRISTIAN
REGENERATION,
OR, THE
NEW-BIRTH,

Offered to the Consideration of

CHRISTIANS AND DEISTS.

By *WILLIAM LAW*, M. A.

LONDON:
Printed for J. RICHARDSON, in *Pater-noster-Row.* 1739.

OF THE
Nature and Necessity
OF
REGENERATION,
OR, THE
NEW-BIRTH.

MAN was created by God *after his own Image*, and in *his own Likeness*, a living Mirror of the *Divine Nature*: where Father, Son, and Holy Ghost, each brought forth their *own Nature* in a *creaturely Manner*.

(2.) As the Son, who is begotten of the Father, is the *Brightness* of the Father's Glory, and the Holy Ghost proceedeth from the Father and the Son, as an *amiable, moving Life of both;* so it was in this created Image of the Holy Trinity. In it, the Father's *Nature* generated the Nature of the *Son*, and the Holy Ghost proceeded from them both, as an amiable, moving Life of both.* *This* was the *Likeness* or *Image of God*, in which the first Man was created, a *true Offspring* of God, in whom the *Divine Birth* sprung up as in the Deity, where Father, Son, and Holy Ghost saw themselves in a *creaturely Manner*.

(3.) In the Divine Nature the Father cannot possibly be separated from the Son, nor the Holy Ghost from both, or either of them. But *such Separation* could come to pass in the Trinity, become *creaturely*, or in the created living Image of the Trinity.

(4.) If such Separation could not have happened, Man *could not* have fallen out of *Paradise;* for so long as this Image of the Holy Trinity continued *unbroken*, so long it must be in Paradise, Heaven, or the Kingdom of Divine Joy.

(5.) But that this *Separation* could happen in this created Image of the Trinity, *viz.*, that the *Birth* of the *Son*, and the Arising or Proceeding of the Holy Ghost, could be *separated* or

---

* See *An Appeal to Deists, Arians, &c.*, c. i., pp. 45-58.

lost, is also certain; because Man is actually fallen out of Paradise into this *poor, wretched, perishable* World.

(6.) Whilst Man continued an *unbroken Image* of the holy Trinity, he was necessarily in Paradise, in the open Enjoyment of the Kingdom of God. He stood indeed upon the *Earth*, and with the *same outward* World about him, as we do now; but Paradise was *over* all, the *Cover* of all; and therefore he neither *saw* nor *felt* either his own *outward* Body, or the Things of this *outward* World, in the *manner*, as we *now* see, and feel them. His own dark, gross, heavy, fleshly Body, which appeared after the Fall, and the *naked Grossness, Heaviness, Darkness, Discord, Contrariety*, and *Enmity*, of the Elements of this *outward* World, the Strife of *Heat* and *Cold*, of *Storms* and *Tempests*, were Things *suppressed* in Paradise, and as *entirely* hid from his Eyes, as the Darkness of the Night is hid from our Eyes by the Light of the Day.

(7.) This is plainly taught us in the holy Scripture, where it is said of our first Parents in Paradise, before the Fall, that 'they were naked, and were not ashamed.' And again, after the Fall, it is said, 'their Eyes were opened,' and 'they saw they 'were naked,' and through Shame sought for a Covering. It is not said, they *saw* their Nakedness in Paradise, but that *though* they were naked, that is, had such Bodies as afterwards *appeared* to be naked, *yet* they were not ashamed, And the Reason of their not being ashamed, was because that Nakedness was *not then visible*, could not *then show* itself, but was *concealed* and *covered* from *them* by their *paradisiacal* Glory; but as soon as by Sin, they *died* to the paradisiacal Life and Glory, then they *saw* their Nakedness, which Sight filled them with Shame and Confusion.

(8.) From these two Passages of Scripture it is most plain, first, that *another sort* of Seeing, or another Sight of Things, was opened in *Adam* after the Fall, than *that* which he had before it: For he *then first* saw his *own Nakedness*, and therefore *first* also then saw the *outward World*, with *such Eyes* as he saw his own Body, that is, in the same State of *Nakedness*, as he saw himself, destitute of its paradisiacal Glory. *Secondly*, That before his Fall, his *Seeing* was *divine*, by means of a *divine Light*, shining forth from the Kingdom of God, that was then not *hid*, but powerfully opened *within him*. It was then with him, as with the heavenly City, of which St. *John* says, 'It had 'no need of the Sun, neither of the Moon to shine in it; for the 'Glory of God did enlighten it, and the Lamb is the Light 'thereof.' Rev. xxi. 23. *Thirdly*, That after the Fall, when the Image of the holy Trinity was *broken* in him, this divine Light *departed* from him, and he was left to the *firmamental Light* of this World, to the Light of *Beasts*, to see himself, and all other *outward* Things, in *no other* Light and Glory, but such as the *Sun*, *Stars*, and *Elements*, cast upon one another. Thus he stood with regard to this *outward* World, a *poor Prisoner* of this earthly Life, as much under the Power and Slavery of the Elements, as his Fellow-creatures the *Beasts*.

(9.) Paradise being departed from the Earth (which before kept all in harmony) now Discord and Contrariety broke forth in *all* the Elements, and Animals upon it. The *Elementary* Nature *in* Man, and Beasts, was in the *same* Disorder with the *outward* Elements and Stars. From this time *Storms* and *Tempests*, *Thunders* and *Lightnings*, *Earthquakes*, and all sorts of Strife and Contrarieties through all temporal Nature; and in *Man*, and other *Animals*, arose the *same Disquiet;* for the Elements *in* and *without* man, were of the same Nature, and therefore acted upon one another. Hence, Heat, Cold, Pain, Sorrow, Fear, Disquiet, Diseases, Sickness and Death, came upon Man, fallen *out of* Paradise *into* this World.

(10.) This was the State of the World, and of Man in it, after that *Paradise* was *retired* from it; when, instead of the *Light* and *Glory* of Paradise, which before made it all *Peace* and *Unity*, and a sweet Habitation of Divine Joy, it had now only the *Light* of the *Sun*, which could only keep the Elements in *such Harmony*, and *Discord*, as we now see in the World. Thus stood Man in this *outward* World; let us now look at the *inward* State of his Soul, and see what *Condition* he was of, in the inward, and spiritual World.

(11.) We have before shown, that Man was created a *living Image* of the holy Trinity in Unity, that the *Divine Birth* arose in him, and *that* Father, Son, and Holy Ghost, saw themselves in him, in a *creaturely Manner*.

Now by his Transgression *this* Image of the Holy Trinity was broken; the Generation of the *Son*, or *Word*, and the Proceeding of the Holy Ghost in him, were at *an End;* in the *Day* that he sinned, in *that* Day he died *this Death*. And therefore *what* was he as to *his Soul?* *What* must be said of it? It was something, *that* was deprived of *that Birth*, which was the *Brightness of its Glory*, and which should be that to it, which the *Son* of God *is* to the Father; it wanted *that Spirit*, which was its *amiable Life*, and which was to be that to it, which the *Holy Ghost is* to the Father, and the Son.

Yet the Soul was *still* a Life, an *imperishable Life, that* could not be *dissolved*, or *cease* to be. Now seeing *every Life*, whether spiritual or corporeal, consists in *Fire*, or rather is Fire; therefore we may say of the Soul in this State, *that* it is a spiritual dark *Fire*-breath, an *Anger-Fire, that must* heat, and torment itself with its *own inward burning* Strife, and yet be *unable* to reach, touch, or obtain any Spark of *Light* and *Love,* to make its *Fire-Life* sweet and amiable, or such a Flame of Fire, as *Angels* are said to be.

(12.) This was the *State* of the Soul after the *Fall,* when the *Birth* of the Son of God, and the *Proceeding* of the Holy Ghost, were *no more* to be found, or felt in it. It was in the *State* and *Condition* of the Devils, who in their *fallen* Nature, are from *Flames* of *Love,* become this spiritual, dark, raging, aching *Fire-breath,* that can draw *no Light* of *Love* into it.

And the Reason why, even the most profligate Persons do not *fully know,* and perceive their Souls to be in this miserable State, *a dark Root of self-tormenting Fire,* is this, because the Soul, though thus fallen, was still *united to the Blood* of an human Body, and therefore the *sweet,* and *cheering Light* of the Sun, could reach the *Soul,* and do *that* for it in some *Degree,* and for some *Time,* which it does to the *Darkness, Sharpness, Sourness, Bitterness,* and *Wrath* that is in *outward* Nature, that is, it could *enlighten, sweeten,* and *cheer* it in a certain Degree.

But as this is not its *own* Light, that is, does not *arise in* the Soul itself, but only reaches it by *means* of the Body; so if the Soul hath in *this time* got *no* Light of its *own,* then, when the Death of the Body breaks off its *Communion* with the Light of this World, the Soul is left a *mere dark, raging* Fire, in the State of Devils.

And if all the Light of this World was to be *immediately* at once extinguished, *all human* Souls *that* were not in some *real Degree* of Regeneration, would immediately find themselves to be nothing but the rage of *Fire,* and the Horror of *Darkness.*

(13.) Now, though the Light and Comfort of this *outward* World, keeps even the worst of Men from any *constant, strong* Sensibility of *that* wrathful, fiery, dark, and self-tormenting Nature, *that* is the *very Essence* of every fallen, unregenerate Soul; yet every Man in the World has, more or less, *frequent* and *strong* Intimations given him, that *so* it is with him, in the *inmost* Ground of his Soul.

How many Inventions are some People forced to have recourse to, to keep off a certain *inward Uneasiness,* which they are *afraid* of, and know not *whence* it comes? Alas, it is because there is a *fallen Spirit,* a *dark aching* Fire within them, which has never had its *proper Relief,* and is trying to *discover* itself, and calling out for *Help,* at every *Cessation* of worldly Joy.

Why are some People, when under heavy *Disappointments,* or some great *worldly Shame,* at the very Brink of Distraction, unable to bear themselves, and desirous of Death of any kind? 'Tis because worldly *Light* and *Comforts*, no longer acting *sweetly* upon the *Blood*, the soul is *left* to its own *dark, fiery raging* Nature, and would destroy the Body at *any* rate, rather than continue under such a *Sensibility* of its own *wrathful, self-tormenting Fire.*

Who has not at one time or other felt a Sourness, Wrath, Selfishness, Envy, and Pride, which he could not tell *what* to do with, or *how* to bear, rising up in him *without* his Consent, casting a *Blackness* over all his Thoughts, and then as *suddenly* going off again, either by the Cheerfulness of the *Sun*, or *Air*, or some *agreeable* Accident, and again, *at times*, as suddenly returning upon him? Sufficient Indications are *these* to every Man, that there is a *dark Guest* within him, concealed under the *Cover* of Flesh and Blood, often *lulled asleep* by worldly *Light* and *Amusements*, yet such as will, in spite of everything, show itself, which if it has not its *proper Relief* in this Life, must be *his Torment* in Eternity. And it was for the sake of this *hidden* Hell within us, that our Blessed Lord said when on Earth, and says now to every Soul, 'Come unto me, all ye that labour and are heavy laden, 'and I will give you Rest.'

For as the Soul is become this *Self-tormenting* Fire, *only* because the *Birth of the Son* of God was *extinguished* in it by our first Parents; so there is *no other* possible Remedy for it, either in Heaven or Earth, but by its coming to this Son of God, to be *born again* of him.

Oh, *poor Unbelievers*, that content yourselves with this Foundation of *Hell* in your Nature, and either seek for *no* Salvation, or, what is worse, turn your Backs with Disregard on the *one only* Saviour, that God himself can help you to!

Think not of saving yourselves. It is no more in your Power, than to save the fallen Spirits that are in Hell; you can no more do the one than the other. Talk not of the *Mercy* and *Goodness* of God; his Mercy is indeed *infinite*, and his Goodness above all Conception; but then the *Infiniteness* of it consists *in this*, that he of his own mere Mercy found out, and offered this Saviour to all Mankind, because in the Nature of Things, nothing less than this Saviour could redeem them.

Therefore to rely upon a Mercy of God, that is not *within* the Christian Scheme of it, is to rely upon a *Fiction* of our own Minds; because *all* the Mercy that God can show to Mankind, *all* that his *omnipotent Love* can do for them, is *done* and *offered* to them in, and through the Redemption of Jesus Christ.

If either *Devils*, or *lost* Souls could *possibly* be annihilated, neither of them would by the Goodness of God, be suffered to exist in *Misery*, for Misery's *sake*. But a Man may as well expect that his Soul shall be annihilated through the Goodness of God, though *Annihilation* is impossible, and what cannot be done, as to expect to be saved through the Divine Goodness, without the Mediation of the Son of God, when the *Birth* of the Son of God in the Soul, is the *one only* Salvation, that the Omnipotence of God can bestow upon him.

Therefore to choose or rely upon *some other* Goodness of God besides that, which he has offered to us in Jesus Christ, is the most dreadful Mistake that can befall any Man, and must, if persevered in, leave him out of the *Possibility* of any Kind, or Degree of Salvation. For as the Son of God is the *Brightness* and *Glory* of the *Father*, so no Soul made in the *Likeness of God* is capable of any Degree of *Brightness* and *Glory*, but so far as the *Birth* of the Son of God is in it; therefore to reject *this Birth*, to refuse *this* Method of Redemption, is to reject *all the Goodness*, that the Divine Nature itself hath for us.

(14.) But to return. I have shown in few Words the *original Dignity and Glory* of Man's Creation and State in Paradise, and the lamentable *Change*, that the Fall has brought upon him.

From a divine and heavenly Creature, he is so wretchedly changed, as to have *inwardly* the Nature, and dark Fire of the Devils, and *outwardly* the Nature of *all* the Beasts, a *Slave* of this outward World, living at all *Uncertainties*, amongst Pains, Fears, Sorrows, and Diseases, till his Body is forced to be removed from our Sight, and hid in the Earth.

Now from this short View of *what* Man is fallen *from*, and what he is fallen *into*, we may see at once in the *strongest Light* the divine *Excellency* and absolute *Necessity* of those Doctrines of our blessed Lord, calling us to *all Kinds* of renouncing the *World*, to so *many Ways* of denying all the Passions and inclinations of Flesh and Blood.

Were the World, as it *now is*, and we, as we *now are*, in the *very first* State in which God made it and us, there would be some Foundation for saying, as some do, 'What are all these 'Things for, if they are not to be enjoyed? Why have we these 'Passions and Inclinations, if they may not be gratified?' But *all these* Questions are *fully* answered, as soon as it is known, that the *first State* of Things is quite altered; that we were not created to be in this World in the *Manner* we are *now* in it; that Paradise was our *first State*, where we should have stood in divine *Strength* and *Ability*, *insensible* of any Evil from *outward* Nature; that *Sin* destroyed this *first State* of Things, destroyed the *Divine Life* in the Soul, and removed *Paradise* from off the Earth;—that Man, cast out of Paradise, came as a *Malefactor*

of Christian Regeneration. 143

into this *outward* World, to be punished and scourged by all its *divided, warring* Elements; that by his falling *into* this World, it got the *same* Power over him, as over the Beasts, that are its proper Inhabitants, and of the same Nature with itself; that *thus* fallen *under* its Dominion, it continually breathes its *own corrupt Nature* into him, feeds him with such *Husks* as the Swine eat, and proposes *such* Pleasures to him, as make him *unwilling*, and *unable* to regain his first Divine Life.

Now, as soon as this is known to be the *Condition* of Man, thus fallen from a *Divine Life* under the Dominion of this World, then all the *renouncing, self-denying* Doctrines of the Gospel, appear to have the *utmost* Reason and Necessity in them; then it appears to be as much our Happiness, to *deny* the Tempers and Inclinations of this earthly Nature, and to be delivered from the *Power* of its Pleasures over us, as to be delivered from the Power of *Death* and *Hell*.

And the most *sober Reason* thus acquainted with the Nature of our Fall, must be *forced* to consider *this World* as having merely the Nature of an *Hospital*, where People *only* are, because they are *distempered*, and where *no* Happiness is sought for, but that of being *healed*, and made fit to *leave* it.

(15.) To proceed: That I have not stated Man's first Dignity too high, is evidently plain from the Scripture Account of it. It is a fundamental Truth of our Religion, that he was created in *Paradise* for a Life *suitable* to it. But Paradise is a *Divine Habitation*, still existing *where* it was at the first, though not *visible* to Eyes which see *only* by the Light of the Sun, and is the Habitation of such as have attained their *first* paradisiacal Nature; it was in this Paradise, that our Saviour, through a Miracle of Love, promised to be with the Thief on the Cross.

It is also a fundamental Truth of Scripture, that Man was created to be *immortal, incapable* of Death, and of everything *that* had any *Likeness* to it, so long as he continued in the Perfection of his State. That it was *Sin alone* which brought Sorrow, Pain, Evil, Distress, Sickness and Death upon him.

But if this be a Truth *that* cannot be denied, then it must be equally true, that before he sinned, he must have stood in *such a Paradise*, as kept everything in the outward World *entirely under* him, so *that* neither *Fire* nor *Water*, nor any other Element, could have the least Power over him. But if Fire, the fiercest of the Elements, had not the least Power of touching his Body in any *hurtful Manner*, or of causing *any Pain* to it; then it must be granted, *that* Paradise *covered*, and *governed* the Power of all the Elements of this outward World; that Man lived in it as an *absolute* Lord over it; and therefore it undeniably follows, that the *Manner*, in which he *now* is under the Power of the Elements, capable of receiving Pain and Evil from them, is a State that he *was not in*, till Sin took Paradise from him, and left him in the *same* poor Condition, that we *now* are in, capable of receiving Pain and Death, from almost everything that is about us.

That Man in Paradise lived in this World *insensible*, and also *incapable* of any Evil from it, superior to all its Elements, is plain from the Tree of *Knowledge* of *Good and Evil*.

For how could it be more plainly told us, that outward Things, the *Stars* and *Elements* could not *affect* his State, or make any *Impression* upon him, than by telling us, that he had no Knowledge of Good and Evil in this World, till he had eaten of that Tree? Is not this directly telling us, that before such eating, he was above the *Nature* of this World, that it had not Power to operate upon him, or give him any *Sense* or *Feeling*, of what there was of Good or Evil in it.

Now that he was created to be, and to continue thus a Lord over all temporal Nature, superior to all the influences and Effects of the Stars and Elements, is also plain from the Prohibition given him, not to eat of this Tree of Knowledge.

But he was not content with this happy Superiority above the Evil and Good of outward Nature. His Imagination, helped on by the Devil, longed to look into, to know and feel the secret working Powers of that outward Nature, which it was his Happiness, and Paradise to be insensible of.

When God forbade his eating of the Tree of Knowledge of Good and Evil, it was the same thing as if he had said, *Fall not into the outward World, under the Dominion of its Stars and Elements, but keep thy State in Paradise.*

When Man disobeyed God, and took the Fruit of the Tree into his Body, which brought the Nature and Power of the Stars and Elements into it; this is not to be considered, as that single Act of eating, but it signifies as much as if he had said; *By eating this Fruit, I desire to come within the Influences of the Stars and Elements, and to be made sensible, and feeling of the Good and Evil that is in them.*

Therefore, small as the Action seems to be at the first View, and of a very limited Nature, it was his *refusing* to be that, which God created him to be; it was his *express, open, voluntary* Act and Deed, by which he chose to *fall into* this outward World, in the Manner we now are in it.

Therefore it was not the mere eating of a Fruit, *that* brought *Adam's* Misery upon him, but it was the eating a Fruit, as his *chosen Means* of entering into this World.

God himself was not *angry* at all, or at a small Act of eating a Fruit, and so in *Anger* turned Man out of Paradise, into a World *cursed* for that Sin. But Man freely and voluntarily chose, against the *Will*, and *Command* of God, to be in the World in its *cursed State*, unblessed by Paradise: For he chose to enter into a *Sensibility* and *Feeling* of its *Good* and *Evil*, which is directly choosing to be, where Paradise is not; for nothing that is in Paradise, can be touched, or hurt by anything of the outward World. Therefore the first State of Man was a state of such Glory, and heavenly Prerogatives, as I have above related; and his Fall, was a Fall into, or under the Power of this outward World.

(16.) If it be also further asked, What *sufficient* Proof there is, *first*, that the *Likeness* and *Image* of God, in which Man was created, signified thus much, that Father, Son, and Holy Ghost, each brought forth their *own Nature* in him, and in him saw themselves in a *creaturely manner?* And then, *secondly*, that by the *first* Sin, this *Birth* of the Son of God, and *Proceeding* of the Holy Ghost was *extinguished* and *lost* in the Soul of Man? It may be answered, that these great Truths stand attested by *undeniable* Evidence of Scripture.

First, from the *Means* and *Manner* of our Redemption. For there is nothing that can so *fully*, and *justly* show us the *true Nature* of our Fall, as the Nature and Manner of our Redemption. And it seems highly suitable to the Wisdom of God to let the *first*, be but in part discovered, till the latter showed and proved itself in an undeniable manner. And this, no doubt, is the Reason why *Moses* is suffered to write *no more* of the Nature of the Fall of Man, or *what* it implied, than he has done. Because the Time for a plain Insight into that Matter, was not *then* come, and it was to lie as much a Secret, as to the true Nature of it, as the *Nature* and *Manner* of our Redemption then did; which was then only *obscurely* declared, by an *Enmity* between the *Seed* of the Woman, and the *Seed* of the Serpent.

But when the Seed of the Woman showed itself to be the *Son of God*, the Second Person of the holy Trinity, *united* to our human Nature; then the Nature of our Fall, and *what* we fell from, and what was the Seed of the *Serpent* in us, manifested themselves in the *same Degree* of Certainty. And therefore it is very unreasonable to hold, that we ought to say *no more* of our first State before the *Fall*, of its *Dignity* and *Perfection*, and what was *lost* by the Fall, than what is *openly* and *expressly* declared by *Moses*. For as it seemed good to the Divine Wisdom to *conceal* the Mystery of our Redemption and Salvation for many Ages, and to let *Moses* only discover it under a Declaration of a *Serpent-destroyer;* so there was a *Fitness*, and even *Necessity*, that the *Nature* and *Degree* of our Fall should be kept in the same Degree of *Secrecy*, then *only* to be discovered with a sufficient Degree of Plainness and Certainty, when our *Redemption* and *Salvation* came plainly to be laid open. The Religion of the *Jews* was suited to *that State* of Things and Times in which they lived; neither the Mysteries of the *Creation*, nor *Redemption*, were then discovered; Things *past*, and Things to come, had then only their *Figures, Shadows,* and *Types.*

But when the Son of God became *incarnate*, and showed forth in the plainest Manner, the *Nature, Manner,* and *Necessity* of our Redemption through *his Blood,* and a *Life* received *from him,* then the *Nature* and *Degree* of our *Fall* became equally *plain* and *manifest;* and everything that he has told us of the Nature and Necessity of a *new* or *second Birth* from him, was *so much* told us of our *first Birth* in Paradise.

For the Nature and Greatness of our Redemption, must show the Nature and Greatness of our Fall. These Things have such a necessary Correspondence, as cannot be denied, but by a Mind utterly indisposed to receive Conviction.

If our Redemption proposed to restore to us a *Divine Sight*, would not this be a sufficient Proof, that by the *Fall* we had *lost* some *Divine Manner* of seeing? So, if *God himself* takes our Nature upon him to *redeem* us, and it be declared that *nothing*, but this *uniting* the Divine Nature to the human, can be *our Redemption*, can we want a Proof, that the Divine Nature existed in *some manner* in us, before the Fall?

Now it is a plain, manifest Doctrine of the holy Scriptures, that Man by the Fall is in *such a Condition*, that there was *no help* or *Remedy* for him, either in the Height above, or in the Depth below, but by the *Son of God's* becoming incarnate, and taking the fallen Nature upon him. If this *alone* could be the Remedy, does not this enough show us the Disease? Does not this speak plainly enough, *what* it was that Man had lost by his Fall, namely, the *Birth of the Son* of God in his Soul; and therefore it was, that only the Son of God in so mysterious a manner, could be his Redeemer?

If he had *lost* less, a *less Power* could have redeemed him. If he had lost something *else*, the Restoration of *that* something, would have been his Redemption.

But since it is an *open, undeniable* Doctrine of the Gospel, that there can be *no Salvation* for Mankind but in the *Name*, and by the *Power* of the Son of God, by his being united to the fallen Nature, and so raising his *own Birth* and *Life* in it, is it not *sufficiently* declared to us, that *what* was lost by the Fall, was the *Birth* of the Son of God in the Soul?

Secondly, This same Doctrine is not left to be drawn from any Consequences of Things, but is in express Words taught us, when it is said, that we must be *born again from above,* born *of God;* for this is expressly telling us *what Birth* we have lost, and is only saying, that the first Birth is to be restored, or that the Divine Birth is to arise, or to be brought again into us, as *at the first,* when the *living* Image of the Holy Trinity was brought forth *in us.*

What this *new regained* Birth is, we are plainly told by St. *Peter,* that is a being *born again of an incorruptible Seed by the Word,* that is, the eternal *Word,* or *Son* of God. Which Divine Word being only in the Soul as a *Seed,* is to restore by degrees the *first Birth* of the Word, or *Son* of God in the Soul. Which is Proof enough that *this* was the State of the Soul in its Creation, that *this Birth* was then in it, and so was an *Image* of the Holy Trinity; and that the *Death* which *Adam* died in the Day that he sinned, was the *losing* this holy Birth from his Soul. And on this Account it was, that nothing could restore him, but that which was able to restore *this Birth* again to his Soul, and make it again *such* an Image of God, as that Father, Son, and Holy Ghost, might *therein* see themselves again in a *creaturely Manner,* and dwell in it, and it in them.

Thirdly, The *Holy Ghost* is in the Scriptures declared to be the *Sanctifier,* or *Renewer* of Holiness in the Soul, and this in such a manner, that *all* the Motions and Operations of the Soul, so far as they are *without* it, and *unmoved* by it, are so far *unholy,* and *unable* even for a good Thought.

Now how could our Thoughts or Operations be *unholy* in themselves, and want the Sanctification and *Renewing* of the Holy Ghost, unless *this* Holy Spirit had first existed in us, and by our Fall had been separated from us?

Had not the *Birth* of the Holy Ghost *arisen* in us at our Creation, we could no more be *unholy* for want of it, than the *Beasts* are, nor any more *now* have wanted to be *renewed* by it, than the *Beasts* that never had it. But since there is now *no Sanctification* or Redemption for us, but by having the Holy Ghost as a *free Gift* of God breathed again into us, it is *no less* than a Demonstration, that we had before we fell, this Holiness by the *Nature* which God gave us *at first;* and that the Holiness of our *Creation* consisted in *this,* that the Holy Spirit then *proceeded,* or *arose* forth in our Soul, as the Birth of the *Son of God* did; and that it might for the same Reason be then called the Holiness of our *Nature,* as it is now after the Fall, called a Holiness by *Gift* or *Grace.* For if we are now to be born again *of the Spirit* by Grace, does not this tell us, that we had *this*

Birth of the Spirit in us at the *first*, and that then it was the Birth of our *Nature* by *Creation?*

Fourthly, These same great Truths are evidently signified to us in the fullest manner by our *Baptism*, and the *Form* of it. Our Baptism is to signify our seeking and obtaining a *new Birth*. And our being baptized in, or into the *Name of the Father, Son, and Holy Ghost*, tells us in the plainest manner, *what Birth* it is that we seek, namely, *such* a new Birth as may make us again what we were at first, a *living real* Image or *Offspring* of the Father, Son, and Holy Ghost.

It is owned on all hands, that we are baptized into a Renovation of *some Divine* Birth *that* we had *lost?* and that we may not be at a loss to know *what* that Divine Birth is, the *Form* in Baptism openly declares to us, that it is to regain that first **Birth** of *Father, Son*, and *Holy Ghost* in our Souls, which at the *first* made us to be *truly* and *really* Images of the *Nature* of the Holy Trinity in Unity. The *Form* in Baptism is but very imperfectly apprehended, till it is understood to have *this* great Meaning in it. And it must be owned, that the Scriptures tend wholly to guide us to *this* understanding of it. For since they teach us, a Birth *of God*, a Birth *of the Spirit*, that we must obtain, and *that* Baptism, the appointed *Sacrament* of this New Birth, is to be done into the *Name of the Father, Son, and Holy Ghost*, can there be any doubt, *that* this Sacrament is to signify the *Renovation* of the Birth of the Holy Trinity in our Souls? And that therefore *this* was the holy Image *born* or *created* at first, when God said, 'Let us make Man in our Image, after our own Like-'ness,' that is, *so* make him, that we may *see ourselves*, our own Nature in him, in a *creaturely Manner*.

What an harmonious Agreement does there *thus* appear, between our *Creation* and *Redemption?* and how finely, how surprisingly do our *first* and our *second* Birth answer to, and illustrate one another?

At our first Birth it is said thus, 'Let us make Man in our 'Image, after our own Likeness'; when the Divine Birth was *lost*, and Man was to receive it again, it is said, 'Be thou baptized 'into the Name of the Father, Son, and Holy Ghost': Which is saying, Let the *Divine Birth*, be brought forth again in thee, or be thou born again *such* an Image of Father, Son, and Holy Ghost, as thou wast at first.

These Considerations all taken from the plain Words, and acknowledged Doctrines of Scripture, do, I think, sufficiently declare and prove to us, these great Truths of the *last Importance*, namely, that the Image in which Man was created, was *such*, as in which, the Holy Trinity saw *itself*, or its *own Nature* in a *creaturely Manner*, in which the Father's *Nature* generated the Nature of the *Son*, and the Holy Ghost *proceeded* from them both, as the amiable moving Life of both.

That by *Adam's* Sin, this holy Image of the Holy Trinity was *broken*, and in *such* a Manner, that the *Birth* of the *Son* of God, and of the *Holy Spirit*, was *no more* in it, and that therefore in a *stupendous Mystery* of Love, the *Son of God* united himself to our *fallen* Nature, to recover, and restore to it, *all that* it had *lost*, and in *such* a Manner, that it might *never* be lost again to all Eternity.

As soon as it is observed and known, that our *Fall* consisted in the *losing* of the Birth of the Son of God in our Soul, and consequently the *proceeding* forth of the Holy Spirit in it, there appears a surprising Agreeableness and Fitness, in the Means of our Redemption, namely, that we could *only* be saved by the *eternal Son* of God; that he only could save us, by taking *our Nature* upon him, and so uniting it with him, that his *Life*, or *Birth* might again *arise* in us, as at the first, and so we become again a perfect living Image of the Holy Trinity.

(17.) Now the Reason why I have gone thus far in inquiring into the Dignity of *Man's original* State, and searched thus deep into his *lamentable Fall*, is this, to point out to the Reader the *true Nature* of the Christian Religion, and the infinite *Importance* of it; which Religion is administered by God, as our *only Relief* from our sad Condition; and that he may at one View see the Height and Depth of Divine Love, which has had so great Care of Mankind.

I persuade myself, no one can *see* these Truths, in the *Manner* that I have represented them, without being in *some degree* inclined to believe them; and in the *same degree* stirred up to act in Conformity to them.

We know nothing *truly* of the Nature of the Christian Religion, and our *deep Concern* in it, but so far as we see into the Nature of our *first* State in the Creation, and our *present* State by the Fall. And as this Knowledge is in some degree necessary, so is it also in some degree obvious to every Man.

Every Man has a *Consciousness* within himself, that a *Perfection in all Kinds* of Virtue *becomes* him; this Consciousness obliges him to set the best Foot forwards, and to put on the *Appearance* of all the Virtue that he can. Now what else is this, but an *inward strong Testimony* of his own Mind, declaring to him, that *Perfection* was his *first* State, and that because his Nature *once* had it, he can neither lose the *agreeable* Idea of it, nor quit his *Pretences* to it; so that every Man carries in his *own Breast*, in the Depth of his *own Frame* and Constitution, a strong

Proof of all those Truths, that I have deduced from Scripture. For I have not been speaking of things *foreign* or *strange* to us, but of things *sensible* felt within us, and spoken to us, by the whole Form of our Nature.

(18.) The *Condition* in which I have represented our Soul to be by the *Fall*, a mere *dark Fire-breath*, of an *hellish* Nature, showing itself in every Man more or less by its Fruits, by such *Eruptions* and Breakings forth of *dark Passions*, but hiding itself under an outward Appearance of *Good*, and a feigned Civility or Rectitude of Manners, is what every Man must be forced to own to be more or less in himself.

For this is the State of every Man's Soul, because it has lost the *Birth of the Son* of God in it, and so is only as a strong Root of a *fiery Life*, unenlightened, and unblessed by *that holy Word*, which is the *Brightness of the Father's Glory*.

This dark Root of a *fiery, self-tormenting Life*, which is the *whole Nature* of the fallen Soul, destitute of the Birth of the Son of God in it, is a Life *that* subsists in *four Elements*, as the Life of this World hath its four Elements.

Now the four Elements of this *dark, fiery Soul*, or fallen Nature, are, (1.) A restless *Selfishness;* (2.) A restless *Envy;* (3.) A restless *Pride;* and, (4.) A restless *Wrath* or *Anger*. I call them the *Elements* of the fallen Soul, because they are *that* to it, which the four Elements of this World are to the Life of the Body.

Now these four Elements which nourish and keep up the Life of the fallen Soul, are also the four Elements of *Hell*, in which the Devils dwell; they can no more *depart* from, or *exist out* of these Elements, than an earthly Life can *depart* from, or exist without the four Elements of this World, *Fire, Air, Water,* and *Earth*.

Now, as the Soul, by the losing of the Birth of the Son of God in it, is become an aching *dark Root* of Fire, that has this restless *Selfishness*, restless *Envy*, restless *Pride*, and restless *Wrath* in it, which are the four Elements of *Hell;* so by its being *in* these, or having them *in it*, it is come to pass, *that* evil Spirits have *such* Communion with it, and so great *Power* over it.

Every *stirring* of the Soul in the Element of *Pride*, is a *moving* in the Devil's *Element*, where he *is*, and has Power to *join* and act with *it;* every *Motion* in the Element of *Envy* or *Wrath*, is so far impowering him to *enter* into the Breath of our Life, and *settle* his fiery Kingdom in us.

And thus in *every one* of these four Elements, so far as we *willingly* are in their Sphere of Activity, and act and stir *according* to them, *so far* we become *Members* of the Devil's Kingdom, and have him for our *Leader*, and *Guide*. How watchful therefore ought we to be of our Hearts, how fearful of *consenting to,* or not *enough* resisting every Motion of these Elements within us, since every voluntary yielding to them, is *opening* the Kingdom of Darkness in our Souls, and giving the Devil Power to infuse his wretched *Nature* into us. And we have still further Reason for this Fear and Watchfulness, if it be considered, that as no one of the *Elements* of this outward World could *be,* or *subsist,* if the other three *were not,* because they are the *mutual Cause* of one another ; so it is in these other Elements, if we live in *one,* we live in *all ; Selfishness* cannot *be,* or *subsist* without *Envy,* nor *Pride* without *Wrath* and *Selfishness,* nor any *one* of the four, without carrying the *other* three in its Bosom ; therefore we must have the same Fear of *any* one, as of them all, for the *Name* of every one is *Legion.*

Could we see, as we see outward Objects, what a dreadful Misery these four Elements bring upon our Souls, we should shun and fly from everything that gave *Life* and *Strength* to them, with more Earnestness, than from the most violent Evils that could threaten our Bodies ; we should choose to burn in any *Fire,* rather than in that of our own *Wrath* and *Pride,* any Poverty of outward Life, rather than *that* of our own *pinching Envy,* any *Prison,* rather than to be *shut* up in our own dark *Selfishness.* For all *outward Fires,* Chains, Torments, Slaveries, Poverties, are but *transient Shadows,* of the tormenting, fiery, dark Slavery of an *unredeemed* Soul, left, and given up to these four Elements of Hell.

And the Reason why they are not a Hell to *profligate Men now* upon Earth, is, as has been said, because we *now* live in *Flesh* and *Blood,* under the *cheering* Influences of the *Sun,* and the Diversion and Amusement of *outward Things,* and in several *Forms of Happiness,* which our Imaginations play with in time. This Wandering of the Imagination through its *own Inventions* of Delight, hinders the poor Soul from feeling *what it is,* in its own Nature ; and therefore, though ever so much a *Slave* of these Elements, it only feels or perceives the Torment of them *by Fits,* and on certain *Occasions.* And yet sometimes it is seen, that one or other of these Elements awakens so violently, as to become *intolerable,* and to give a true and plain *Foretaste* of the Condition and Nature of Hell in the Soul that feels it.

Here again, I cannot help observing by-the-by, the wondrous Excellency and Divine Nature of the Gospel Religion, which knowing our *Fall* to consist in this *darkened Fire* of the Soul, dwelling in *these Elements* of Hell, has set before us such amazing Representations of *Humility, Meekness,* and *Universal Love,* as the Imagination of Man could never have thought of ; namely, the *Humility*, *Meekness*, and *Lowliness* of the Son of God, who left his Glory, to take upon him the Form of a Servant for our Sakes; the *great Love* of God towards us Sinners, in giving his only begotten Son to redeem us, and the Love of God the Son, in laying his Life down for us, *that* we might imitate this amazing *Humility*, *Meekness*, and *Divine Love*, and love one another as he has loved us. These are *Mysteries* of Love and Mercy that are set before us, to quench the *fiery Wrath* of our fallen Nature, and to compel us, if possible, to abhor our own dark Passions, and in Humility and Meekness become Lovers of God, and one another.

(19.) Now so far as we, by true Resignation to God, die to the Element of *Selfishness* and *own Will*, so far as by *universal* Love, we die to the Element of *Envy*, so far as by *Humility* we die to the Element of *Pride*, so far as by *Meekness* we die to the Element of *Wrath*, so far we get *away* from the Devil, enter into *another* Kingdom, and leave him to dwell without us in his own Elements.

These are not *Fictions* of a *visionary* Imagination, but sober Truths, spoken by the Word of God in Scripture, and written and engraven in the Book of every Man's *own Nature*.

No Man since the *Fall*, but is a living Witness to these Truths; to *deny* them, is to *own* and *prove* them: for we could not tell a *Lie*, or resist the Truth, but because we have this *dark Enemy* to Truth hidden in our Bosom.

(20.) Now the greatest Good that any Man can do to himself, is to give leave to this *inward Deformity* to show itself, and not to strive by any Art or Management, either of Negligence or Amusement, to *conceal* it from him. *First*, Because this Root of *a dark Fire-life* within us, which is of the Nature of Hell, with all its Elements of *Selfishness, Envy, Pride,* and *Wrath*, must be in some sort *discovered* to us, and *felt* by us, before we can *enough* feel, and enough groan under the Weight of our Disorder. Repentance is but a kind of *Table-Talk*, till we see so much of the Deformity of our inward Nature, as to be in some degree frightened and terrified at the Sight of it. There must be some kind of an *Earthquake* within us, something that must *rend* and *shake* us to the bottom, before we can be enough sensible, either of the State of Death we are in, or enough desirous of that Saviour, who alone can raise us from it.

A *plausible Form* of an outward Life, that has only learned *Rules* and *Modes* of Religion by *Use* and *Custom*, often keeps the Soul for *some time* at ease, though all its inward *Root* and *Ground* of Sin has never been *shaken* or *molested*, though it has never tasted of the *bitter Waters* of Repentance, and has only known the Want of a Saviour by *Hearsay*.

But Things cannot pass thus : Sooner or later, Repentance must have a *broken*, and a *contrite* Heart; we must with our blessed Lord go over the Brook *Cedron*, and with him sweat great Drops of Sorrow, before he can say for us, as he said for himself, ' It is finished.'

Now, though this Sensibility of the Sinfulness of our *inward Ground*, is not to be expected to be the *same* in *all*, yet the *Truth* and *Reality* of it must, and will be in all, that do but *give way* to the Discovery of it ; and our Sinfulness would ever be in our Sight, if we did not industriously turn our Eyes from it. If we used but half the Pains, to find out the Evil that is *hidden* in us, as we do to *hide* the Appearance of it from others, we should soon find, that in the midst of our *most orderly Life*, we are in Death, and want a *Saviour*, to make our most apparent Virtues to be virtuous.

It is therefore exceeding good and beneficial to us, to discover this *dark, disordered Fire* of our Soul ; because when rightly known, and rightly dealt with, it can as well be made the Foundation of *Heaven*, as it is of *Hell*.

For when the *Fire* and *Strength* of the Soul, is sprinkled with the *Blood* of the Lamb, then its Fire, becomes a Fire of *Light*, and its Strength is changed into a Strength of triumphing *Love*, and will be fitted to have a Place amongst those *Flames of Love*, that wait about the Throne of God.

The Reason why we know so little of Jesus Christ, as our *Saviour, Atonement*, and *Justification*, why we are so destitute of *that Faith* in him, which alone can change, rectify, and redeem our Souls, why we live starving in the Coldness and Deadness of a formal, historical, *hearsay-Religion*, is this ; we are Strangers to our own inward *Misery* and *Wants*, we know not that we lie in the Jaws of *Death* and *Hell;* we keep all things quiet within us, partly by outward Forms, and Modes of Religion and Morality, and partly by the Comforts, Cares and Delights of this World. Hence it is that we consent to receive a Saviour, as we consent to admit of the Four Gospels, because only Four are received by the Church. We believe in a Saviour, not because we feel an absolute want of one, but because we have been told there is one, and that it would be a Rebellion against God to reject him. We believe in Christ as our Atonement, just as we believe, that he cast seven Devils out of *Mary Magdalene*, and so are no more helped, delivered, and justified by believing that he is our Atonement, than by believing that he cured *Mary Magdalene*.

True Faith, is a coming to Jesus Christ to be saved, and delivered from a *sinful Nature*, as the *Canaanitish* Woman came to him, and would not be denied. It is a Faith of *Love*, a Faith of *Hunger*, a Faith of *Thirst*, a Faith of *Certainty* and firm *Assurance*, that in Love and Longing, and Hunger, and Thirst, and full Assurance, *will lay hold* on Christ, as its loving, assured, certain and infallible Saviour and Atonement.

It is this Faith, that breaks off all the Bars and Chains of Death and Hell in the Soul; it is to this Faith, that Christ always says, what he said in the Gospel, 'Thy Faith hath saved 'thee, thy Sins are forgiven thee; go in Peace.' Nothing can be denied to this Faith; all things are possible to it; and he that thus seeks Christ, must find him to be his Salvation.

On the other hand, all things will be dull and heavy, difficult and impossible to us, we shall toil all the Night and take nothing, we shall be tired with resisting Temptations, grow old and stiff in our Sins and Infirmities, if we do not with a strong, full, loving, and joyful Assurance, seek and come to Christ for *every Kind*, and *Degree* of Strength, Salvation and Redemption. We must come unto Christ, as the Blind, the Sick, and the Leprous came to him, expecting *all* from him, and nothing from themselves. When we have this Faith, then it is, that Christ *can do all his mighty Works in us.*

(21.) From the foregoing Account anyone may be supposed already to see the *Nature* and *Necessity* of Regeneration, or the New Birth. It is as necessary as our Salvation. By our *Fall*, our Soul has lost the *Birth of the Son of God* in it; by this Loss it is become a *dark, wrathful, self-tormenting Root* of Fire, shut up in the four hellish Elements of *Selfishness, Envy, Pride*, and *Wrath;* considered as a fallen Soul, it cannot stir one Step, or exert one Motion but *in*, and *according* to these Elements; therefore it is as necessary to have this Nature *itself* changed, and to be born *again* from above, as it is necessary to be delivered from Hell, and eternal Death.

For these Elements are Hell, and eternal Death itself, and not *without*, or standing at a *distance* from us, but Hell and Death springing up in the *Forms*, and *Essences* of our fallen Nature; they are the *Serpent* that is in *us*, and constitute that *gnawing Worm which never dieth*; for they mutually *beget*, and mutually *torment* each other, and so constitute a Worm, or *worming Pain*, that never dieth.

Now as this *Hell, Serpent, Worm*, and *Death*, are all *within us*, rising up in the Forms and Essences of our fallen Soul; so our *Redeemer*, or *Regenerator*, whatever it be, must be also equally *within us*, and spring up from as great a Depth in *our Nature*. Now the Scripture sufficiently tells us, that it is only the *promised Seed of the Woman*, the eternal *Word*, or *Son* of God made Man, that can *bruise* this *Head*, or kill this Life of the *Serpent* in us;

therefore *this Seed* of the Woman must have its Dwelling in the *Ground* and *Essence* of our Nature, because the Serpent is *there*, that a new Life of a *new Nature* may arise from *this Seed* within us; and therefore it is plain, that *Regeneration*, or the *New Birth*, is, and can be *no other* thing, but the *recovering of the Birth of the Son of God* in the fallen Soul.

And this is what the Scripture means by the Necessity of our being *born of God, born again from above*, born of the *Spirit*. Hence also we see in the clearest Light, the Meaning of all those Passages of Scripture, where we are said to be *in Christ*, that Christ is *in us;*—that we must *put on* Christ;—that he must be *formed* in us;—that he is *our Life;*—that we must *eat his Flesh and drink his Blood;*—that he is our *Atonement*, that his *Blood* alone *cleanseth* us from all our Sins; that we have *Life* from him, as the Branches have Life from the *Vine;*—that he is our *Justification*, or *Righteousness;* that in him we are *created again* to good Works; that *without him* we can do nothing, and have *no Life* in us: All these, I say, and the like Sayings of Scripture, have a wonderful Congruity and Plainness in them, and fill the Mind with the most excellent and solid Truths, as soon as it is known, that Regeneration is *absolutely* necessary, and that this Regeneration signifies, the *recovering* of the *Birth* of the Son of God in the Soul.

(22.) And as it does this Justice to so great and concerning a Part of Scripture, so it sets the *whole Scheme* of the Christian Salvation in the most agreeable and engaging Light, and such as is enough even to compel everyone, to embrace it with the utmost Earnestness. The Mystery of this Salvation is still preserved, and yet hereby so *unfolded*, that every Man has as much Reason to desire to be *born again*, and to believe that the *Son* of God can *only* bring forth this Birth in him, as to believe that God made him, and can alone make him happy.

A *Mediator*, an *Atonement, Regenerator*, thus understood, must be as agreeable and desirable to every human Mind, and as much according to his *own Wishes*, as to be delivered from the *Uneasiness* and *Disquiets* of a Nature, which he finds himself not *Master* of, nor able to fix it in a State of *better* Enjoyment.

What is it that any *thoughtful*, serious Man could wish for, but to have a *new Heart*, and a *new Spirit*, free from the *hellish*, self-tormenting Elements of *Selfishness, Envy, Pride*, and *Wrath?* His *own Experience* has shown him, *that* nothing *human* can do this for him; can take away the *Root* of Evil *that* is in him; and it is so *natural* to him to think, *that* God alone can do it, *that* he has often been tempted to *accuse* God, for suffering it to be so with him.

Therefore to have the *Son of God* come from Heaven to redeem him by a Birth of his own Divine Nature in him, must be a way of Salvation, highly suited to his *own Sense, Wants* and *Experience;* because he finds, that *his Evil* lies deep in the very *Essence* and *Forms* of his Nature, and therefore can only be removed by the arising of a *New Birth,* or Life in the first Essences of it.

Therefore an *inward Saviour,* a Saviour, *that is God himself,* raising his own *Divine Birth* in the fallen Soul, has such an *Agreeableness* and *Fitness* in it, to do for him *all that* he wants, as must make every *sober* Man, with open Arms, ready and willing to receive such a Salvation.

(23.) Some People have an *Idea,* or Notion of the Christian Religion, as if God was thereby declared so full of *Wrath* against *fallen* Man, that nothing but the *Blood* of his only begotten Son could satisfy his *Vengeance.*

Nay, some have gone such *Lengths* of Wickedness, as to assert, that God had by *immutable Decrees* reprobated, and rejected a *great Part* of the Race of *Adam,* to an *inevitable* Damnation, to show forth and magnify the *Glory* of his Justice.

But these are miserable Mistakers of the Divine Nature, and miserable Reproachers of his great Love, and Goodness in the Christian Dispensation.

For *God is Love,* yea, *all Love,* and so all Love, *that nothing* but Love can come from him; and the Christian Religion, is nothing else but an *open, full* Manifestation of his *universal* Love towards *all* Mankind.*

As the Light of the *Sun* has only *one common* Nature towards all Objects *that* can receive it, so God has only one common Nature of *Goodness,* towards all created Nature, breaking forth in infinite Flames of Love, upon every Part of the Creation, and calling everything to the *highest* Happiness it is capable of.

God so loved Man, when his *Fall* was *foreseen,* that he chose him to Salvation in Christ Jesus, *before* the Foundation of the World. When Man was actually fallen, God was so *without* all Wrath towards him, so full *of Love* for him, that he sent his only begotten Son into the World to redeem him. Therefore God has *no Nature* towards Man, but *Love,* and all *that* he does to Man, is Love.

(24.) There is no *Wrath* that stands between God and us, but what is awakened in the *dark Fire* of our own fallen Nature; and to quench *this Wrath,* and not *his own,* God gave his only begotten Son to be made Man. God has *no more* Wrath in him-

---

* See *Spirit of Prayer* .

self *now*, than he had *before* the Creation, when he had only himself to love. The precious Blood of his Son was not poured out to *pacify* himself (who in himself had *no Nature* towards Man but *Love*), but it was poured out, to quench the *Wrath*, and *Fire* of the fallen Soul, and kindle in it a *Birth* of Light, and Love.*

As Man lives, and moves, and has his Being in the *Divine Nature*, and is supported by it, whether his Nature be good or bad; so the *Wrath* of Man, which was awakened in the *dark Fire* of his fallen Nature, may, in a *certain Sense*, be called the *Wrath of* God, as *Hell* itself may be said to *be in* God, because nothing can be *out of* his Immensity; yet this Hell, is not God, but the dark Habitation of the Devil. And this Wrath which may be called the *Wrath* of God, is not God, but the fiery Wrath of the fallen Soul.

And it was solely to quench *this Wrath*, awakened in the *human* Soul, that the *Blood* of the Son of God was *necessary*, because nothing but a *Life* and *Birth*, derived from him *into* the human Soul, could change this darkened Root of a *self-tormenting Fire*, into an amiable Image of the holy Trinity, as it was at first created.

This was the *Wrath, Vengeance,* and *vindictive* Justice *that* wanted to be satisfied, in order to our Salvation; it was the Wrath and Fire of *Nature* and *Creature* kindled only in itself, by its departing from due Resignation, and Obedience to God.

When *Adam* and *Eve* went trembling behind the Trees, through *Fear* and *Dread* of God, it was only *this Wrath* of God awakened in them; it was a Terror, and Horror, and Shivering of Nature, *that* arose up *in themselves*, because the *Divine* Life, the *Birth* of the Son of God, which is the *Brightness* and *Joy* of the Soul, was departed from it, and had left it, to feel its own *poor miserable* State without it. And this may well enough be called the Wrath, and Justice of God upon them, because it was a Punishment, or painful State of the Soul, *that* necessarily followed their *revolting* from God.

But still there was *no Wrath*, or painful *Sensation, that* wanted to be *appeased*, or *satisfied*, but in *Nature* and *Creature;* it was only the Wrath of *fallen* Nature, *that* wanted to be changed, into its *first State* of Peace and Love. When God spoke to *them*, he spoke only Love; *Adam, where art thou?* And he called him, *only* to comfort him with a promised Redemption, through a *Seed of the Woman,* a Spark of the WORD of Life which should reign in him, and his Posterity, till all Enemies were under their Feet.

---

* See *Spirit of Love*, part ii., p. 50, &c.

God therefore is all Love, and nothing but Love and Goodness can come from him. He is as far from Anger in himself, as from Pain and Darkness. But when the fallen Soul of Man, had awakened in itself, a wrathful, *self-tormenting Fire*, which could *never* be put out by itself, which could never be relieved by the *natural* Power of *any* Creature whatsoever, then the Son of God, by a Love, *greater than* that which created the World, became Man, and gave his own *Blood*, and *Life* into the fallen Soul, that it might through his *Life in it*, be raised, quickened, and *born again* into its first State of inward Peace and Delight, Glory and Perfection, never to be lost any more. O inestimable Truths! precious Mysteries, of the Love of God, enough to split the hardest Rock of the most obdurate Heart, that is but able to receive one Glimpse of them! Can the World resist such Love as this? Or can any Man doubt, whether he should open all that is within him, to receive such a Salvation?

O unhappy Unbelievers, this Mystery of Love compels me in Love, to *call* upon you, to *beseech* and *entreat* you, to look upon the Christian Redemption in this amiable Light. All the Ideas that your own Minds can form of Love and Goodness, must sink into nothing, as soon as compared with God's Love and Goodness in the Redemption of Mankind.

I appeal to nothing but the State of your own Hearts and Consciences, to prove the *Necessity* of your embracing this Mystery of *Divine Love*. I will grant you all *that* you can suppose, of the Goodness of God, and that no Creature will be finally lost, but what *Infinite Love* cannot save.

But still, here is no *Shadow* of Security for *Infidelity;* and your *refusing* to be *saved* through the *Son* of God, whilst the Soul is in the *redeemable State* of this Life, may at the Separation of the Body, *for* aught you know, leave it in *such* a Hell, as the infinite Love of God *cannot* deliver it from. For, *first*, you have no *Kind*, or *Degree* of Proof, that your Soul is not that *dark, self-tormenting, anguishing* and *imperishable Fire*, above-mentioned, which has lost its *own proper* Light, and is only comforted by the Light of the *Sun*, till its Redemption be effected. *Secondly*, You have no *Kind*, or *Degree* of Proof, that God himself *can* redeem, or save, or enlighten this *dark Fire-Soul*, any other Way than, as the Gospel proposes, by the *Birth* of the Son of God in it. Therefore your own Hearts must tell you, that for aught you know, *Infidelity*, or the *refusing* of this Birth of the Son of God, may, at the End of Life, leave you in *such* a State of *Self-torment*, as the infinite Love of God can no way deliver you from.

You build much upon certain *clear Ideas*, founded in the Nature and Fitness of Things; but I beseech you to consider, that here in this *great Point*, on which all depends, you have no Ideas at all; for you have not *one* clear, or even *obscure* Idea, that your Souls cannot be in this *disordered State*, or *that* they can be set into a right Order, without the Birth of the Son of God brought forth in them.

But to return.

(25.) What has been already said of the *Nature* of Regeneration, may sufficiently show us, how greatly it is *mistaken*, when it is said to signify only a *moral Change* of our Tempers and Inclinations.

Tempers and Inclinations are the *Fruits* of the new-born Nature, and not the Nature itself; and as *Fruits* and *Flowers* are entirely distinct, and different from the *Root* and the *Tree*, and necessarily suppose the Root and the Tree, before they can be brought forth; so good Tempers and Inclinations are as distinct from, and posterior to that Nature, which is to produce them, as its Fruits.

And if *good Tempers* rightly purified, could really arise, or be brought forth in us, without a *Change* first made in the *Root*, or *Nature*, that is to bring them forth, it would be no Absurdity to say, that Men may *gather Grapes of Thorns, or Figs of Thistles*.

But if our blessed Lord has declared this, to be contrary to the Nature of Things, and has further said, that *the Tree must first be made good, before* it *can* bring forth good Fruit; then we can with sufficient ground of Assurance say, that our *Nature* must first be *made good*, its *Root* and *Stock* must be new made, or regenerated again, before it can bring forth good Fruits of moral Behaviour.

(26.) Angels are justly represented to us, as *Flames of Love*; now every Flame must have a *hidden Fire* for its Root, from which it has its Subsistence; and the *spiritual flaming* angelical Nature, must have a spiritual *Fire* concealed under it. Now let it be supposed, that in an Angel this *Flame of Love* was extinguished, and that there then *only* remained that inward *Root* of a spiritual Fire. Let it be supposed, that this spiritual Fire that has lost its *Flame* of Love cannot cease to *be*, and to be a *fiery Spirit*; that it cannot, by any Properties of its Fire *kindle itself* in its first *Flame of Love;* that all its own Stirrings can produce no one Thought, Motion or Desire, but what solely tends either to *Selfishness, Envy, Pride*, or *Wrath;* that it can of itself no more come out of this State, than *Fire* locked up in a *Flint*, can of itself become a *Flame;* could it be said, that this Angel had only lost *some moral* good Dispositions? Must it not be said, to have lost that *Nature*, from which alone, its good

Tempers could proceed? Let it be further supposed, that God, by a Miracle of Love entered into the *fiery Root*, or Essence of this fallen Angel, and by a *new Birth* made it again to be a *Flame of Love ;* could it be said, that it had gained nothing by this new Birth, but only a Change of *some moral* Tempers? Must it not be said to have gained a new Nature, a *Flame of Love*, instead of a *dark Fire?* and from this new Nature, its angelical and good Tempers can alone proceed.

(27.) But the representing the New-Birth, as signifying *only* a Change of moral Behaviour, is not only thus *false* and *absurd* in itself, but is also exceeding prejudicial to true *Conversion*, and saps the *Foundation* of our Redemption.

That it is highly prejudicial to *true Conversion*, is most evident from this, that it hides and suppresses the *real Nature* of our fallen State, and the true Greatness of the *Love* and *Mercy* of God in our Redemption. Now these two things it inevitably does in a great Degree, and therefore the Hurt that it does us, is more than can be well imagined.

And it is owing to this Cause more than to any other, that even amongst People of sober Behaviour, Religion is only a superficial thing, that has no true *Depth* in them, because they have never understood the true *Depth* of Religion, nor conceived, in how deep a manner, their Nature is concerned in it.

A *Heathen* may say, that by going to such a *Neighbourhood*, or marrying into such a *Family*, or falling into Acquaintance with *such a Man*, he obtained an entire *Change in his moral Behaviour*. Now if Christians are told, that this is the *true, and only* Meaning of their *new Birth* in Christ Jesus, namely, a great Change in their moral Behaviour, a thing that happens to *Heathens*, by the *ordinary Occurrences* of human Life, it is no wonder, that they live all their Lives, Strangers to true *Humility*, and *Penitence*, are never truly *converted* to God, or have any *just Sense* of his *infinite Mercy*, in the manner of their Salvation.

For if they are to believe, that to be *born of God*, born from *above*, born of the *Spirit*, born of an *incorruptible Seed* of the *Word of God*, signifies no more than this now mentioned, must not this naturally lead them, to take *everything* that is said of God and Christ, in the *Mysteries* of their Redemption, in a Sense as much *below* the Expression, as this of the New Birth? Must it not naturally lead them to think, that all Scripture-Doctrines, have more of *Height* and *Mystery* in the *Expression*, than in the *thing* itself? and that there is no need to *fear*, or *hope*, or *believe*, or *trust*, or *resign*, or *love*, or *seek*, or *do*, or *bear*, or *give*, or *suffer* according to the *apparent* Language, and *plain* Expression of the Gospel? And thus, the Words of him that spoke as never Man spoke, have all their *Spirit* and *Life* taken from them ; and we may be said to have the Words of Christ, as though we had them not.

(28.) The whole Nature of the Christian Religion, stands upon these *two great Pillars*, namely, the Greatness of our *Fall*, and the Greatness of our *Redemption*. In the full and true Knowledge of these Truths, lie all the Reasons of a deep *Humility*, *Penitence*, and *Self-denial*, and also all the Motives and Incitements, to a most hearty, sincere, and total *Conversion* to God. And everyone is necessarily more or less of a true Penitent, and more or less truly converted to God, according as he is more or less deeply, and inwardly sensible of these Truths.

And till these *two* great Truths, have awakened, and opened our Minds for the full Reception of the Divine Light; all Reformation and Pretence to Amendment, is but a *dead*, and *superficial* thing, a mere Garment of Hypocrisy, to hide us from ourselves, and others.

Nothing can truly awaken a Sinner, but a true Sense, of the deep inward Possession, and Power that Sin has in him. When he sees, that Sin *begins* with his *Being*, that it rises up in the *Essences* of his Nature, and lives in the *first Forms* of his Life, and that he lies thus chained, and barred up in the very Jaws of Death and Hell, as unable to alter his own State, as to create another Creature ; when along with this Knowledge he sees that the *free Grace* of God, has provided him a Remedy *equal* to his Distress, that he has given him the holy *Blood* and *Life* of Jesus Christ, the true Son of God, to enter *as deep* into his Soul, as Sin has entered, to change the *first Forms*, and *Essences* of his Life, and bring forth in them a *New Birth* of a Divine Nature, which is to be an immortal Image of the Holy Trinity, everlastingly safe, blessed, and enriched in the Bosom of Father, Son, and Holy Ghost; when a Man once *truly knows, and feels* these two Truths, he may be said, truly to know, and feel so much of the Power of Christ brought to Life in him. And there seems to be no more, that you need do *outwardly* for him. The Voice of his inward Teacher is so ever speaking, so ever heard, and loved within him, that you can say nothing to him *outwardly* of any *Humility, Penitence*, or *Self-abasement*, but what is less, than his own wounded Heart suggests to him. Humility can only be feigned or false, before this Conviction. He can now, no more take any Degree of Good to himself, than assume any Share in the Creation of Angels ; and all *Pride* or *Self-esteem* of any kind, seems to him to contain as *great a Lie* in it, as if he was to say, that he helped to create himself.

You need not tell him that he must turn unto God with all his

Strength, with all his Heart, all his Soul, and all his Spirit; for all that he can offer unto God, seems to him already less than the least of his Mercies towards him. He has so seen the exceeding Love of God, in the *Manner* and *Degree* of his Redemption, that it would be the greatest of Pain to him, to do anything, but upon a Motive of Divine Love. As his Soul has found God to be *all Love*, so it has but one Desire, and that is, to be itself *all Love* of God. This is the *Conviction* and *Conversion,* that necessarily arises from a full, inward *Sensibility* of these Truths; the Soul is thereby wholly consecrated to God, and can like, or love, or do nothing, but what it can, some way or other, turn into a Service *of Love* towards him. But where the Weight and Power of these Truths is not livingly felt in the Heart, there it is not to be wondered at, if Religion has no Root, that is able to bring forth its proper Fruits.

And if the Generality of Christians, are a Number of *dead, superficial* Consenters to the *History* of Scripture-Doctrines, as unwilling to have the *Spirit,* as to part with the *Form* of their Religion; loath to hear of any kind of *Self-denial,* fond of *worldly Ease, Indulgence,* and *Riches,* unwilling to be called to the *Perfection* of the Gospel, professing and practising Religion, merely as the *Fashion* and *Custom* of the Place they are in, require; if some rest in *outward Forms* of Religion, others in certain *Orthodoxy* of Opinions; if some expect to be saved by the Goodness of the *Sect* they are of, others by a certain Change of their *outward Behaviour;* if some content themselves with a *lukewarm* Spirit, and others depend upon their *own Works,* these are *Delusions,* that must happen to those, who do not know and feel, in some good Degree, the *true Nature* of their own *fallen* Soul, and what a *Kind* of Regeneration can alone save them.

But all these Errors, Delusions, and false *Rests,* are cut up by the Root, as soon as a Man knows the *true Reason* and *Necessity* of his wanting so great a Saviour.

For he that knows the Ground and Essences of his Soul to be so many *Essences of Sin,* which form Sin as they form his Life, entirely *incapable* of producing any Good, till a *Birth* from God has arisen in them; such a one can neither place his Redemption, where it *is not,* nor seek it coolly and negligently, where *it is.*

For knowing, that it is the *Hell within* his own Nature, that only wants to be destroyed, he is intent only upon bringing Destruction upon that; and this secures him from *false Religion.*

And knowing, that this *inward Hell* cannot be destroyed, unless God becomes his *Redeemer,* or Regenerator in *the Ground* of his Soul; this makes him *believe* all, *expect* all, and *hope* all from his Saviour Jesus Christ alone.

of Christian Regeneration. 163

And knowing that all this Redemption, or Salvation, is to be brought about in the inmost *Ground and Depth* of his Heart, this makes him always apply to God, as the God of *his Heart;* and therefore what he offers to God is his *own Heart;* and this keeps him always *spiritually* alive, wholly employed and intent upon the *true Work* of Religion, the fitting and preparing his Heart for all the Operations of God's Holy Spirit upon it. And so he is a true *inward Christian*, who, as our blessed Lord speaks, has the *Kingdom of God within him*, where the State and Habit of his Heart continually, thankfully, *worships the Father in Spirit and in Truth.*

(29.) Having sufficiently shown the Nature and Necessity of Regeneration, that it consists *solely* in the *Restoration* of the Birth of the Son of God in the human Soul, it must be plain from thence, that it is solely the Work of God, he being alone able to effect it; and that Man can have no other Share in it, but that of complying with the Terms, on which it is to be received of God.

It may be proper to inquire, When, and how this great Work is done in the Soul?

The Mercy and infinite Goodness of God, has chosen all Mankind to Salvation in Jesus Christ, before the Foundation of the World. Now this eternal Decree of God, took place upon the *Fall* of *Adam;* and as he was admitted into the Terms of Christian Salvation *immediately* after his Transgression, so all Mankind, as being in his Loins, were taken into the same Covenant of Grace, and what was then done to *Adam*, was done to him, as the *common Parent* of Mankind.

The *Bruiser* of the Serpent given to *Adam*, as his Saviour, was not a *verbal Promise* of something *only*, that should come to pass in future Ages to redeem him, and which left his Soul in the same State of inward Darkness, Disorder, and Weakness in which it found him; but it was a *redeeming Power*, which by the Mercy of God, was treasured up in his fallen Nature, which was to resist and overcome the *Wrath* and *Death*, and awakened *Nature* of Hell, *that* was in his Soul; and from *that* Time of God's accepting him to a Salvation, through the Seed of the Woman, he was saved by the Power of Christ *within him*, as really, as those that lived, and believed in Christ, after he had been incarnate. As nothing can save the *last* Man, or become his *Righteousness*, or Redemption, but the Divine Nature of Jesus Christ, *derived* into his Soul, so nothing else could be Righteousness, Redemption, or Salvation to the first Man.

All Men therefore *that* ever were, or shall be descended from *Adam*, have *Jesus Christ* for their Saviour, as *Adam* had, they receive the Promise made to him, and receive by *that* Promise, that which he received by it, they have a Seed of the Woman, an *incorruptible Seed* of Life, springing up in the *first Essences* of their Life, which is to *oppose* and *resist* the Seed of the Serpent, or the *diabolical* Nature that is in them also. And therefore no Son of *Adam* is *without* a Saviour, or can be *lost*, or entirely *overcome* by the Evil, that the Fall has brought upon him, but by his *own turning* away from this Saviour *within* him, and giving himself up to the Suggestions, and Workings of the *evil Nature*, that is in him.

(30.) This Mystery of an *inward Power* of a Salvation *hidden* in all Men, has had just such degrees of *Obscurity* and *Manifestation*, as the Nature, and *Birth*, and *Person* of the Messiah have had; that is, as the Nature and Person of Jesus Christ, as an *Atonement, Saviour* and *Redeemer* of Mankind, were for several Ages of the World only *obscurely pointed* at, and typified by the Religion of the *Jews ;* so this *Seed* of a New Birth, or *saving Power* of Christ hidden in the Souls of all Men, was, through the same Ages, under the *same Veil*, and Obscurity.

But when the eternal Son of God became incarnate, and manifested to the World the Mysteries of his *Nature, Person*, and *Office*, when it was publicly declared, that he was the *Life* and *Light* of the World, the *only Source* of Goodness in every Creature, the 'Light that lighteth every Man that cometh into the 'World'; that we must all be *born again of him*, be born again *from above*, be born of the Spirit, and *that* everyone was to profess the *owning, seeking* and *desiring* this Divine Birth, by a *Baptism* into the Name, or Nature, of Father, Son, and Holy Ghost; then it became *plainly* manifest, what Christianity *was* from the Beginning, and in *what Manner* Jesus Christ was the Saviour of *Adam*, and what it was that he received, by receiving a *Bruiser of the Serpent*, into the first Essences of his Life.

Therefore when Jesus Christ came into the World, declaring the *Necessity* of a New Birth, to be owned, and sought, by a *Baptism* into the Name of Father, Son, and Holy Ghost; this was not a *new* Kind, or Power of Salvation, but only an *open* Declaration of the *same* Salvation, *that* had been till then, only *typified*, and veiled under certain *Figures* and *Shadows*, as he himself had been. And Men were called not to a new Faith in him, as *then first* become their *inward Life*, and *Light*, but to a more *open* and *plain* Acknowledgment of him, who from the Beginning, had been the one Life and Light, and only Salvation of the first Man, and all that were to descend from him.

(31.) Now the Things required on our Part, towards the raising and bringing forth this new Birth in us, are *Repentance*, and

of Christian Regeneration. 165

Faith. These are to be the *continual Support* of our Regeneration, carrying it on to the End of our Lives.

But now though Repentance and Faith are to *bring forth*, and carry on our Regeneration; yet they are themselves the Effect and Fruit of it, *viz.*, of that *first* Seed or *Light* of Life, which God *willed* to be in *Adam*.

For had not God of his own *free Grace*, chosen *Adam* and *Eve* to Salvation in Jesus Christ, by doing inwardly in the deep, and darkened Essences of their fallen Souls, something like that, which he did to the 'Darkness which was upon the Face of the 'Deep,' when he said, 'Let there be Light' in it; *Adam* and *Eve*, and all their Posterity, had been *inwardly*, as to their Souls, only of the Nature of the Devils, full of their *dark* and *fiery* Dispositions, shut up in their Elements, *incapable* of any Thought or Motion, but what tended to *Selfishness, Envy, Pride*, and *Wrath*.

Neither they, nor any of their Posterity, could have brought forth *any Degree* of Humility, Resignation, Love, Faith, Hope, or Desire of God; but had lived *hardened* and *fixed*, in the abovenamed *Elements* of Hell, full of their *own perverse Will*, without all *Conscience*, or *Instinct* of Goodness.

And therefore when God of free Grace, provided that falling Man should fall into a State of Redemption, that is, into a *Possibility* of being God's Creature again; this was effected by God's *treasuring* up, or *preserving* in him a Seed of *the Woman*, a *remaining* Spark of his first Divine Life; which first Divine Life, was *then*, Christ in him, his *full Birth* of Glory, as certainly, as *Christ in us*, is now our Hope of Glory.

St. *Paul* says, 'God hath chosen us in Christ Jesus, before the 'Foundation of the World.' Now from this eternal, foreseeing Goodness of God towards Mankind, it is, that a *Root* or *Remains* of the first Divine Life, called a *Seed of the Woman*, the *ingrafted* WORD, a *Kingdom of God*, a *Pearl of great Price*, a *Treasure hid in a Field*, was fore-ordained to be preserved, and treasured up, though hidden under that Death, which *Adam* died in Paradise. And thence it was, that the Goodness of God, could direct distressed *Adam* to this Comfort, *viz.*, 'The Seed of 'the Woman shall bruise the Head of the Serpent'; not a foreign Seed, to be sown into thee *from without*, but a remaining, preserved Seed of thy *first Life* of Christ, which through the Divine Love for thee, is hidden, and securely treasured up under thy own fallen earthly Nature, as a *Pearl* hidden in thy own Field, a *Principle* of Holiness, a *Touch* of Love, the *Pledge* of Immortality, and *Fund* of everlasting Happiness. For this heavenly Pearl, called by St. *Peter*, 'the incorruptible Seed of 'the WORD,' shall surely come forth again out of its state of *hiddenness* and *Death;* shall quicken and revive into its first Glory, through Christ, who is, and ever shall be, the RESURRECTION, and LIFE of all that, which was hid and lost in the Death, that *Adam* died.

(32.) And here it is, that we see again how 'God is Love,' *universal Love* towards all Mankind, having put all into a State of Redemption. For if all Men, as Sons of *Adam,* are by the *free Grace* of God made Sons of the *second Adam,* and, as such, have a *Seed* of Life in them from him, in order to be raised up to a Perfection of the new Man in Christ Jesus; and if this *Seed* of a New Birth, or *Light* of Life, is the *general,* and *preventing Grace* of all Men, that enables them so to act, as to obtain God's *assisting Grace,* in the Renewal of their Hearts and Minds, then it is a glorious and undeniable Truth, that there is no *Partiality* in God, *no Election* of one People to *Mercy* in Christ Jesus, and *Dereliction* of another to their *own helpless* Misery, but that *all* Men, have a *general Call,* and a *general Capacity* to obtain their Salvation ; and that as certainly as all *fell* and *died* in *Adam,* so *all* were *restored* in his Restoration.

(33.) Now as the first *Power* and *Ability* of our having one good Thought, or Desire of turning to God in *Penitence* and *Faith,* is the Effect of this first Seed of a New Birth in all Men ; so this Seed of a New Birth is *quickened, strengthened,* and *brought forth* to its full *Stature* or *highest* Degree of Perfection, by Acts, or rather Habits of Repentance and Faith.

So that Faith and Repentance are the *Life* of the new Man, or the Acts by which it *grows,* and is *brought* forth into its proper State of Perfection. There is no *Difference* between Faith and Works, in this *inward new-born* Man. Its Faith is its Works, and its Works are its Faith. For Faith is its *turning to God,* and its turning to God, is its *Aversion,* or *turning from* all Evil ; so that Faith and good Works, are only two Considerations of *one* and the *same thing,* or of one and the same State of mind, in the *new-born Man.*

(34.) This *Seed* of the New Birth, that is God's free, and foreordained Gift to Man, as the *Power* that is to redeem him, is the *Reason* and *Foundation* of that Language in Scripture, of a *new,* inward and *spiritual* Man, and of an *old, natural,* and outward *rational* Man, and of the Enmity between the one and the other ; in which Enmity, the whole Warfare, and Trial of the Christian Life, consist.

The Seed of the New Birth, is the inward and *new* Man, which is to grow up into that spiritual and holy Man, which was *first created* in Paradise.

This inward Man, is alone the *Subject* of Religion and Divine Grace; he only *is of God, and heareth God's Word ;* he only hath Eyes to *see*, and Ears to *hear*, and a Heart to *conceive* the Things of God.

This is he alone, *that is born of God, and cannot sin*, because he has no Sin in his Nature. This is he alone, *that overcometh the World*, because he is of a Divine Nature, and is both contrary to the World, and above it. This is he alone, that can love his Brother as himself, because the Love of God is alone alive, and abideth in him.

The *old, natural* Man, or the *rational* Man of this World, is the *dark fallen* Nature, enlightened *only*, and solely with the *Light* of this outward World ; it is the diabolical Nature, only softened with *Flesh* and *Blood*, quieted and comforted with the Light of the *Sun*, by this Light, he can only see the *outward Images* of Things, whether *Divine* or *human*, and can only *reason, dispute*, and *wrangle* about his own shadowy Images, but can know no more of God, and the Things of God, than such *dead Images* can represent unto him.

The *old* or *natural* Man, may be an *Historian*, a *Poet*, an *Orator*, a *Critic*, a *Politician*, or worldly wise Man, *&c.*, all this Skill and Art lies within his reach ; the *Fire* of his Soul, *kindled* only by the Light of the *Sun*, may do all this. But notwithstanding all these *Trappings* and *Endowments*, he is wholly shut up in his own dark Prison of *Selfishness, Envy, Pride*, and *Wrath ;* his *Virtues, Piety*, and *Goodness* can be only *such*, as give no Disturbance to these *four Elements* of the fallen Nature.

He is an *Animal*, full of earthly, sensual Passions and Tempers, and can only favour such things as can gratify their Nature.

Here, and here only, lies the *true, solid*, and *immutable* Distinction, between the *old* and the *new* Man, and the plain Reason, why the *Life* of the one, is the *Death* of the other.

(35.) Now in this essential Difference, between the *old* and the *new* Man, we may at one View, see a clear and solid Ground of Distinction, between what is called a bare *historical*, and *superficial* Faith, which cannot *save* the Soul, but leaves it a Slave to Sin, and that *living* and *real* Faith, which effecteth our Salvation, and sets us in the glorious Liberty of the Sons of God.

Human *Reason*, or the *natural* Man of this Life, can believe and assent to this Truth, that Christ is our Saviour, and that we are to be saved by a Righteousness from him, as easily, as it can assent to any other Relation, or Matter of Fact. But whilst it is human Reason *only*, that *assents* to this Truth, little or nothing is done to the Soul by it ; the Soul is under much the same Power of Sin as before, because only the *Notion*, or *Image*, or

History of the Truth is taken in by it; and *Reason* of itself can take in no more.

But when the *Seed* of the New Birth, called the *inward* Man, has *Faith* awakened in it, its Faith is not a *Notion*, but a real, *strong, essential Hunger*, an attracting, or *magnetic Desire* of Christ, which as it proceeds from a *Seed* of the *Divine* Nature in us, so it attracts and unites with its *Like*, it lays hold on Christ, puts on the Divine Nature, and in a living and real Manner, grows powerful over all Sins, and effectually works out our Salvation.

And therefore it is justly called a *Divine Faith*, not only because of its Divine Effects, but chiefly because it arises from that, which is *Divine within us*, and by its *attracting* Hunger, and Thirst after that Fountain of Life, from whence it came, becomes essentially united with it; breathes by that SPIRIT, and lives by that WORD which eternally *proceeds out of the Mouth of God*. Of this Faith alone it is, that our Lord speaks, when he says, 'whoso eateth my Flesh and drinketh my Blood, hath eternal 'Life.'

When this Faith is thus awakened, and sprung up in the inward Man, then we may be said to have a *saving Faith*, or a *saving Knowledge* of Jesus Christ.

(36.) From these *two Sorts* of Faith here mentioned, we may very plainly see and perceive, why there is such a *Misunderstanding* between two *Sorts of Believers*, and why they speak a Language so unsatisfactory, and *disgustful* to one another.

Busy inquisitive *Reason*, learned enough in its *own Sphere*, grammatically skilled in Scripture-Knowledge, looking no further, or deeper into the *Things of God*, than a *Dictionary* can guide it, cannot bear the Language of the regenerate, inward Man, but condemns it as *fanatical*, and *enthusiastic;* not considering, that this *rational Man*, which is made the Judge of *Salvation*, is that very individual *old Man with his Deeds*, that we are by the Religion of the Gospel, to be *saved*, and delivered from; and that we should have no occasion for a *new Seed* of a Divine Life in us, no occasion to be *born again of God*, but because *this natural Man* of human Reason, can neither *see* nor *hear*, nor *feel*, nor *taste*, nor understand the Things of God, as they are in themselves.

(37.) From this Difference between the *new*, and the *old* Man, which is a Difference as *real*, as that between Heaven and Earth, several Lessons of great Instruction may be learnt.

When Religion is in the Hands of the *mere natural* Man, he is always the worse for it; it adds a *bad Heat* to his own *dark Fire*, and helps to inflame his four Elements of *Selfishness, Envy, Pride*, and *Wrath*. And hence it is, that worse Passions, or a worse Degree of them, are to be found in Persons of great

of Christian Regeneration.

religious Zeal, than in others *that* make no Pretences to it. History also furnishes us with Instances of Persons of great *Piety* and *Devotion*, who have fallen into great *Delusions*, and deceived both themselves and others. The Occasion of their Fall was this; it was, because they made a *Saint* of the *natural Man*. My Meaning is, they considered their *whole Nature*, as the *Subject* of Religion, and Divine Graces; and therefore their Religion was according to *the Workings* of their *whole* Nature, and the *old Man* was as busy, and as much delighted in it, as the *New*. And hence it was, that Persons of this Stamp, all inflamed, as they seemed to be, with Piety, yet overlooked in their own Lives, such Errors of moral Behaviour, as the first Beginners in Religion, dare not allow themselves in.

Others again, perhaps truly awakened by the Spirit of God, to devote themselves wholly to Piety, and the Service of God, yet making too *much haste* to have the *Glory* of Saints, the Elements of fallen Nature, *Selfishness*, *Envy*, *Pride* and *Wrath*, could *secretly* go along with them. For to seek for *Eminence*, and Significancy in Grace, is but like seeking for Eminence and Significancy in *Nature*. And the *old Man* can relish Glory, and Distinction in *Religion*, as well as in *common Life*, and will be content to undergo as many *Labours*, *Pains*, and *Self-denials*, for the sake of religious, as for the sake of secular Glory. There is nothing safe in Religion, but in such a Course of Behaviour, as leaves *nothing* for corrupt Nature to *feed*, or *live* upon; which can only then be done, when every Degree of *Perfection* we aim at, is a Degree of *Death* to the Passions of the natural Man.

(38.) It may now perhaps be said, if Regeneration is so *great* a Matter, if it signifies the *Restoring* to the Soul its first *paraaisaical* Light, or the Renewing of the *Birth* of the Son of God in it; surely so great a Thing, and transacted *within* us, must not only be known and felt, *when* it is *brought about*, but must be known and felt in some *strange*, and *extraordinary* Manner.

It may be answered, *first*, That all Mankind may in a certain and good Sense, be said to be in some degree Sharers of this Regeneration, as having in them a *Seed* of Life, *that* is contrary to their corrupt Nature; which *Seed* they partake of, as Heirs of the first Grace, granted to *Adam* in the *ingrafted Word*. This first Seed, or *Light* of Life, *which lighteth every Man that cometh into the World*, is the *first Seed* of the New Birth; which Birth stands in this Life, as a *Tree* or Plant in the Soil, and is only in a State of growing during this Life. For was the *New Birth*, with regard both to Soul and Body, ever totally *finished* in anyone, he would be as certainly in Paradise, as *Adam* was, and be as much above the Power of the Elements of this World, as *Adam* was at his Creation. *Secondly*, All Christians are in a *higher* and *further* State of Regeneration, by the *Grace* of Baptism into the Name of the Holy Trinity. By Baptism, they profess themselves Disciples of Jesus Christ, in his Kingdom of Grace, to seek for Life, Righteousness, and Sanctification in him; to live by his Spirit, in Conformity to his Doctrine, Life, Sufferings and Death, in a continual Resistance of the Corruptions of their Nature, the Temptations of the World and the Devil.

This Profession faithfully kept, is their *Progress* in the Way of Regeneration. Some only outwardly make this Profession, and so only have the Name of Christians. Some make it in a much better manner; yet being very defective in their Conformity to the Life and Doctrines of Jesus, live and die far short of that Purification, or Renewal of the inward Man, which the Religion of the Gospel proposes.

Others renouncing all for Christ, and following his *Counsels*, as well as his *Precepts*, arrive at high Degrees of Regeneration, and experience such a Life *in* Christ, or such a *Manifestation* of Christ in them, as others less faithful to their Master, must be Strangers to.

To ask therefore by what *strange* or *extraordinary* Effects, the Work of the New Birth is to be *known*, and *felt* to be *done* in the Soul, is a very improper, and useless Question. Because Regeneration is not to be considered as a Thing, *done*, but as a State that is *progressive*, or as a Thing, *that* is continually doing.

(39.) If it be further asked, What are then the certain *Marks*, or *Effects* of a *highly advanced* Degree of Regeneration, which Christians are to *look for?*

It may be answered, This Question is not useful: *First*, Because there is no Obligation upon anyone, to *know* and *feel* the Height, or Advancement of his State. *Secondly*, Because the *Inquiry* after such Knowledge, and inward *Feeling* of it, is very dangerous. *Thirdly*, Because it can be no hurt to anyone's Piety and Holiness, to take it to be *lower* than it really is. *Fourthly*, Because nothing keeps up our Progress in the Way of Regeneration, let it be in what Degree it will in us, but our *constant Fidelity* in conforming to the Doctrines, Life, and Death of Jesus Christ. *Fifthly*, Because this Question directs, and turns People's Minds to the seeking after *certain Effects*, merely from *Ideas* and *Descriptions* of them, when their Minds should only be set upon the *Causes* that are to produce them.

Thus, supposing it to be true, that an *Assurance of Salvation*, or Continuance in Grace, was a *genuine Effect* of a certain Degree of Regeneration; Christians should not be directed to seek for *this Assurance*, as a certain *Mark* or *Effect* of such a

Degree of Regeneration, for this is directing them to seek for this Effect from their *ownselves*, and not from the *State* of their Regeneration.

For their Minds and Imaginations will be naturally upon the *Stretch*, how to work themselves up into this Pitch of *Assurance*, and so it will be something, *that* they have seized upon by their *own Will*, and not received as the *genuine Effects* of their State in Grace. Whereas, supposing (but not granting) this Assurance to be the *proper* Effect of a certain Degree of the New Birth, yet it is an Effect that is not to be sought for *beforehand*, but only to be received when its *proper Cause* has produced it.

(40.) It is a great Error, to fix any certain Marks or Effects to *such a Degree* of Regeneration; for its Effects will be various in *different* Persons, from a Variety of Causes, both on the Part of God, and Man.

The truly pious Christian, in whom the Holy Ghost dwelleth as in his Temple, is indeed in a State of *high Acquiescence* in God; but he wants no more to have this Acquiescence turned into an *Assurance* of his own Mind, that he *cannot fall* from his State of Grace, than he wants to have the Promises of God made sure to him, by the Promise of some mortal Man.

And if it pleases God to impress strongly and plainly upon his Mind, that his Salvation is secured, he receives it, as he does everything from God, with a grateful Mind; yet will he not *rest* in it, or receive it as a *Sign* of his *high Regeneration*, but rather as a Sign that God saw his *Weakness* stood in need of it; and so will pass over it, and return to an *humble, total* Resignation of his whole *Soul, Spirit*, and *Body*, both for Time and Eternity, into the Hands of God, through Faith in the Merits of his Saviour Jesus Christ.

Least of all can such a one call peremptorily upon others, for *such* an Assurance as he has had, or condemn their *Resignation* and *Peace* in the want of it; he will be more afraid of thus *meddling* with the Things of God, than of being a *Busy-body in other Men's Matters*.

(41.) The only useful Question in this Matter, is this, How a Man may know that he is in the *Way* of Regeneration, that he is spiritually *alive*, and *growing* in the inward and new Man?

It may be answered, Just as the *State, Nature*, and *Life* of the *natural* Man makes itself to be *known*, and *felt*. The Soul of Man, or that which is the *Subject* both of the *old* and *new* Nature, is not two, but *one Soul*. The Fire of the Soul, or that *spiritual Fire* which is the Soul itself, is kindled or enlightened by the Light of the *Sun ;* this makes the *natural Man*, and from whence the *Imagination, Will, Desires, Thoughts*, and *Inclinations* of the natural Life arise.

The same individual *Fire-soul*, enlightened by the *Son of God*, makes the true *new Man*, from which Soul *thus enlightened*, the Imagination, Will, Desires, Thoughts, and Inclinations of the New Man arise. So that the same Proofs are to be expected in both Cases, the spiritual Man is to know that he is alive in the same manner, as the natural Man knows and feels his Life. In these things, in the Imagination, Will, Desires, Thoughts, and Inclinations, consists the Life of each Nature ; and what are more than these, are to be considered as the outward Fruits and Effects of each Nature.

(42.) Now though the natural Life in all Men is *one* and the *same*, yet there are under it Variety of *Complexions*, which makes Men of the same Nature, almost infinitely different from one another. Now the Matter is just thus with the spiritual Man, or in the inward World. As many different Complexions arise in the Soul, enlightened by the Son of God, as in the Soul, enlightened by the *outward Light* of this World.

For the outward World is but a *Glass*, or *Representation* of the inward ; and everything and Variety of things in temporal Nature, must have its *Root*, or hidden *Cause*, in something that is more inward.

It is therefore a well-grounded, and undeniable Truth, that the new spiritual Man hath his *particular Complexion*, as sure as the outward and natural Man hath. Hence it is, that there has been so great a Difference, in the *Form* and *Character* of the most eminent and faithful Servants of God ; one could think of nothing but *Penitence* and penitential *Austerities ;* another all inflamed with the *Love* of God, could think or speak of nothing else ; some have been driven into a *holy Solitude*, living as *John* the *Baptist ;* others have been wholly taken up in Works of Charity, loving their Neighbour even more than themselves. A great Variety of this kind, has been always found amongst those, who were most truly devoted to God, whose Variety, is not only not hurtful in itself, nor displeasing to God, but is as much according to his Will, and the Designs of his Wisdom, as the Difference between *Cherubims* and *Seraphims*, or the Variety of the *Stars* in the Firmament.

Every *Complexion* of the inward Man, when sanctified by *Humility*, and suffering itself to be tuned, and struck, and moved by the Holy Spirit of God, according to its particular *Frame* and *Turn*, helps mightily to increase that Harmony of Divine Praise, Thanksgiving, and Adoration, which must arise from different *Instruments*, *Sounds*, and *Voices*. To condemn this *Variety* in the Servants of God, or to be *angry* at those who have not served him, in the Way that we have chosen for ourselves, is but too plain a Sign, that we have not enough renounced the Elements of *Selfishness*, *Pride*, and *Anger*.

(43.) From this Variety of Complexions both in the inward and outward Man, we may make some useful Observations. And the first may be this, that every Man whose Complexion is strong in him, as to one particular Kind, is vehemently inclined to imprint the same upon others, and that others of the same Kind, are naturally disposed to catch and receive it from him. But I shall consider this Matter only with regard to Religion. Let it be supposed that Men of a certain *Complexion*, have taken upon them to try the religious State of others by these Questions: Are you sure that you should be able to die a *Martyr*? Do you find certain strong Resolutions, not in your *Head*, or your *Brain*, but in your inward Man, that you would not refuse a *Martyrdom* of any kind? Have you the *Witness* of the Spirit within you, bearing witness with your Spirit, that you are in this State?

Now, it is beyond all Question, *that* an *Examination* of this Kind, or a *Demand* of such a Faith, can have no better Foundation than *Complexion*. Who do you think would be most likely to come into this Faith? First, It would be those that were most *unlikely* to keep it. It would be those who knew the *least* of themselves, and whose Piety had more of *Heat* than of *Light* in it. It would be *those*, whose outward Man was of the *same Complexion, that* was *Sanguine*, capable of a *false Fire*, and willing to have the *Glory* of Resolutions, and fine Persuasions at so easy a Rate. Let it now be supposed, that People of another Complexion should put such Questions as these: Do you *know* and *feel* that all your Sins are forgiven you? Do you know *when* and *where*, or at what *Time*, and in what *Place*, you received this Forgiveness? Do you know *when* and *where* you ceased to be one of those Sinners *called to Repentance?* And became one of those *Whole*, that *need not a Physician?* Have you an *absolute Assurance* of your Salvation, and *that* you cannot *possibly* fall from your State of Grace? Now who may be thought to be the most likely to come into this Religion?

First, Not he who is deeply *humble, that* abhors *Self-Justification*, and truly knows the *Free Grace* of God. Such a one would say, I believe the Forgiveness of Sins, with as much Assurance, as I believe there is a God; I believe that Jesus Christ does now to all those who have a *true*, and *full* Faith in him, *that* which he did to those who *so* believed in him, when he was upon Earth. That he forgives their Sins, as immediately, as certainly, as fully, as when he said by an outward Voice, 'Thy Sins are forgiven 'thee.' I believe that in *this Faith* lies all our *Strength*, and

Possibility of growing up in the inward Man, and recovering that Image and Likeness of God, in which we were created; that to *this Faith* all things are possible, and *that* by this Faith, every Enemy we have, whether he be within us, or without us, may, and must be entirely overcome. I believe, that to Repentance and Faith in Christ, Salvation is made as *secure*, and as absolutely *assured*, as *Paradise* was made *secure* to the Thief upon the Cross, by the express Word of our Saviour. I believe that *my own* Sins, were they greater, and more than the Sins of the whole World, would be wholly expiated, and taken away by my Faith, in the *Blood* and *Life* of my blessed Saviour.

But if I now want to add *something* of my own to this Faith, if this great and glorious Faith is *defective*, and saves me not, till I can add my *own Sense*, and my *own Feeling* to it, at such a *Time* or *Place*, is not this saying in the plainest Manner, that *Faith alone* cannot justify me? Is not this making *this Faith* in the Blood of Christ *defective*, and *insufficient* to my Salvation, till a *Self-Satisfaction*, an *own-Pleasure*, an *own-Taste*, are joined with it? Might it not better be said, *that* Faith could not justify me till it had Works, than that it cannot justify me without these inward *Workings, Feelings, Witnessings*, of my own *Mind, Sense*, and *Imagination?* Is there not likely to be a more hurtful *Self-seeking*, a more hurtful *Self-Confidence*, a more hurtful *Self-Trust*, a more dangerous *Self-Deceit*, in making Faith to depend upon these inward *Workings* and *Feelings*, than in making it depend upon outward good Works of our own?

Secondly, No one who was *truly resigned* unto God in *all things*, would come into these Questions; for to be resigned unto God in *all things*, and yet seek to be *not resigned* to him, in these *great Matters* above mentioned, is a Contradiction.

Such a one would say, I seek not to have an inward *Sense* and *Feeling* of the Certainty of these things, because that would be departing from that *pure, entire, full,* and *naked* Faith in God, and Resignation of myself to him, which alone can justify me in his Sight, and make me capable of the Operations of his Holy Spirit. He can only then, do all his good Pleasure in me, when I have no *own Will*, no *Self-seeking;* this total Resignation of myself to him, is the one only *immediate Disposition*, or *Capability* of enjoying God himself with all his infinite Treasures. Particular *Impressions*, sensible *Convictions*, strong *Tastes*, high *Satisfactions*, though they may be often the good Gifts of God, yet if they are much sought for, or *rested* in, they minister Food to a spiritual *Self-love*, and Self-seeking, and lay the Foundation of spiritual Pride; and so become a Wall of Partition between God and the Soul. For the Soul may be as fully fixed in Selfishness, through a Fondness of Sensible Sweetness, pious Motions, and delightful Enjoyments in spiritual things, as by a Fondness for earthly Satisfactions.

Thirdly, No one, whose Heart was truly touched by a *pure* and *perfect* Love of God, could come into these Questions. For this Love cannot seek for *Self-comfort* in the Answer of such Questions as these.

Such a Person would say, My Religion consists in living *wholly to my Beloved*, according to *his* Satisfaction, and not *my own*. What God wills, that I will; what God loves, that I love; what pleases God, that pleases me. I have no desire to know anything of myself, or to feel anything in myself, but that I am an *Instrument* in the Hands of God, to *be*, to *do*, and *suffer*, according to his good Pleasure. I am content to know that I *love* and *rejoice* in God *alone*, that he is what he is, and that I am what he pleases to make of me, and do with me.

(44.) Seeing then it appears that the truly *humble* Man, the Man that is wholly *resigned* to God, and the *pure Lover* of him, are not likely to come into the Religion of these Questions, let us now see who may be supposed ready to receive it.

First, All young Persons, whose Passions had not yet been much *awakened*, or spent their *Fire;* who had but little Experience of *themselves*, and the Deceitfulness of their *own Hearts;* for everything in their Nature, would help them to like, love, and obtain such an *Assurance*, Strength of *Conviction*, inward *Feeling*, as is here required.

Secondly, All restless *Self-Lovers*, who were uneasy with themselves, and everything else, who could find nothing in Religion, or common Life, that enough pleased them; these would be easily persuaded to work themselves up into a Belief, that their Sins were forgiven them at *such* a *Time*, or that Christ took an entire Possession of them at *such a Place*. For hearing that true Religion consisted *solely* in this, and that they only wanted it, because of their want of Faith in it, they would naturally embrace this, as the shortest Way to Comfort and Rest *in themselves*, in their own *Self-convictions*.

Thirdly, All Persons of a *sanguine*, *tender*, and *imaginary* Complexion, would be likely to strike in with the Religion of these Questions. For such Persons receiving everything *strongly*, and having a Power of believing and imagining almost in any degree, as they please, they would not find it hard, to comply with Doctrines so suited to their Nature, and which indulged that in them, which wanted most to be indulged, a sanguine Imagination.

Fourthly, All those who so *blaspheme* God, as to make him from all Eternity *absolutely* to elect some to an *irresistible* Salvation, and absolutely to *reprobate* others to an *unavoidable* Damnation. For there could be no subsisting under such an horrid Belief as this, but by those, who through a blind *Partiality*, strong Bias of *Self-love*, and *Self-esteem*, can work themselves up into a *full Assurance*, inward *infallible Feeling*, that they are in the Number of the absolutely elected from all Eternity.

Lastly, These Questions are a great *Bait* to all kinds of *Hypocrites*, who must find themselves much inclined to enter into a Religion, where they may pass immediately for *Saints*, upon their *own Testimony*, and stand in the highest Rank of Piety, and of Interest in Christ, merely by *their own* laying Claim to it.

(45.) Suppose it was to be asked Christians, as *necessary* to their Salvation, Do you believe and know that you have the *Self-denial* and *Mortification* of *John* the *Baptist?* Have you an inward Conviction that you have a *Zeal* equal to that of St. *Paul?* Have you an *Assurance* that your Love is full as *high* as that of *John* the *Evangelist?* That your *Penitence* is equal to that of *Mary Magdalene?*

Could these Questions, with any Warrant from Scripture, be put to all Christians, as Terms of their Salvation?

Yet there is as much Foundation in the Gospel, for putting such Questions as these, and making the Salvation of Christians to depend upon them, as for asking them, on the same Account, *When*, and *where*, they *felt* their Sins were forgiven them? When and where they felt Christ to take an entire Possession of them? When and where they felt themselves made *sure* of their Salvation, and *incapable* of falling from their State of Grace?

For what is all this but calling, hastening, and stirring up People to seek for Self-Justification, and compelling them to *think highly*, and affirm *rashly* of themselves, in order to be saved? Why might it not be as well to call upon them to say, I feel myself as *good* as St. *Paul*, as *pious* as St. *John*, as to say, I *feel* that my Salvation is *secure*, and that I *cannot* fall from my State of Grace? Is not this making Faith in *one's self*, as good, as necessary, and as beneficial to us, as Faith in *Christ?*

Would it not be as well, nay better, to make good Works of *our own*, necessary to true Faith, than to make Self-Justification, which is not a good Work, to be the very Essence and Perfection of it?

The Matter will not be much mended by saying, that this *Feeling* and *Assurance* is acknowledged to be the *pure Gift* of God, and so cannot be called *our own*, or our *own Justification*. For if I have not this Gift of God, till I *pronounce* it myself, till my *own Feeling* and Assurance *confirms* it to me, I am self-justified, because my Justification arises, from what I *feel* and *declare* of myself.

(46.) How strangely must they have read the Gospel, who can take a *naked implicit* Faith, and an *humble total* Resignation of our *Spirit, State,* and *Life,* into the Mercy and Goodness of God, to be not only a *poor* and *imperfect,* but a *reprobate* State; or *that* a Man has no true and *saving Faith,* till it is an *infallible own-Feeling,* and *Self-Assurance?* What must such People think of our Saviour dying upon the Cross, with these Words in his Mouth; 'My God, my God, why hast thou forsaken me!' Will they say that this is a *dangerous* State? Is the *Spirit* of Christ here to be *renounced?* Will they say, that no *new-born* Christian can die in this Manner? Or that if he does, he is not in a State of Salvation?

To know no more, and to seek to know no more of our Salvation, *than* we can know by an *implicit* Faith, and *absolute* Resignation of ourselves to God in Christ Jesus, is the true *saving Knowledge* of Christ, and such as keeps us in the highest Degree of Fitness to receive our perfect Salvation.

(47.) I hope it will here be observed, that I no way depreciate, undervalue, or reject any particular *Impressions,* strong *Influences,* delightful *Sensations,* or heavenly *Foretastes* in the inward Man, which the holy Spirit of God may at times bestow upon good Souls; I leave them their just Worth, I acknowledge them to be the *good Gifts* of God, as special *Calls,* and *Awakenings* to forsake our Sins, as great *Incitements* to deny ourselves, and take up our Cross, and follow Christ with greater Courage, and Resolution.

They may be as *beneficial,* and *useful* to us in our spiritual Life, as other Blessings of God, such as *Prosperity, Health, happy Complexion,* and the like. But then, as *outward Blessings,* remarkable *Providences,* religious *Complexion,* and the like, may be very serviceable to awaken us, and excite our Conversion to God, and much assist the spiritual Life; so they may very easily have a contrary Effect, serve to fill us with *Pride,* and *Self-satisfaction,* and make us esteem ourselves, as *greater Favourites* of God, than those that want them. Who may yet be led to a *higher Degree* of Goodness, be in a *more purified* State, and stand *nearer* to God in their *poor, naked,* and *destitute* Condition, than we in the midst of great Blessings.

It is just thus with regard to those *inward Blessings* of the spiritual Life. They are so many *Spurs, Motives,* and *Incitements* to live wholly unto God; yet they may instead of that, fill us with *Self-satisfaction* and *Self-esteem,* and prompt us to *despise* others that want them, as in a *poor, mean,* and *reprobate*

State; who yet may be *higher* advanced, and stand in a *nearer* Degree of Union with God, by *Humility*, *Faith*, *Resignation*, and *pure Love*, in their inward *Poverty* and *Emptiness*, than we who live *high* upon spiritual *Satisfactions*, and can talk of nothing, but our *Feasts of fat Things*.

All that I would here say of these inward *Delights* and *Enjoyments*, is only this, They are not *Holiness*, they are not *Piety*, they are not *Perfection*, but they are God's gracious *Allurements*, and *Calls* to seek after Holiness and spiritual Perfection. They are not to be sought for, for their *own sakes*; they are not to be prayed for, but with such a perfect *Indifference* and *Resignation*, as we must pray for any earthly Blessings; they are not to be *rested in*, as the Perfection of our Souls, but to be received as *Cordials*, that suppose us to be *sick, faint*, and *languishing*; and ought rather to convince us, that we are as yet, but *Babes*, than that we are really *Men* of God.

But to demand them in others, to make them uneasy under the Want of them, full of Search and Endeavour how to come at them, and satisfied in the Enjoyment of them, is as great a Mistake in itself, and as prejudicial to true Piety, as to make *outward Blessings* of Providence, Marks of Salvation, or *worldly Poverty*, *Pains*, and *Distress*, to be Proofs, that we are *not born* of God.

'There are indeed Impressions and Communications from God,
'which are more necessary and essential to the pious Life of the
'Soul, than the Impressions of the *Sun* are to the comfortable
'Life of our outward Man. And he that prays for nothing else
'but these Divine Communications and Impressions, who thinks
'of nothing else, trusts in nothing else, as able to comfort,
'strengthen, and enrich his Soul; he that is thus all Prayer,
'all Love, all Desire, and all Faith, in these Communications and
'Impressions from above, is just in the same State of *Sobriety*,
'as he that only prays that God would not *leave him to himself*.
'For he that is without anything of *these Communications* and
'Impressions of God upon him, is in the same State of *Death*
'and *Separation* from God, as the Devils are.'*

These *Impressions* or *Operations* of God upon our Souls, are of the Essence of Religion, which has no Goodness in it, but so far as it introduces the *Life*, *Power*, and *Presence* of God into the Soul. The praying therefore for Impressions of *this kind* from God, is only praying that we may not be *left to ourselves*; to pray always for these with Faith, and hunger and thirst after

---

* Demonstration of the gross Errors, &c., in the *Plain Account of the Sacrament*, p. 287.

them, is only praying earnestly, that the *Kingdom of God may come, and his Will be done in us.*

For the Soul is only so far cleansed from its Corruption, so far delivered from the *Power* of Sin, and so far purified, as it has renounced all *own Will,* and *own Desire,* to *have* nothing, *receive* nothing, and *be* nothing, but what the *one Will* of God chooses for it, and does to it.

This, and *this alone* is the true Kingdom of God *opened* in the Soul, when stripped of all Selfishness, it has only *one Love,* and *one Will* in it, when it has no Motion or Desire, but what branches from the Love of God, and resigns itself wholly to the Will of God.

There is nothing Evil, or the Cause of Evil to either Man, or Devil, but his *own Will;* there is nothing *Good* in itself, but the *Will of God:* he therefore who *wholly* renounces his *own Will,* turns away from *all Evil;* and he who gives himself up wholly to the Will of God, puts himself in the Possession of all that is good.

(48.) It may freely be granted, *that Conversion* to God, is often very *sudden* and *instantaneous,* unexpectedly raised from Variety of Occasions. Thus, one by seeing only a *withered Tree,** another by reading the Lives and Deaths of the *Antediluvian Fathers,* one by hearing of *Heaven,* another *Hell,* one by reading of the *Love,* or *Wrath* of God, another of the *Sufferings* of Christ, may find himself, as it were, *melted* into Penitence all on a sudden. It may be granted also, that the greatest Sinner, may in a *Moment* be converted to God, and feel himself wounded in such a Degree, as perhaps those never were, who had been turning to God all their Lives.

But then it is to be observed, that this *Suddenness* of Change, or *Flash* of Conviction, is by no means of the *Essence* of true Conversion, and is no more to be demanded in ourselves, or others, than such a Light from Heaven, as shone round St. *Paul,* and cast him to the Ground. *Secondly,* That no one is to expect, or require, *that* another should receive his Conversion, or Awakening, from the same Cause, or in the same Manner, as he has done, that is, that *Heaven,* or *Hell,* or the *Justice,* or *Love* of God, or Faith in Christ, either as our *Light,* or our *Atonement,* must needs be the *first Awakening* of the Soul, because it has been so with him. *Thirdly,* That this Stroke of Conversion, is not to be considered, as signifying our *high State* of a New Birth in Christ, or a *Proof that* we are on a sudden made *New Creatures,* but *that* we are thus suddenly *called,* and *stirred* up to look after a

---

* *Frere Laurent.*

Newness of Nature. *Fourthly*, That this *Sensibility*, or *manifest Feeling* of the Operations of God upon our Souls, which we have experienced in these first Awakenings, is not to be expected, or desired, to go along with us, through the Course of our Purification. *Fifthly*, That Regeneration, or the *Renewal* of our first Birth and State, is something entirely *distinct*, from this first *sudden Conversion*, or *Call* to Repentance ; that it is not a Thing done in an *Instant*, but is a certain *Process*, a *gradual Release* from our Captivity and Disorder, consisting of several *Stages* and *Degrees*, both of Death and Life, which the Soul must go through, before it can have thoroughly put off the old Man. I will not say that this must needs be in the *same Degree* in all, or that there cannot be any Exception to this. But thus much is true and certain, that Jesus Christ is our *Pattern*, that *what* he did for us, *that* we are also to do for ourselves, or, in other Words, we must *follow him in the Regeneration*. For what he did, he did, both as our *Atonement*, and *Example*, his Process, or Course of Life, Temptations, Sufferings, denying his own Will, Death, and Resurrection, all done, and gone through, on our Account, because the human Soul wanted *such a Process* of Regeneration and Redemption ; because, only in such a *gradual Process*, all that was lost in *Adam*, could be restored to us again. And therefore it is beyond all doubt, *that* this *Process* is to be looked upon, as the stated Method of our Purification.

It is well worth observing, that our Saviour's *greatest Trials*, were near the End of his *Process* or Life, that he then experienced the *sharpest Part* of our Redemption. This might sufficiently show us, that our *first Awakenings* have carried us but a little way ; that we should not then begin to be *self-assured* of our *own Salvation*, but remember, that we stand at a great Distance from, and in great Ignorance of our severest Trials.

To sum up all in a Word : Nothing hath separated us from God but our *own Will*, or rather our own Will is our Separation from God. All the Disorder, and Corruption, and Malady of our Nature, lies in a certain *Fixedness* of our own Will, Imagination, and Desire, wherein we live to ourselves, are our own *Centre* and *Circumference*, act wholly from ourselves, according to our own Will, Imagination, and Desires. There is not the smallest Degree of Evil in us, but what arises from *this Selfishness*, because we are thus, *All in All* to ourselves.

It is this *Self*, that our Saviour calls upon us to deny ; it is this Life of *Self*, that we are to *hate* and to *lose*, that the Kingdom of God may arise in us, that is, that God's Will may be done in us. All other Sacrifices that we make, whether of worldly *Goods, Honours*, or *Pleasures*, are but small Matters, compared to that Sacrifice and Destruction of *all Selfishness*, as well *spiritual*, as natural, that must be made, before our Regeneration hath its perfect Work.

There is a Denial of our *own Will*, and certain Degrees even of *self-denying Virtues*, which yet give no Disturbance to *this Selfishness*. To be humble, mortified, devout, patient in a *certain Degree*, and to be persecuted for our Virtues, is no *Hurt* to this Selfishness; nay, *spiritual-self* must have all these Virtues to subsist upon; and his Life consists, in *seeing, knowing* and *feeling* the Bulk, Strength, and Reality of them. But still in all this Show, and Glitter of Virtue, there is an *unpurified Bottom* on which they stand, there is a *Selfishness*, which can no more enter into the Kingdom of Heaven, than the Grossness of Flesh and Blood can enter into it.

What we are to feel, and undergo in these *last Purifications*, when the *deepest Root* of all Selfishness, as well spiritual as natural, is to be *plucked up*, and torn from us, or how we shall be able to stand in *that Trial*, are both of them equally impossible to be known by us beforehand.

It is enough for us to know, that we *hunger and thirst after the Righteousness* which is in Christ Jesus; that by Faith we desire, and hope to be in him new Creatures; to know, that the *greatest Humility*, the *most absolute Resignation* of our whole selves unto God, is our *greatest* and *highest Fitness*, to receive our greatest and highest Purification, from the Hands of God.

FINIS.

www.ingramcontent.com/pod-product-compliance
Lightning Source LLC
Chambersburg PA
CBHW051929160426
43198CB00012B/2082